CHICKEN SOUP FOR THE SOUL®

Celebrating People Who Make a Difference

Jack Canfield
Mark Victor Hansen
Peter Vegso
Theresa Peluso

Health Communications, Inc.
Deerfield Beach, Florida

www.hcibooks.com
www.chickensoup.com

We would like to acknowledge the many publishers and individuals who granted us permission to reprint the cited material. (Note: The stories that were penned anonymously, that are in the public domain, or that were written by Jack Canfield, Mark Victor Hansen, Peter Vegso, or Theresa Peluso are not included in this listing.)

Rescue of Little Naomi. Reprinted by permission of Gloria Cassity Stargel. © 2005 Gloria Cassity Stargel.

Gertrude's Stuff. Reprinted by permission of Rhonda Richards-Cohen. © 2006 Rhonda Richards-Cohen.

Rock Island Angel. Reprinted by permission of Susan A. Karas. © 2006 Susan A. Karas.

Good Samaritans in Disguise. Reprinted by permission of Sallie A. Rodman. © 2006 Sallie A. Rodman.

Full Circle. Reprinted by permission of Margaret Frezon. © 2006 Margaret Frezon.

(Continued on page 315)

Library of Congress Cataloging-in-Publication Data

Chicken soup for the soul celebrating people who make a difference / Jack Canfield ... [et al.].
    p. cm.
    ISBN-13: 978-0-7573-0667-9 (trade paper)
    ISBN-10: 0-7573-0667-5 (trade paper)
    1. Caring.   2. Helping behavior.   3. Spirituality.   I. Canfield, Jack, 1944–
BJ1475.C45 2007
177'.7—dc22   2007041646

Publisher: Health Communications, Inc.
               3201 S.W. 15th Street
               Deerfield Beach, FL 33442–8190

Cover design by Andrea Perrine Brower
Inside book formatting by Theresa Peluso and Dawn Von Strolley Grove

This book is dedicated to those
who seek proof that love and compassion
are alive and well in our world today.

Contents

2. A MATTER OF ATTITUDE

3. CHARACTER AND COURAGE

4. MOVING FORWARD

Acknowledgments

Compiling, editing, and publishing a book requires the energy and expertise of many people. First, a huge thank-you to our families who support us with love and encouragement. Thank you Inga, Christopher, Travis, Riley, Oran, Kyle, Patty, Elisabeth, Melanie, Anne, Melinda, Hayley, and Brian.

Behind the scenes are dozens of talented, enthusiastic staff members, freelancers, and interns who keep the wheels turning smoothly at Chicken Soup for the Soul Enterprises, Self-Esteem Seminars, Mark Victor Hansen and Associates, and our publisher, Health Communications, Inc. (HCI).

Patty Aubery and Russ Kalmaski share this journey with love, laughter, and endless creativity.

Patty Hansen has handled the legal and licensing aspects of each book thoroughly and competently, and Laurie Hartman has been a precious guardian of the Chicken Soup brand.

Michelle Adams, Noelle Champagne, D'ette Corona, Lauren Edelstein, Jody Emme, Teresa Esparza, Jesse Ianniello, Tanya Jones, Debbie Lefever, Barbara LoMonaco, Mary McKay, Dee Dee Romanello, Gina Romanello, Veronica Romero, Brittany Shaw, Shanna Vieyra, Lisa

Williams, and Robin Yerian support Jack's and Mark's businesses with skill and love.

We appreciate the work of HCI's editorial department, directed by Michelle Matrisciani, and the HCI creative team, led by Larissa Hise-Henoch, whose efforts make each book special. And thank you to the rest of the staff at HCI, who for their sheer number must go nameless, who get all of our books into readers' hands, copy after copy, with dedication and professionalism.

Readers around the world enjoy Chicken Soup for the Soul in more than thirty-six languages, for which we can thank Claude Choquette and Luc Jutras at Montreal Contacts, The Rights Agency.

While we were compiling this book, the stories shared by hundreds of writers moved and inspired us, and we thank you for sharing such personal experiences with us. We regret that we couldn't publish every story, and we hope that the essence of each person's experience and message has been captured somewhere in these pages.

We sincerely appreciate the efforts of the volunteer readers: Eloisa Bracken, Noelle Epstein, Beverly Fine, Gay Lewis, Marsha Louden, Kathleen Nevins, Janet Posner, Shamya Rudolph, Theresa Sanders, Gloria Torres, Amy Traub, Rachel Weisenfeld, Barbara Wellington, Susie Yau, and Julia Zafer, who dedicated their time to help us select the stories in *Celebrating People Who Make a Difference*.

And, last but certainly not least, thank you to our readers and loyal Chicken Soup for the Soul fans. Your support and enthusiasm for the Chicken Soup series keep us motivated and dedicated to changing lives, one story at a time.

Introduction

The second most destructive hurricane in history, surpassed only by Katrina in 2005, was Andrew, which made landfall as a category 5 storm in Dade County, Florida, on August 24, 1992. Essentially, that's my backyard.

However, just a few miles away from the storm's narrow path, it was nearly impossible to surmise that a catastrophic event had happened—except, of course, for the continuous drone of low-flying Hueys and C130s, and the endless convoys of National Guard and Army trucks streaming southbound down the turnpike to the epicenter. Clearly, now we all understood what the term "natural disaster" meant: life had changed. For some it would never be the same.

In times such as those, we couldn't afford to concentrate on the negative. In times such as those we craved—we absolutely needed—good news. We needed it shouted from podiums, rooftops, front pages, and breaking news bulletins; but that seldom happened. Instead, we saw sensational images of disaster or turmoil, and we read more about the worst actions of a few than we ever did of the many good and kind. In times such as those we needed an antidote to the six o'clock news. I didn't know it in 1992, but that was the beginning of *Chicken Soup for the Soul, Celebrating People Who Make a Difference*.

Mahatma Gandhi once said, "Be the change you want to see in the world." Think about that. Chances are you often see where change is needed, but do nothing. Why not? Perhaps, individually, we seldom feel empowered or effective to create change. But what if we didn't focus on the larger, daunting picture? What if we weren't dealing with natural disaster on a grand scale, but with the person in need next door? What if we simply did what Gandhi suggested and became the change we want to see? What might happen then?

Something that sounds so simple but with so much potential just can't be simple or easy, right? Well, the people you are about to meet in this book will prove it's easier than you think. They aren't heroes, they aren't superhuman. But they *are* powerful, wealthy people who held someone else's welfare in the palm of their hands, albeit not in the generally accepted sense of those words.

The people in this book are everyday people who performed uncommon deeds. Their actions were undertaken without thinking about what was is in it for them, or even if they were putting themselves at risk. Universally, they believed that helping others, that acknowledging another person's value, that recognizing someone else's potential, their challenges, or pain was as essential as taking a breath. They became the change they wanted to see. How much more powerful and wealthy would you want to be?

These are stories about the small kindnesses, the ordinary things that have extraordinary meaning for the people to whom they happened, the quintessential defining moments in life, that ripple of a butterfly wing. This book represents a thank-you to all the unknown people who should have been recognized. It's a chance for the good news to be told. And it proves that the expression of compassion is a powerful agent for change. It is what makes us human.

What I hope you'll discover in reading these stories is that giving makes you happier, helping someone is fulfilling, and that seeds planted early in life result in a bountiful harvest of service to others. If you are inspired to fulfill your intrinsic potential and embrace the change you want to see, this world will indeed be a better place— because of *you*.

Theresa Peluso

Share with Us

We would love to hear your reactions to the stories in this book. Please let us know what your favorite stories were and how they affected you.

We also invite you to send us stories you would like to see published in future editions of Chicken Soup for the Soul. You can send us either stories you have written or stories written by others. Please send submissions to:

Chicken Soup for the Soul
P.O. Box 30880
Santa Barbara, CA 93130
Fax: 805-563-2945

You can also access e-mail or find a current list of planned books at the Chicken Soup for the Soul website at www. chickensoup.com.

We hope you enjoy reading this book as much as we enjoyed compiling, editing, and writing it.

1

A HELPING HAND

We have stopped for a moment to encounter each other. To meet, to love, to share. It is a precious moment, but it is transient. It is a little parenthesis in eternity. If we share with caring, lightheartedness, and love, we will create abundance and joy for each other, and this moment will have been worthwhile.

Deepak Chopra, M.D.

Rescue of Little Naomi

Nothing in the world can take the place of persistence.

Calvin Coolidge

Darkness was closing in as I maneuvered my old Dodge Charger down the treacherous road around Blood Mountain toward home after my shift at Union County Medical Center in Blairsville, Georgia.

Beep! My pager startled me. I answered to hear, "You're to call this number in Dahlonega."

"Dahlonega?" I wondered aloud, fear taking hold. Duane was taking the children hiking toward Dahlonega. But they should have been home hours ago! I dialed the number. "Lumpkin County Sheriff's Office." Suddenly I felt sick to my stomach.

"This is Mirna Whidden," I said, panic building. "What's wrong?"

"You need to get down here right away."

I started to cry. "Tell me what's wrong."

"Mrs. Whidden, one of your children is missing."

My heart stopped. *Dear God, help me.*

I don't recall the hour's ride to Dahlonega. Unanswered questions pounded inside my head. *Which child? What happened? A kidnapping?*

I bolted out of the car smack into a bevy of media people with cameras and microphones in hand.

The sheriff rushed out and escorted me into his office. "Where are my babies? I want to see my babies!" I was becoming hysterical.

Finally I heard him say, "Matthew and Rachel are back there in an office, playing with a computer and eating cookies. But your youngest—the two-year-old—is missing."

"Naomi! Naomi is missing? What are you saying? Someone took my baby?" By now, I had lost all control.

"Your husband said she wandered off while they were hiking. She's lost in the forest."

"Lost? Naomi is lost in the forest? My baby is out there all alone in those mountains? It's cold out there. And dark. And raining. And there are wild animals! We've got to find her! Take me there!"

"We have crews out there searching, Mrs. Whidden. It will be best if you stay here."

"Where is my husband? I want to see Duane!" I needed Duane, desperately. I needed his steadying strength.

"Mr. Whidden is here, but you can't see him right now. We're questioning him, trying to find out what happened."

By nine o'clock, the officers surrendered to my frenzied pleas and drove me out through rugged terrain to the Chattahoochee National Forest. We passed a roadblock, then came to a stop where an old logging trail snaked precariously around the side of a mountain.

"This is where Mr. Whidden parked his car this morning," the officer told me. "He said the children stopped to play in a clearing about a mile and a half down this trail. He took his eyes off them for a minute and little Naomi disappeared."

I called out across the black forest, "Naomi—Naomi—Mommy's here, baby. Come to Mommy." My voice was devoured by the vast darkness.

Far away, across the valley, I saw a long line of lights moving slowly through the trees. *The searchers! Dear God, please help them find my baby.*

Beautiful little Naomi had just turned two. Naomi, with the precious pixie smile and big brown eyes, her light brown hair tied with a bright ribbon on top of her sweet head. *Please, God, send your angels to look after Naomi.*

In the patrol car, I could hear communication between the staging area and searchers in the woods. The radio's every crackle made me hold my breath. At one point an Army helicopter was brought in, giving me hope. Its heat sensors located two coon hunters and a deer. But no little girl.

Then search dogs arrived. In teams of two, they were led down the logging trail, not making a sound. "The dogs will find her if anything can," someone stated. But they didn't.

I shivered in the night air as the temperature dipped down to forty degrees. "Naomi. . . . " *Please, God, if they don't find her right away, put her into a deep sleep so she won't feel anything. So she won't feel fear or cold or pain. And especially, dear Lord, so she won't feel Mommy and Daddy abandoned her.* It just about killed me to think she might feel we didn't love her.

When Duane was finally brought out to the site at three in the morning, we held each other and cried.

Soon after, the sheriff drove us home to get Naomi's bed linens so the dogs could pick up her scent. There, in the baby crib, her little brown teddy bear waited. I couldn't watch as the men donned rubber gloves, removed her sheets and pillowcase, and placed them in a plastic bag.

With the coming of daylight, I just *knew* they would find Naomi. But as the hours ticked by and steady rain cast a dreary pall, I experienced an indescribable mental agony.

Eventually, my anguished prayers began to include, *Lord, I don't need to know the why of this. And whether I like the result or not, help me to accept it. But, Lord, most of all, I pray you will give Naomi peace in her little heart.*

By early afternoon on Saturday, almost twenty-four hours since Naomi had disappeared, hope dwindled for the more than 200 professionals and volunteers who were combing the forest. One more sweep and the searchers would abandon their efforts. Kip Clayton and his volunteer unit, the Habersham County High Angle Rescue Team, were making their final sweep when he led his search team to the outer limit of their assigned area. Reluctantly, he turned to start back but "something" told him to go an additional 250 yards. He did. "I turned and took two steps. She was lying five feet in front of me." Shocked, he yelled to his teammates, "I see her!"

Kip feared little Naomi was dead. She was lying so still, face down in wet leaves and mud. "Just as close up against a log as she could get." Then a tiny whimper—almost like a sigh—came from the little soaked body. "She's alive!" he shouted into the radio. "She's alive!"

At the same time, Al Stowers, a physician specializing in pediatric trauma medicine, who had recently received special training in hypothermia, arrived at the staging area to volunteer. Because the last search for Naomi was coming to an end, Dr. Stowers was turned away. Just as he put his car into gear and was about to drive away, someone ran toward him. "Don't leave. We've found her! She's alive!" Dr. Stowers reached the ambulance just in time to see it was a "load and go" situation. "I'm right behind you," he called out to the driver as they both sped off toward the local hospital.

In the patrol car, Duane and I heard Kip's shouts over the radio—"She's alive! She's alive!" Relief and gratitude filled my being. "Oh, Duane. She's alive."

"They're rushing her to an ambulance," an excited officer told us. "We'll meet them at St. Joseph!" We beat them
there.

As they hurried Naomi into the ER, I called out to the
little form in the huge cocoon of blankets, "Naomi, baby.
Mommy and Daddy are here. We love you!" We prayed.

The doctor pronounced Naomi's condition critical. She
was unconscious, swollen, and blue. Her temperature registered only 74 degrees; her heart rate just 70 beats per
minute. "I doubt if she could have survived out there
another two hours," Dr. Stowers told us.

Ordering warmed intravenous fluid for Naomi, Dr.
Stowers and the local medical team worked feverishly to
stabilize her enough for transport to Egleston Children's
Hospital in Atlanta for more intensive care. Dr. Stowers
asked the director of nurses, "Can you get me a pediatric
nurse to travel with us?" Gail Blankenship, a highly skilled
nurse with regular weekend duty in Atlanta, just
happened not to have left home for work.

An hour later, Sherrie, the respiratory specialist, sat at
Naomi's head, operating the breathing bag; an EMT at her
left checked equipment; Gail, the pediatric nurse, was at
Naomi's right, keeping the IV tubes functioning; and Dr.
Stowers, at her feet, watched the heart monitor. They
positioned me so I could talk to her and pat her little head,
barely visible above the heated-air blanket.

Naomi's temperature remained precariously low, and
she continued to be unresponsive. But when I gently laid
my index finger in her hand, she weakly, very weakly,
closed her little fingers around it. Midway to Atlanta,
Naomi's eyes fluttered, and she murmured, "Mama." We
all gasped. I continued to gently stroke her forehead,
whispering, "Naomi, baby. Mommy's here."

Then a faintly audible, "Mama, song."

I knew what she wanted. I started singing softly, "Jesus

loves me! This I know, for the Bible tells me so." Sherrie sang, too. And then, unbelievably, little Naomi—through swollen and chapped lips—tried to join in. I looked around at the circle. Dr. Stowers made no effort to hide the tears spilling down his face. Nor did we.

Dear Jesus, who loves Naomi, thank you, thank you, thank you!

On arrival at Egleston, Naomi's condition was still listed as critical. She was not yet fully conscious—indeed she slept through most of Sunday. But on Monday she woke up her normal self. As her dad laughingly describes it, "She perked right up and trashed the room." Later that day, she *walked* to the car. Our little family came home— together.

I can never say thank-you enough to all those who took time from their busy lives to rescue little Naomi. They have my undying gratitude and my prayers that they will be blessed beyond measure. I will never wonder whether or not God hears and answers prayers, for only God and his ministering angels could have orchestrated such a miraculous set of circumstances. Yes, he hears. And answers.

Mirna Whidden
as told to Gloria Cassity Stargel

Gertrude's Stuff

The best things in life aren't things.

Art Buchwald

"Thank you for putting up with my eccentricities," she said.

"Oh, I don't mind so much." *Tell the truth.* "There is one thing that kind of bothers me."

"Hum?"

"It's when you go through trash cans."

Silence.

"Why do you do that?"

"Well," she reasoned, "that's when people give me money. Five bucks. Twenty bucks, once."

Shrewd, I thought. *Not crazy.*

"Besides, I find lots of valuable stuff."

"Like what?"

She smiled a wide, toothless smile. "One time, I was diggin' around at the supermarket and I found a fast food bag with six packets of catsup in it!"

My great aunt Gertrude and I were sitting on her back porch, sorting through old papers, canned food, and cardboard that she had stashed in metal trash cans for safe-keeping. She was hunched over a feed sack filled with old mail. I studied the hand-knit orange hat she wore, in spite of the heat, to cover her matted gray hair. She had on a man's shirt. The breast pocket was stuffed with so many pencils and paper towels, they stayed put as she bent down.

For as long as anyone could remember, Aunt Gertrude was weird. She loved radios and telescopes, not cooking and sewing. She hadn't worn high heels since her gradua-tion from Parsons Junior College in 1936. She followed Edgar Cayce and other mystics down a path of woo-woo that caused our strict Methodist relatives to call her crazy. But by far her biggest sin was that she never threw any-thing away. Nowadays, what was "wrong" with Aunt Gertrude would be diagnosed as obsessive-compulsive disorder, and she would receive treatment for it; then, we just referred to her as eccentric and left her alone.

She had not asked for my help. In fact, she barely knew me. I started writing to her the day we buried my grand-mother. And she wrote back—volumes: life stories, bits of wisdom, journal entries. We had journaling in common. And we were both single women. Even though it was an unlikely friendship, my thirty-something to her eighty-something, we were kindred spirits. Later, she would tell me that she kept it going because, "You were the only one who hugged me at my sister's funeral." That small kind-ness would change my life.

A few years and many letters passed between us. Then Aunt Gertrude's across-the-street neighbor called me. "It's time," Joe said. "Someone in the family has got to come take her out of that house. She doesn't want to go." He was insistent. My aunt had stopped bathing after an army of court-ordered Boy Scouts with garbage bags convened in her yard to help bring her property into compliance with city code. An inexperienced volunteer driving a bulldozer broke the water line and Gertrude never had it fixed. She had taken to hauling water from the garden hose for drinking, cooking, and filling the toilet tank.

Joe and Janette had helped for as long as they could: delivering groceries, mowing her front yard, and inviting her for dinner. When Gertrude's license was revoked, they drove her to doctor's appointments—if she would clean up in their bathtub first.

The morning I made up my mind to leave Dallas, I talked to God. "I'll move to California to take care of my great-aunt; but, I want a dog, a house with a fenced yard, and a garden," then added, "and a partner." It was more of an ultimatum than a prayer. "I'll do this good deed, but I'm getting something I want out of it, okay, Almighty?" Of course, I was joking. I wanted to believe that we all have someone who will be there for us in our old age. For Gertrude, that someone was me.

My father came from Illinois to drive the moving truck the 1,500 miles to Roseville and to move me into a falling-down rented house that overlooked a horse pasture. A week later, Gertrude moved in with me.

For months, I worked by myself knee-deep in debris at Gertrude's house, sorting treasure from trash: old newspaper, *toss*; photograph of my mother as a baby, *save*. It was like an archaeological dig: layer upon layer of magazines, flat boxes filled with buttons and coins, watches, and dry pens. I unearthed letters from 1919 and Christmas cards from the Depression. I uncovered a nest of chicken eggs in the living room, about three feet down, vintage— early eighties if the newspaper stratum was accurate. More bags, boxes, old transistor radios, and acid-bubbled batteries.

And there were antiques, like prescriptions dated before printers and plastic, when headache remedies came in tins, nerve pills in wooden cylinders, and laxatives in blue glass bottles. Each Saturday the narrow path through the house widened. But at this rate we would both be dead before I finished.

One evening a man in my Bible study group announced that he was moving into a new apartment on Saturday and could use a hand. About eight people showed up—in no time the job was done. I knew then that I had to do the unthinkable: *ask for help.* At the next meeting, I explained that I had come to Roseville to be my great-aunt's caregiver and that she had filled her house with so much stuff it was uninhabitable. It was awful, dangerous work, but if anyone was available on Saturday, I would really appreciate help. I looked around the group and my nervousness subsided. They were smiling.

"Community Services is donating a Dumpster," I added. "I have maps . . . and if you come, bring work gloves." On the way home I bought extra garbage bags, dust masks, and bottles of water. *That wasn't too hard. But will anybody show up?*

On the designated day, I arrived early to open the house. I dragged a few full garbage bags to the Dumpster. Doubts crowded in. *You're asking too much.* I had been taught that it is better to give than it is to receive. Here I was, begging others to give to me. I sat on the crumbling front step, feeling guilty. *You couldn't handle Gertrude's stuff alone. You failed.*

At five minutes after ten, when I was sure that no one was coming, a car parked across the street. Peace swept over me as the first volunteer walked toward the house. Soon, another car arrived. Joy swelled up to tears. Then another pulled up. In a matter of minutes, twenty people were standing with me in Gertrude's front yard.

Maybe it is better to give than it is to receive. But I learned a valuable lesson that day. If you can put aside your pride and ask for what you need, when help comes it brings with it an unexpected blessing—love.

Ask. Receive. Could it be that simple? I asked God for a dog, a house with a fenced yard, a garden, and a partner. One month before I moved to help Gertrude, I was walking in the park when a stray puppy was run over by a car. As I carried the injured dog back to my apartment, someone offered to drive me the final mile. Two years later, I returned to Dallas with Aunt Gertrude to marry the man who had helped me. We live in a house with a fenced yard and that dog can jump it. The garden thing isn't working out too well. *God?*

Rhonda Richards-Cohen

Rock Island Angel

Nothing is as frightening as ignorance in action.

Johann Wolfgang von Goethe

"What if I forget my solo?" I said, practicing my ballet steps for the umpteenth time.

"Everyone has a guardian angel, Susie." Mom winked. "Your angel will guide your feet."

"Oh, Mom, you're just saying that to make me feel better." Still, I squeezed my eyes tight and tried to imagine what my angel would be like, probably graceful and light, dressed in white, with fluffy wings, and a halo. Oh, how I wanted to believe it was true.

Just like I'd wanted to believe that I would be the next Margot Fonteyn. She had been magical in the *Nutcracker Suite.* I was spellbound as the lights in the theater dimmed, the music swelled, and the curtain went up. From that moment, I dreamed of becoming a prima ballerina. So the next year, when I turned five, Mom enrolled me in Miss Daphne's School of Dance.

Finally, after ten years of classes, Miss Daphne took me

aside and said, "Susan, this will be your last recital with our studio. It's time you moved on to more serious lessons."

More serious lessons? Me? I was thrilled, of course, but it would mean traveling into the windy city of Chicago. That was almost an hour from our sleepy town of Tinley Park, so I'd have to take the train. To quell my nerves, Dad went along the first few times to show me the ropes. By the third trip, I was feeling quite grown-up, so I stated boldly, "You don't have to ride with me today. I can go by myself."

"I don't know. I'm not sure if I want my little girl alone in the big city."

"Aw, Dad, I'm not a baby anymore," I said as the train's whistle blew. "I'm fifteen now!"

My dad yelled out, "Be careful," as I hopped aboard and waved good-bye.

I easily found the dance studio and quickly changed into my black leotard, pink tights, and toe shoes. I stared at my reflection in the mirror as I drew my hair into a bun. *See, Dad, I told you I wasn't a baby.* I danced and got lost in the piano music, until, *tap, tap, tap,* Madame Bender clacked her cane against the wooden floor.

"That will be all for today. *Allez-vous en*—quickly now, go change."

With my head held high, I walked out of the studio; I was on my way to becoming the prima ballerina I'd always dreamed of. I made it about a block before I realized how dark it was. Suddenly the city was a spooky place, with lots of murky alleys and streets that all looked the same. My eyes darted from one street sign to the next. I wondered where the confident girl of this morning had gone. I tucked my fear inside my warm down jacket as I raced for LaSalle Street. It couldn't be much farther now!

Finally, I spotted the familiar sign "Rock Island Railroad" above the doors of the cavernous building. I just about cried as I hurried over to the ticket counter.

"One way to Tinley Park," I said in a small voice.

"That will be a dollar twenty-five."

I reached for the fare nestled safely in the bottom of my dance bag and gasped. My bag! Oh no, I must have left it at the studio! The ticket clerk drummed his fingers on the counter. I quickly stepped out of line, the red heat of embarrassment warming my cheeks.

Now what? It was dark outside. No way did I want to run all the way back to Wabash Avenue. Besides, I knew Madame Bender would be long gone. She'd rushed us all out of class. *"Vite, vite, cheries,"* she'd said, herding us out the door. She rushed me so much I'd left without my bag. An announcement crackled over the public address system, "The six fifteen to Tinley Park will be boarding on track three in fifteen minutes; fifteen minutes to boarding time."

My stomach somersaulted. That's my train! Throngs of people pushed around me in a rush to catch their trains. Then a terrible thought hit me. *What if this was the last train of the night?* I raced for the stairs. Should I just board and hope the conductor would let me slide? My temples throbbed as I plunked down on a bench and cried.

"What's the problem here, dearie?"

Startled, I looked up, swiping the tears from my eyes. A rumpled old man with bushy white hair sat down beside me. I shrank back. *Never talk to strangers.* Hadn't my parents always told me that? But I was desperate, and his deep blue eyes sparkled with compassion.

"I left my money at the dance studio, and my train is leaving soon. I don't even have change to call my parents, and we live way out in the suburbs." My chest heaved as I struggled to choke out the words between sobs.

"That ain't no problem. Let's just go over and get you a ticket. You'll be home in no time."

I wiped away the last of my tears as I studied the old man. His coat was shabby and his shoes had holes in them. It didn't look like he could afford a cup of coffee, let alone a train ticket. He looked like a street person—one of those poor homeless souls who huddled under the stairs and panhandled coins just to survive.

"C'mon, darlin', you can still make the train," he gestured with a gnarled hand.

What if he just wanted to lure me away from the crowds and then kidnap me?

Nah, he looked harmless. And those kind eyes. I felt safe, almost as if I were with my grandpop.

"Okay," I sniffled. True to his word, he shuffled up to the ticket counter.

"Where to, young lady?" he asked me, a crooked smile lighting his face.

"Tinley Park."

He turned to the agent. "One way to Tinley Park, please."

"That'll be a dollar twenty-five," the agent barked. He punched a button and sent the ticket shooting out of the slot.

The old man wheezed as he reached into the worn pocket of his trousers. I figured his hand would come up empty, then I'd be sunk. I stared intently, willing the money to appear. He slowly pulled out coin after coin, counting each one before sliding them under the window.

He turned and handed me the ticket. "Here you go, honey." His blue eyes shimmered, and I felt warm all over. "Now get on that train and get home safe."

I tucked the ticket safely into my pocket, trembling with relief. "I don't know how to thank you mister...." I looked up. He was gone! I turned in a slow circle, searching the station, but he was nowhere to be seen.

With hardly a moment to spare, I collapsed onto a seat

on the train, then it hit me. Mom was right. I really did have a guardian angel. He wasn't anything like I'd imagined. No fluffy wings or halo. And definitely not dressed in white. But he was there for me just when I needed him.

Susan A. Karas

Good Samaritans in Disguise

*K*indness *makes a fellow feel good, whether it's being done to him or by him.*

Frank A. Clark

"Al, you better watch that tank." My mother smiled at my father and motioned toward the gas gauge. "You know you're not used to this new car yet."

"Honey, relax. I know what this baby can do," my dad replied, pacifying my mother and applying more pressure on the accelerator. He was driving our new dual exhaust 1955 tan and white Ford Fairlane. How he loved that dual exhaust. I ignored the banter between my parents. I was lost in my own little world, my blond hair flying in my face, pretending I was Annie Oakley. I had on my red cowgirl hat and my new leather holster, complete with cap gun, as we sped down the highway. We were cruising across the big state of Texas on our way to California when the car gave a gasp, coughed, and coasted to a stop.

"Are we out of gas, honey?" my mother asked.

"Sure sounds that way, but I could have sworn we'd get better mileage than this. Yup, it's on empty. We've got ourselves a problem," my father replied. That was the under-statement of the century. Cotton fields lined both sides of the highway as far as the eye could see. They seemed to go on for miles. We hadn't seen a car for a very long time, and we'd passed the last town an hour ago. "Don't you worry your pretty head," my dad said, looking at me. "Someone will be along soon." But he didn't sound very sure about that. My father got out and put the car's hood up. "This will let them know we're in trouble," he explained to me.

My mother proceeded to produce a snack of homemade chocolate chip cookies. Her solution to any problem was comfort food. After about an hour, we saw dust in the distance. A car was fast approaching, going the same direction we were. My father jumped to his feet, waving his arms wildly. He smiled as the car got closer. In my cowgirl mind, I thought he wanted them to know we were the friendly hombres, not the bad guys out to do them harm. I think, in reality, he was just secretly pleased to see another soul on this lonely highway.

My father swore softly under his breath as the car tooted its horn and whizzed on by. What had started for me as a fun adventure, pretending to be Annie Oakley stranded in the badlands, was now becoming a tad scary. Dusk was approaching and we had been sitting a couple of hours. Then we heard it. A faint noise in the distance.

It sounded like men singing at the top of their lungs. It got louder, and pretty soon we saw a beat-up old truck meandering slowly down the highway toward us. The whole truck seemed to float along surrounded by songs sung in Spanish, punctuated by lots of exuberant whoops and hollers.

"Get in the car immediately and lock your door," my mother instructed me sternly. "Al, you better get in here, too. We can't be too careful out here in the middle of nowhere." My father just stood by the car door, tension making the veins on his forehead stand up and salute.

The wooden-sided truck came to a halt right beside him. Mom and I held our breath. Would they hold us up? What would happen to us? We were at their mercy.

"*¿Habla Español?*" the driver called out his window at my father.

"No," my father shouted back, shaking his head.

Through gesturing and some small English pronouns, my father managed to convey that we needed a ride to a gas station. The next thing I knew, my mother and I were sitting inside the truck next to the driver, and my father was in the back riding with the men. They sang us all the way to the nearest town, twenty-five miles back down the road they had just come.

We pulled into the gas station, and one of the men lifted me down from the truck. He offered my mother his hand as she stepped down onto the floorboard. "*Gracias,*" I said, the only word I knew in Spanish. His eyes lit up and he smiled.

My father thanked them profusely and offered to give each man some money. None of them would take a dime. My dad asked the man at the gas station, who spoke some Spanish, to tell them he really wanted to repay them. When he did, they all laughed and shook their heads no. The gas station owner said they were very proud men, even though they labored in the fields all day under the hot Texas sun.

We expected them to leave, but they sat and waited while my father filled an old container with a couple gallons of gas. When he finished, they motioned for us to get back into the truck. My father gave the owner a puzzled look.

He laughed. "It's dark and they want to make sure you get back to your car safely, so they're driving you back."

We rumbled back down the highway to our car. The last we saw them, they were singing and driving away into the night. When I look over my pictures from that trip, I see a young girl in an Annie Oakley hat with a holster at her side who learned a valuable lesson that day. There are Good Samaritans everywhere, even if they come disguised in an old pickup truck.

Sallie A. Rodman

Full Circle

The true meaning of life is to plant trees, under whose shade you do not expect to sit.

Nelson Henderson

We'd been roaming the city for hours, dragging heavy suitcases and anxiously searching for a place to stay. It was July 7, 2005, and eighteen members of my church and I were on our way home to New York from a mission trip in Nairobi, Kenya. After an eight-hour flight, we touched down at Heathrow Airport, ready for a few days of rest in London before continuing on to New York. We were tired, and now we were frightened. Just a few hours earlier, as we were riding toward King's Cross station on the Piccadilly subway line, what locals call "the tube," everything ground to a halt.

Workers urgently directed us to evacuate the subway immediately. Confused, we joined the throng of passengers crushing out the doors and emerging onto the streets. There, hundreds of others, also evacuated from their trains, ran up and down the sidewalks. It looked like a scene from an action movie. Sirens blared and traffic tangled in all directions. *Dear Lord, what has happened here?* I wondered.

"What's going on?" I asked everyone I saw.

"A bomb!" someone said.

"Terrorist bombings," another passerby explained, his eyes wide. "One bomb blew up a double-decker bus. Another went off at the King's Cross station."

King's Cross—that was where we had been headed! We were only a handful of stops away. If we had been a few minutes earlier, our trip would have taken a sudden, tragic turn.

The subways were down, all buses had stopped running, and taxis and car rentals were nowhere to be found. After walking and lugging our bags for hours, we realized there was no way we could get across town to our hotel. We needed some place to rest, regroup, and touch base with our families across the Atlantic. With the afternoon waning, we'd have to settle for anything we could find.

"Do you have any rooms?" I asked over and over, my voice growing hoarse. We were turned away everywhere. We found vacancies only in large hotels with sky-high prices, far out of reach on our modest budget. When we passed a small local hotel—Cromwell Crown Hotel— something told me to give it a try.

"We've been wandering for hours," I told the lady behind the desk. "We've just returned from a mission trip in Kenya and we're very tired. Can you help us?"

As I explained my plight to the desk clerk, a man stepped next to me, seemingly out of nowhere. His expressive dark eyes revealed that he understood our predicament. "What can you afford?" he asked.

"Not much," I replied soberly.

He looked at us thoughtfully for a moment and then nodded. "I can help."

I didn't quite believe it. "Thank you very much. We're

very grateful," I said, finally releasing my heavy bags.

But his response surprised me. "No, I am grateful. It is my turn to help you," he said. "You see, I am from Kenya."

It had been an honor to serve in Kenya, and we had been more than compensated by the loving gratitude of the people we helped there. But through this man's generosity, we were shown again that our efforts had mattered. We marveled that we were led to just the right hotel and, even half a world away, to someone from Kenya who had reached out and helped us. Just when we needed it most, when the city's peace was shattered and our nerves were raw, we felt God's touch and blessing.

Harry Heintz as told to Peggy Frezon

A Child's Gift

It is not fair to ask of others what you are unwilling to do yourself.

Eleanor Roosevelt

About a year ago, I was volunteering at a home for elderly women. On this particular day as I prepared to leave for the home, the telephone rang. For a fleeting moment I toyed with the idea of not answering it, but I ran back to the kitchen anyway.

It was my husband. "Sorry, honey, but I have to work overtime. Guess you'll just have to pick up Taylor after school. I'll be home as soon as I can."

Each week I set aside several hours to bring a little joy into the lives of the elderly women. Today I was bringing freshly cut red and yellow snapdragons and mammoth zinnias. As I gathered the bouquets to carry them to the car, I decided that rather than find a babysitter, I would take Taylor with me to visit with the residents.

With my unexpected companion, we started our rounds. After Taylor and I had visited the third or fourth woman, I noticed that just as we were ready to leave each room, my son would hug each woman and whisper something in her ear. Because I wanted to make sure that we had enough time to visit all of the residents, I didn't stop to ask him what he was whispering; but he elicited a huge smile from every lady.

Later that evening, during dinner, my husband asked how my volunteer job worked out with our son in tow.

"It was actually lots of fun," I said. "We were quite a pair. Whatever Taylor said to the ladies, it definitely made them happy." As I stood up to clear the dishes, I stopped and glanced across the table at our son. "What was it that you whispered?"

Looking up at both his dad and me, with his big brown eyes and angelic face, he responded, "I whispered, 'I love you Grandma. And I just wanted you to know that you look soooooo beautiful today.'"

I asked Taylor why he did that.

He responded, "I just knew it would make them feel good."

Pamela Strome-Merewether

Santa's Elves

The best place to find a helping hand is at the end of your own arm.

Swedish Proverb

When my husband and I first met, I was an anti-Christmas Scrooge. I associated the season with negative baggage from my past. Brian, on the other hand, had a great Christmas family; everyone decorated and the holidays were a special time. When we fell in love, it was time to leave my inner Scrooge behind.

Each Christmas Brian strung outdoor lights on every inch of the house, and we decorated a tree that reached our thirteen-foot ceilings. Faithfully, we claimed a couple of tags from the Salvation Army's Angel Tree or bought toys for the Toys for Tots campaign. I would pick a girl, and Brian would pick a boy. All very impersonal and "safe."

One year an eight-year-old named Latisha had written "piano," "piano," "piano" for her three choices on her Angel card. When I saw that, I felt the Scrooge within shift. Each year since, I imagined the look on Latisha's face when she unwrapped an electronic keyboard (sorry,

Mom) on Christmas morning. She'd be on her way to college by now, and I wonder if she really learned how to play that piano.

In one of those dot.com boom years, we were feeling flush with an unexpected windfall of a few extra dollars at Christmastime. Not having children of our own, we decided to splurge and make the holidays really special for some kids who wouldn't otherwise have a Christmas. It was time to close that "safe" distance. I wanted to feel more connected to the kids whose name we picked. Ideally, we wanted to "adopt" a family who knew the real meaning behind Christmas. Although we didn't want to send a message that Christmas was only about things, we understood that children expect Santa to visit on Christmas. As luck would have it, we got just what we asked for. (Santa was already at work.)

We live in an affluent county in Florida. It's a generous community, rich (no pun intended) with philanthropic individuals and organizations. When my friend Anne discovered the Youth Activity Center (YAC), an after school and summer program serving children from low-income families, she knew that people within the community could make a difference for these financially strapped families. When she called and asked if I could marshal my coworkers for a mission, I found many willing volunteers.

First, we got a list of the names, genders, sizes, and ages of the over one hundred children YAC served, as well as any brothers and sisters in the home. Next, we decided that every child would get a complete outfit of new clothes, shoes, socks, and at least one toy. We made up our own angel tree and strategically located cards around our building for employees to take. For example, one person would buy shoes for Miguel, another would buy him pants and a shirt, while another employee would purchase the toy. Within a week, boxes and bags began to accumulate, so I set about organizing and logging who got what to be sure every child got something.

A week before our "wrap and tag marathon," I went over the list of items received, grabbed my Christmas-loving husband, and headed for the stores to take care of what we still needed. Our first hurdle was figuring out how the sizes and the ages worked together. One card said a ten-year-old boy wore a "YS," another ten-year-old specified a "boy's large," yet another twelve-year-old boy needed a size "13 husky." Would a men's small work? How can a size 13 shoe fit an eight-year-old?

Flustered, we decided to tackle the fun stuff first—*toys!* Armed with the List, we walked through the doors of Toys "R" Us. Now this was Santa's workshop! My toy-deprived childhood was in for a healing, while Brian's challenge was buying for the kids—not himself.

After exercising our elf muscles and filling two carts full of toys, we loaded up the car and hit Payless Shoes. A very helpful salesperson explained the mystery of children's shoes sizes and produced a handy sizing chart, which confirmed that Brian and I weren't the only befuddled ones. We quickly made our selections: well-made athletic shoes that the kids would surely outgrow before the shoes wore out. My eyes kept drifting to cute pairs of pink-glittered sneakers with light-up heels, but I knew they were too impractical.

Inspired by our mission, the manager of the store gave us a hefty discount on our purchases; I scurried back down the aisle and grabbed a couple pairs of pink-glittered sneakers.

At Target our strategy was simple; we'd start with the easy stuff (we thought) in the baby/infant aisles and then find our rhythm.

Leave it to marketing geniuses to turn a tiny, little bum into dozens of choices and sizes for diapers, or the need to feed into a plethora of formulas and supplements. As I headed for the cute little onesies, I spotted Brian, a man who could navigate thousands of permutations of screws and bolts in the Home Depot, staring mystified at shelves full of baby stuff. Finally, a compassionate mom with a baby in her cart took pity on Brian and helped him sort through the list of babies in the YAC families. In no time they figured out what the mothers of those infants would appreciate and need.

Our nemeses still waited, all dolled up and merchandised for the holidays—the boys, and girls, apparel departments. I skirted the perimeter, picking up inexpensive watches, jewelry, and purses that I knew any ten- to fifteen-year-old would love. Next, I chose disposable cameras for the sixteen- to eighteen-year-olds—hey, I was kicking it—until Brian came down the aisle pushing a cart full of diapers and formula, wanting to know how I was doing with this age/size thing.

Finally, we devised a plan to defeat the bumbleheads who didn't make it easy for children-challenged shoppers—we'd buy a few of every size and take the pile back to the office and let some children-savvy moms figure out which child should get what size and style. We grabbed more carts and started pillaging racks and shelves. We thought it strange no one seemed to notice us. When we arrived at the checkout with four carts overflowing with merchandise, we discovered why we hadn't attracted any attention with our multiple carts: we weren't alone. An aisle or two over, a man was swiping his credit card for six shopping carts full of clothes and toys. Beyond that a man who looked like a coach was emptying two carts full of workout pants and shirts. Elf fever was epidemic!

Over the next few days, I sorted through the YAC families list. I mixed and matched to be sure that every child had multiple gifts from Santa. We added gift certificates from the supermarket and some books for the parents. The Saturday before the party at YAC, we had our wrap and tag marathon at work. We wrapped hundreds of boxes and tagged them with the name of each recipient. All the gifts were bagged according to family and loaded into large gaylord shipping containers. A pallet jack maneuvered them into the truck that would be Santa's sleigh the following Wednesday.

At the appointed time, the big blue truck from JBD Delivery, followed by cars of my coworkers, pulled up to the small trailer that served as an office, classroom, and meeting area for YAC. Jimmy rolled up the back door of his truck, and we began to uncrate and organize all the families' goodies. We put on our elf hats, our reindeer ears, and popped some holiday music into the CD player. We strung decorations and put out food and beverages. We had asked the program staff to tell the adults to come to the office before picking up their children. We had also asked that the kids be kept busy on the other side of the park so they didn't see what was going on and thereby ruin their Christmas morning surprise.

As each adult arrived at the office, we explained that the presents were gifts from a caring community, then loaded the bags into their trunks and vans. One grandmother who spoke no English, sat on a chair surrounded by bags bearing the names of the six grandchildren she cared for. One of our bilingual employees knelt beside her and asked if there was anything wrong. Tears welled up in her eyes. In Spanish she told him, "Before I came here, I had nothing . . . nothing . . . to give to my babies, but now . . . all of this! God bless you!"

A young woman arrived, very pregnant and very stressed, probably thinking that she had been asked to stop by the office because of some problem. When she walked in and was given her family's gift bags, she dropped onto a chair and cried. She had been upset at having to chose between serving a Christmas dinner or giving one gift to each of her children. This situation was turning what should have been a joyous holiday season into a stressful time and was making this mom sick.

We felt good knowing we had done something worthwhile as we bid one another good-bye after the last child had been picked up and the last bags had been delivered. Some of us headed to our homes, others left to finish shopping for family and friends who maybe had all they needed, but not all we wanted them to have.

That was the Christmas I banished the inner Scrooge for good. Turns out I didn't need expensive therapy, and I didn't need to spend hours pouring my heart out in a support group. All I had to do to enjoy the true spirit of Christmas and have a festive holiday was to be one of Santa's elves.

I'm a ranking member of the Elf Corps today. To the extent we can afford it, Brian and I continue the tradition of giving each year, knowing that even small gestures make a world of difference in a time of need.

Theresa Peluso

Some Enchanted Evening

A day can seem so empty without the opportunity of making a difference in the life of one more person.

Ellie Braun-Haley

Norma, our sixty-five-year-old neighbor, was born with cerebral palsy. She was an only child and lived with her mother and father until their deaths. At the time of her mother's death, Norma was fifty-three and still able to walk around the house and go on outings. Her mother had made sure that the home was handicapped-accessible and that Norma knew about the family finances.

Norma wanted to continue living at home, and with no immediate family left nearer than ninety miles, she was in charge. She went to bed when she wanted, got up when she wanted, and ate what she wanted, which included ice cream and candy for breakfast. Her life was a dream for any kid.

Norma's mother died when my son, Justin, was only five. His grandmother, who lived across the street from Norma, began helping her with light household chores.

Norma quickly became part of our extended family, and she and Justin began a relationship that would extend for the next twelve years. Norma joined our holiday and birthday celebrations. She dressed in her Christmas sweater, and her eyes danced around the room, watching as the children opened their gifts. She acted like a child herself when her lap was full with her own presents.

Norma enjoyed taking drives to look at the houses decorated for the holidays, but she felt it wasn't appropriate for her to decorate her home because her mother had died during the holiday season. The November that Justin became a teenager Norma's ideas about decorating changed.

Justin visited Norma once or twice a week, and he talked her into decorating just a little. No tree inside, but maybe lights outside. A little gradually turned into a beautifully decorated house with pine wreaths, clear lights, and red ribbons. Admirers of her decorations sent Norma Christmas cards, and she continued to add a little more to the decorations each year. One year she announced that she would buy an artificial tree and a Nativity set. With her cleaning lady's help, Norma decorated her house. My husband installed a switch that lit her tree, which she sat by every night.

As the years passed, Norma became more dependent on our family for her day-to-day needs. Justin entered high school, and as with most teenagers and parents, we had our differences, after which he would disappear for hours. But I never worried that he was running away or getting into trouble. He always went to Norma's house and spent time with her. As he complained about our rules, or how we were treating him, Norma would listen and tell him how good he had it and that he should be ashamed to complain. He never became angry with her or argumentative. Some nights after they talked, Norma was sure he would never return. But a few nights would pass and she would hear the garage door open and know that her friend was back.

I realized the strength of their relationship when on New Year's Eve 1999, the eve of the next century, my seventeen-year-old spent the evening with Norma. After my nightly ritual of putting her to bed, he went over for a visit. They ordered pizza, popped popcorn, watched the world usher in 2000 on television, and just before the stroke of midnight they "cracked open" a bottle of Sprite to celebrate. Norma was elated that she had had her own New Year's Eve party with a young man.

In March, Justin's high school Thespian troupe was performing *South Pacific*, Norma's favorite musical, and Justin decided she needed to get out of the house and go to one of the shows. On the appointed Saturday evening, she was ready and excited. My husband escorted her to the auditorium, placed her on the chairlift, and found seats for us at the end of the aisle. When the stage lights went up, she was captivated, listening carefully to every song, her knee bouncing to the rhythm of "Bloody Mary" and her eyes glistening when they performed a rendition of "Some Enchanted Evening."

She recognized Justin onstage by his smile and watched every movement he made. After the show, we joined the crowd edging toward the lobby. At the top of the chairlift stood Justin, waiting in the crowd to meet her. When she reached the top of the stairs, Justin bent down and hugged her and knelt gently by Norma's chair to ask how she enjoyed the performance. That evening was her last social outing. In late May she was admitted to the hospital for surgery and passed away a few days into June.

I am reminded of her often, especially when I look at the collage of pictures on my refrigerator. In the middle is a picture taken the Saturday before she was admitted to the hospital. It is one of a couple ready for a night out on the town, Justin in his prom tuxedo and Norma in her leopard print pajamas, smiling as though she were going to the prom with her "special" young man.

Ellen Bolyard

Compassion on Wheels

If you can't feed a hundred people, then feed just one.

Mother Teresa

On this sultry morning, my delivery partner and I wait outside the church kitchen to pick up the food we'll deliver for Meals on Wheels. We watch volunteers in white aprons and plastic gloves plop fried chicken, mashed potatoes, and green beans into Styrofoam trays. Then Bev and I load the hot and cold containers into the trunk of her car. We will take the food to low-income residents in mobile home parks, and witness lifestyles that make us grateful for our blessings.

Our first delivery is to a woman confined to a wheelchair. "Have you decided on your operation yet?" Bev asks cheerfully.

"The doctors insist I have gangrene and they say I need surgery soon. But I can't justify having my other leg amputated," she replies.

We find our next shut-in asleep on the couch, next to her table of medications. I leave a hot meal that will soon grow cold and put the chilled food in the refrigerator.

Next, we deliver to an elderly couple whose trailer is so stuffed with clutter it looks like a thief ransacked it during the night. We're concerned for their safety in this fire hazard they call home.

The sun blazes high overhead when we deliver to a frail lady who hobbles with her cane to the door.

"My son and his wife live in California," she explains. "They want to visit me, but they have jobs, you know." She complains about the heat and the annoying squeak of the rusty fan.

"Do you have any ice cream today?" she asks.

"I'm afraid ice cream would melt on a day like today," answers Bev.

"I really need some ice cream in this heat. My neighbors are gone, and I can't find anyone to bring me some."

"What kind do you like?" I ask.

"Chocolate," she replies, as if there is no other flavor. A smile spreads across her wrinkled face. "My doctor told me I should eat chocolate ice cream and drink ginger ale whenever I can."

"That's the kind of doctor to have," I reply as we leave.

An hour later, after all the meals are delivered, Bev and I return the empty containers to the church.

As I drive toward my errands, visions of the shut-ins flood my mind. I realize these people are fortunate to have food, shelter, and the family members whose framed portraits adorn their shelves. But I'm concerned about their struggles with health problems, uncomfortable living conditions, and loneliness.

Suddenly, I decide to abandon my errands. I drive to a grocery store and buy a gallon of chocolate ice cream and three six-packs of ginger ale. I have one more delivery.

Perspiration trickles down my face as I knock on the door of the humble trailer. I wait for the lonely lady inside to lean on her cane and open the door. When I show her the goodies inside the bags, her eyes sparkle with delight.

On this sultry day, this little lady is happy as she follows her doctor's orders—eat chocolate ice cream and drink ginger ale whenever she can.

Miriam Hill

Dawn

*Live as if you were to die tomorrow. Learn as if
you were to live forever.*

Gandhi

We originally met as nurse and patient years ago. Then
we started seeing each other at our kids' sporting events.
As multiple sclerosis took its toll on my body, I had to put
my RN career on hold. With the nurse/patient relationship
no longer an awkward barrier, we started hanging out.
Soon, we were undoubtedly the oddest looking pair in
town. For two years, three days a week, we'd get our children off to school, then meet, and have breakfast at a local
coffee shop. There, we would solve world problems, discuss local politics, giggle, and gossip. Our presence was
always met with stares, often with shock, and occasionally
pity. Dawn, just thirty years old, was losing her long battle
with breast cancer. She was bloated by steroids, pale and
pasty from radiation, and bald from chemo. I was also
young, pale, gaunt, and weak, riding an electric wheelchair, or dragging my body around with Lofstrand
crutches. Yet, we found each other hilarious and a

welcome break from all the emotional, mental, and physical stress that illness can bring.

New Hampshire's cold wintry holidays had just passed and we were in the midst of a winter thaw. My buddy and I were leaving the restaurant after a heady discussion on the trip we were about to take, when suddenly Dawn ducked behind me.

"Quick, hide me. There's my mother."

I giggled and shielded her from view. It wasn't that Dawn disliked her mother. She just didn't want to divulge where we were headed lest the woman dissolve into tears. Moms are like that when their daughters are dying.

For the past few months, I had been driving us around town, since Dawn reluctantly agreed that her driving days were past. The cancer that began in her breast six years ago and seemingly had been in remission had accelerated rapidly to include bone, lung, and brain. Some days she didn't even know me. Within three months she had declined from doing town errands and driving to being cared for. I had noticed her shortened attention span, brief episodes of cognitive impairment, and confusion even before she had been informed of brain metastasis. With that new diagnosis came a grave prognosis. It wasn't until today and our previous conversation in the restaurant that Dawn was prepared to deal with end-of-life issues.

"Thank you for helping me with this," Dawn said as I pulled the van into the church's parking lot.

"That's what friends are for," I said hoarsely.

We met the assistant pastor. He knew us well, both being active members in his congregation, but he was clearly surprised at my friend's rapid physical decline. "What do you need help with, Dawn?" he asked.

"My funeral," she said, bluntly. There was an awkward silence.

Slowly, painstakingly, we worked out the details. Dawn

seemed even more confused and detached than she had been an hour before. I reminded her of the Bible readings she selected and songs that she desired to be sung at the service. The reverend's eyes were glistening when he said, "I have seen many things, have heard many stories in this office, but never have I seen the bravery and support of two greater friends. You both are vessels filled with the Holy Spirit."

The following day after the children left for school, I met with Dawn, her husband, Doug, and the home hospice nurse. When the time came, Dawn would live out her final days at home surrounded by friends and family. After the nurse and Doug left, I tried to tidy up the kitchen table, but my body was weak and the dishes slipped from my grasp. As I bent to pick up the broken shards of glass, an even greater crash came from the other room. Dawn had fallen.

We worked together, me leaning back on my crutches for leverage, Dawn grasping the heavy couch. It took a good fifteen minutes to raise Dawn from the floor and ease her onto the couch. Then I called her husband and said she could no longer be alone.

With my nursing background, pastoral care visits to the homebound, hospital visitations, and grief counseling experience, you would think that the parting with my friend would have been smooth and graceful. It wasn't. I was subject to sudden bursts of anger at God, feelings of inadequacy for not being able to help with her physical care, deep depression, and an impending sense of doom and gloom. I was losing a beautiful, wonderful friend in the worst way possible.

When I told her that in spirit she would always be around to watch her kids grow up . . . and that love is eternal and never dies . . . it sounded rehearsed and hollow. When she would whisper, "I love you so very much," my tears would start. She would be visibly pained at my struggle, and then she'd try to reassure me with, "I will miss you."

During a particularly intense exchange, I asked Dawn if just once in a while she would look down on me from heaven and help me on this life journey. With this request, my now-blind Dawn turned her head toward my voice and with perfectly focused eyes looked straight at me and replied, "No!"

Then we both started laughing. Soon, we both began to sob. After a while I tried again. "Please?"

"No," she teased. And so we went off again. Laughter was our signature through sickness, funeral arrangements, and end-stage blindness.

Just a few days prior to her death, Dawn whispered that she had just seen a friend from her cancer support group (who had died months before). Then she said that Jesus was in the room. I told her that both her friend and Jesus would help her pass when she was ready. I asked her if she understood me. She said yes. This was the last conversation we had. She slipped into a coma.

Home alone with my thoughts, I cried and sobbed, wailed and shouted. I thought of distancing myself to save my own health, but I could not. The winter thaw was over, and cold air returned. I tossed and turned in bed, unable to turn off morose thoughts. And then, finally, sleep came. And with sleep came a dream so vivid it seemed real.

In my dream, I was at home serving tea to four women about my age and their many children. It must have been about time for the school bus to arrive, because three of the women left to help their kids into their winter coats. One woman, however, stayed to help me clean up the table. While we picked up dishes, she gave me a litany of her problems. She went on and on, until I felt ready to burst. I wanted to shout that she truly didn't know what real problems were. But she rattled on and on and on. The other women and all the children were gone . . . I was left alone with this annoying woman.

Then I heard a familiar laugh. I looked up, and on my couch sat Dawn. She was young, slim, healthy, and radiant. Her hair was thick and full with golden ringlets tight around her face. She was wearing a sparkling white gown that flowed over her perfect, trim body. She had an amazing big smile and confident twinkling eyes.

"Friends," she said with a pure chuckle, "you sure know how to pick 'em."

I awoke to an early morning phone call. Doug wanted me to come to their home as soon as possible. He sounded lost and sad. I heard sobbing in the background. "Is she gone?" I asked softly.

"Yes," he mumbled. "Just a few moments ago."

As I trudged up toward Dawn's house one last time, snow began to fall. Noises became muffled; the surrounding air silent. And as I held Dawn's still warm hand, I sensed love and new beginnings. For the first time, in a long time, I felt peace.

Diana M. Amadeo

The Heart of San Francisco

If the world seems cold to you, kindle fires to warm it.

Lucy Larcom

Recently, one Monday afternoon, I found myself walking the colorful streets of downtown San Francisco. The sun was shining, the sky cloudless and unsullied, thanks to a chill, gusting wind that made me tighten my baseball cap and stuff my hands into my trouser pockets for warmth.

My wife, Sally, and I were on the first day of a vacation trip that would take us to the Napa Valley wine country. Wine tasting is not one of our favored activities. Instead, we were looking forward to a few rounds of golf and spa activities in weather that would be warmer than we could expect at home under the Central Coast's early summer marine layer of fog.

That morning I had stuffed my wallet at the ATM in our hometown of Pacific Grove, about 135 miles south of the city. We would be meeting our San Francisco-based older son for dinner at a pricey restaurant once evening rolled

around, but we had driven into town early to give ourselves time for window shopping and savoring the sights
and sounds of our favorite California metropolis. We split
up after lunch, Sally to browse the emporiums near Union
Square, while I meandered to our Post Street hotel, making a few purchases of predinner snacks and a bottle of
wine to share with our son before claiming our reserved
table at the restaurant downstairs.

My route took me through the neighborhood known as
the Tenderloin. For the unaware, the term comes from the
brawling days of yore when the police were paid extra to
patrol this area of high crime and lowlife. These days,
according to the guidebooks, the streets are not as clean as
you might wish, and a number of homeless sleep in door-
ways if they are not awake and panhandling. Were I to
write my own guidebook, I would encourage tourists to
stroll the area and enjoy its mix of classy bars, ethnic restaurants, evening jazz locations, mom-and-pop markets, corner sandwich stops, and theatrical sites. If there are
mentally-disabled wanderers, dope peddlers, and prosti-
tutes, they are not obvious to me. On this occasion I got a
chuckle out of a panhandler's cardboard sign that said, "I'll
be honest. I'm just looking for money to cover a few beers."

I had strolled just beyond the upper fringe of the
Tenderloin, at Post and Mason streets across from the
Donatello Hotel, when a sudden wind gust ripped my cap
from my head. I jerked my hands from my pockets in a
vain attempt at catching my cap, and with my left hand
out came my bulging wallet, which I always carry in a
front rather than a hip pocket for comfort and security. I
watched in helpless horror as the wind-borne billfold dis-
gorged its wad of greenbacks and other contents that
swirled in the howling wind before descending yards
away to scuttle down the sidewalk, gutter, and lightly
trafficked street.

I retrieved my hat and empty wallet first, and was wondering how many bills I could chase down, when the parade began. One person handed me the plastic window inserts that had separated from the billfold. A young boy and his younger sister approached me to return my Medicare card and my secondary insurance card that had been doing cartwheels in the gutter. Then came a stream of pedestrians, young and old, male and female, clutching twenty-dollar bills and handing them to me. I uttered a stream of thank-yous and stuffed the bills into my pockets. Last in the parade was a street person I had seen a block or two down the hill I had been climbing.

"Hold on there, my man," she shouted, waving her right hand that held a couple of bills in it. She was dressed rather shabbily, but I focused on her broad smile and the gold tooth gleaming in the lower jaw of her mahogany face. As she approached me, she said, "I found these two twennies blowin' down the road near Taylor Street. I guess you're the litterbug been fouling our streets with filthy lucre."

She handed me the bills, and I tried to give her back one of them. "No, honey, I accepts handouts, but I don't get fat on people's misfortunes. Don't you be givin' away twenny-dollar bills, unless you richer than you look."

I found two singles among the returned bills and pressed them on her with heartfelt, mumbled expressions of gratitude. "Well, that I can gratefully accept," she said. "Now you have yourself a very nice day. And come see me whenever you're in town. I don't stray much from where you first saw me."

A few minutes later I was in my hotel room at the Kensington Park, rummaging in my pockets to assess my financial loss and its effect on our plans for our vacation in the Wine Country. My credit cards and ATM card had fortunately remained in their wallet slots. I had withdrawn

$200 from the ATM that morning and remember having had a couple of twenties and some singles before making the withdrawal. Now, I had twelve, twenty-dollar bills. As nearly as I could calculate, I had not lost a thing except a scrap of paper with some phone numbers that had been in one of the wallet windows, and the two singles I had given to the gold-toothed street lady.

I have no idea whether those other honest and kind people who returned my money were San Franciscans or out-of-town visitors like me, but my faith in humanity moved up several notches, and my affection for what the late Herb Caen used to call Baghdad by the Bay is renewed and redoubled.

My son, wife, and I marveled at my good fortune as we munched hors d'oeuvres before dining that evening downstairs in the Farallon restaurant, under the glowing medusa jellyfish. Still unable to believe my good fortune and the honesty and kindness of people, I tipped the waiter more than my customary amount.

Kerry M. Wood

Wishing to Do More

*It's not how much we give but how much love
we put into giving.*

Mother Teresa

It is said that helping one in need can bring the benefactor great fulfillment. Although I have often found this to be true, it was on a memorable day in Sao Paulo, Brazil, when I met a pair of young brothers whose life struggles left me wishing I could do more to help others.

It all began on what seemed like a normal Sunday afternoon. While we were waiting in the endlessly long grocery line, a young thin boy approached my husband, Joao. He stood with a package of ground beef in his hands as he asked Joao something and then walked away.

Curious, I inquired what the boy wanted. Joao regretfully relayed that the boy wanted him to buy the beef for his family. In Brazil it is not uncommon for a child to beg for money. The problem is that some kids have found this an easy way to get things they want and may not even need to beg. Therefore, people are selective about giving.

"I should have just accepted," he said, shaking his

head. "It was only five reais." (About $2.00.)

I could see how sad turning the boy away had made him feel. Because he was asking for food, and not money, we decided to help out. So Joao brought the boy back to stand in line with us.

Seeing him up close, I noticed a large pink scar on his left cheek. Baggy white shorts and a white shirt hung from his tiny frame. Atop his head rested a white ball cap he had undoubtedly found in the trash.

To break the awkward silence, Joao brought up the ever-popular subject of futebol (soccer). We discovered that Bruno was a good player and had won a few trophies, which he had sold to buy the new tennis shoes that he modestly wore upon his feet.

Because the line was not shrinking quickly, we had an opportunity to learn a lot about this fourteen-year-old. He pointed out his shy younger brother who was waiting by the door with a bag of a few items some other people had graciously purchased for them.

Bruno was the oldest of six kids, all being raised by a single mother, who worked as a housekeeper. Bruno's father had died a few years back while attempting to rob a truck containing food. Since he was the oldest, and his mom worked, Bruno rarely attended school. Instead he remained home to care for his younger siblings. Bruno spoke of these hardships in a nonchalant fashion, for it was all he knew of life.

However, a little smile crossed his face as he proudly announced that he had been on television before. Expecting it was due to soccer, we inquired about his fame. To our surprise it was for a much more heroic reason. His family lived in an area of very poor living conditions, which had caught on fire. Bruno had braved the flames of their home to rescue his baby sister. In the process, he had been burned on his face and chest.

Joao and I had compassionately listened and decided that we could do more than just pay for the beef. We asked Bruno to watch our cart and quickly excused ourselves. We gathered up a *cesta de comida* (a family food box of basic essentials like rice, beans, milk, etc.), sweets, and a drink for the two boys.

The boys graciously accepted the food. We gave them bus fare along with some words of advice from Joao, for he had grown up in humble beginnings in Brazil. Joao explained to them that he had never given up and found a way to attend a U.S. college. He wanted these boys to understand that if they stay out of trouble, they can make it.

The brothers happily rushed off to the bus stop. Joao and I, on the other hand, were left in tearful silence on the drive home. In some way we felt terrible . . . a box of food, how long would that last? It hardly seemed sufficient. We wished we could have done more, but what?

We resolved to return to the grocery store at the same time the following weeks to try to find the boys once more, but with no luck. We were not able to give a lot, but we did give with much love and hope for the brothers and their family. They will forever remain in our hearts and thoughts.

Heather Ekas

The Boss

The quality of a leader is reflected in the standards they set for themselves.

Ray Kroc

The president of the firm I worked at in 1989 wasn't the type of boss who mingled with his employees. He distanced himself, maintaining a somewhat chilly relationship with all but his executive staff. He transmitted any necessary information to the general workforce through this chain of command, never in person. Because of this, he loomed as an unknown entity the everyday staff avoided. Everyone had a vague fear that he was interested in you only if you messed up—and then it was bad news.

My position was one of the marketing assistants, and I hadn't worked at the company for even a full year when my worst nightmare hit. In this world full of random violence, the most horrible suddenly targeted my family. My beautiful daughter was shot and killed. The randomness of the act still reverberates in my heart decades later.

As a single mom of three teenage daughters, I went through all the necessary motions of life by rote, like a zombie, trying to be strong for those around me who were completely falling apart. My only thoughts were on how to get though this terrible time without completely losing my sanity.

Friends suggested I take a leave of absence from work, but I knew I couldn't do that. I needed the money to keep the house going, and I couldn't stand being alone with my thoughts. Instead, I stoically plodded from task to task, handling everything with quiet efficiency, while inside my whole being was screaming. I attended to the legal details. I went to the morgue and to the police station and handled mountains of paperwork. I learned that there was no suspect, and that this case would probably remain as one of the thousands of unsolved shootings that riddle Los Angeles every year.

I went to work each day and never noticed that my workload was growing daily. It took all of my strength to keep up with it. When the day ended, I was so tired I literally came home and fell asleep—sometimes on the couch, still wearing my work clothes. Every day, my desk seemed to be piled with more and more work that had short deadlines. I threw myself into it, and it actually helped move the minutes and hours along.

When the day of the funeral arrived, I made it through the service with my two remaining daughters sobbing at my side. I dreaded going home, knowing that I was finally going to have to face the stark reality of the situation.

Within minutes of arriving at home, a knock sounded on the front door. There, holding a beautiful potted plant, stood the personal assistant to the president of the company.

The card read, "A living piece of hope for your well-being."

The boss and his wife had arranged to care for me during my worst evening on earth. One by one, it seemed as if every single employee from the company arrived. Some brought food, some brought cards, some just brought themselves. I finally broke down and cried in the arms of a woman I barely knew.

Soon, the house was full of people offering support and companionship. Although he and his wife weren't there, I learned that the boss had assigned extra work to me, feeling that "busy" work would keep me from falling apart during this terrible period in my life. He was right. He knew me so well without even really knowing me at all.

Later, I got to know the boss better. One day I asked him why he and his wife hadn't come to the house after he had gone to all the trouble to arrange everything for me and my child—a girl that he had never even known. When asked why his only presence was the plant he sent, he cleared his throat in an authoritative manner and reiterated his standing policy of not "socializing with his employees." Then, he looked away quickly, and I'm sure that I saw him wipe away a tear. I knew he hadn't come because he couldn't trust his emotions, and he had to remain "the boss" at all times.

Many years have passed since I left the corporate world to run my own business, but my old boss and I still keep in touch. I let him know when some of my writing will be published, he sends congratulations, and we send jokes back and forth by e-mail.

We never mention that time in my life, and we never talked about that evening again. The plant he sent is still alive and thriving in my living room window after all these years. Of all the people I worked for in my life, he will always be the one boss who stands apart from the rest. Although he would gruffly brush it off as "no big deal," the compassion, wisdom, and silent strength he offered to me in my darkest hour helped get me back on my feet again and it is something I will never forget.

Joyce Laird

A Wave for Grandpa Bob

Sometimes your joy is the source of your smile,
but sometimes your smile can be the source of
your joy.

Thich Nhat Hanh

The old man sat in a plastic chair, smiling, waving at everyone who passed. They'd honk and wave back. "Every single person waves at me. I don't know why," he explained. "I have no idea who ninety percent of them are."

Every day the eighty-two-year-old, who the neighborhood children called Grandpa Bob, traveled from his bed to his carport and no farther, waving at neighbors as he picked up the daily paper.

He inquired of drop-in visitors how they were doing and put a water bowl out for their dogs. Some of the neighbors were original homeowners from 1967, when the houses went for $15,000 and there wasn't anything but black Angus cattle to the west, where interstates now run.

Other visitors were new faces, often from another country. Grandpa Bob befriended the Haitian family down the block, the Dominicans two doors away, and the Cubans across the street. Their children called him *Abuelo Robert.*

They may have noticed that his arms were bruised purple—he fell four times last year—and that his legs were giving out. They may even have noticed that he kept a portable phone clipped to his three-wheeled walker, just in case he needed to dial 911.

But if they didn't notice, he sure wasn't going to say anything about it. He wasn't going to listen to any doctor, either. "What do I need to go to some doctor for? To find out I'm getting old? I already know that," he would say. "Really, I'm lucky, because I don't have any pain." His calendar was bereft of doctor's appointments. His real medicine? The best neighbors a guy could want.

The first big curveball in Grandpa Bob's life came in 1982 when his precious wife, Hazel, was diagnosed with multiple sclerosis. He was only sixty-two, but he did what he had to do. Bob quit his job as a warehouse manager. He and Hazel began to live off Social Security and what they'd saved.

"I'd do the same thing all over again," he'd say. "If ever there was an angel in this world, it was her. She never spoke bad about anyone, never. You just had to know her."

He spent the next twelve years caring for her, first providing encouragement and an occasional drink of water. Then, as her legs gave out, he pushed her for miles up and down a small park. Eventually he'd carry her to doctor's appointments, then stay awake at night gazing at her during the rare moments she could peacefully sleep.

On July 24, 1994, he said good-bye to Hazel.

Bob shared the pain with his adult son, Robert. Not Robert Jr.—the Parrs gave one boy that name, but he died very young—so this one would be Robert H. He was a cop, and a good one: lots of decorations from the sheriff's office and kind words from almost every peer. He busted scam artists, the people who rip off the elderly.

But then Robert H. felt a little pain in his mouth. Cancer took his tongue, then his larynx. Still, speaking by voice box, he won officer of the month. Finally, he was communicating by typing on a computer, still working until the day he died.

On August 17, 1999, Robert G. Parr said good-bye to Robert H.

"You never get over losing a child," he'd say. "You just don't. But you can go on. Enjoy each day. I've learned in eighty years to take it as it comes."

"It's bad luck losing your wife, but you wouldn't want her back here suffering. There's bad luck to losing a son, but you wouldn't want him back here with no tongue."

Here is where Grandpa Bob's luck turned.

"I don't have neighbors," he'd say. "I have family."

The morning would start with help from Emery, who lived a few houses down. Bob gave him a key a few years ago, so Emery would let himself in and set up the coffee pot.

Bob would pour a cup, and with the help of his walker, move out to his carport to sit and watch traffic. Three open chairs surrounded him, awaiting the day's visitors.

His friend, Sue, would check in daily and buy groceries for him on Thursdays. Her son would do a quick regular cleaning of the pool, which Bob hadn't set foot in since Hazel died. Another neighbor, Roni, would take his clothes to her house and wash them once a week.

His daughter-in-law, Robert H.'s wife, called daily. For a birthday present, she hired Maid Brigade to come in and clean his house monthly, which was plenty because he didn't dirty it up much.

Another neighbor called Meals on Wheels, and the agency's weekly delivery filled the refrigerator. The root beer that Emery would drop off washed it all down.

Grandpa Bob was grateful for the basics and for his neighbors but was even more amazed at how others were so willing to help keep an old man from feeling lonely.

Two Haitian ladies from the Catholic Church, apparently out on a quiet walk one day, befriended him. From then on, they delivered a rosary prayer regularly.

And the sister-in-law of the Dominican friend down the street gave him a spiritual boost, too, making his heart beat a little quicker every time he'd see her station wagon pull up. Out would pour five children, who surrounded him, held his hands, and warbled through a quick hymn and a prayer. They'd be back in their car and on their way, but not before he got five hugs and five kisses. "I really don't know what they're saying," he'd say. "All I know is *Feliz Navidad.*"

Between visitors, he watched the mail for his Social Security check: $788 went quickly after taking out a portion to pay toward the annual $1,048 in house insurance and $1,300 in property taxes. He asked Medicare to pay for an electric wheelchair or buggy, so he could ride down the street, but no luck.

Yes, he'd heard of old folks homes, where the money goes farther and the care is professional. But he never wanted to go there. "I don't want to live in a home. I have a home," Bob would say.

If he lived in a home, he would miss his neighbors. Even the ice-cream man, who would turn down the music to shout "hi" out the window. "Someplace in my life I've just done something right," Grandpa Bob would say. "But whatever it is, I don't know."

But then, on the first Saturday in November, he called a neighbor, and it was serious. An ambulance came and took him to the hospital. He had a form of gangrene. A payback for ignoring diabetes.

He lost a little toe. Then a leg. The neighbors steadily came to visit, and his circle of friends grew even larger: like Amy, the nurse, and Tami from the rehabilitation center.

Back home, the strangers accustomed to his wave began to worry. They taped notes to the plastic chair in his carport, asking of his whereabouts.

By Thanksgiving, he was back in the hospital, wondering where he'd be going and what would happen next.

"I want to go back to my carport," he said one December day. But a week later, he said, "I want to be with my wife and my son."

At 4:11 PM on Christmas Eve, Robert Parr Sr. said good-bye.

The neighbors and his daughter-in-law made all the arrangements, and it was at this time that Grandpa Bob's stubborn streak paid off. You see, he never let them talk him into moving his beloved Hazel's ashes from his home. He had kept them tucked away in a closet all these years, despite neighbors' pleas that Hazel deserved better. So now his ashes would be mingled with Hazel's in a dual brass urn, with the words "Together Forever" engraved on it and kept in a niche across from their sons'.

After Grandpa Bob was put to rest, almost everybody on the block whose lives he had touched—and who had touched him—gathered at the spot where they shared their lives: a breezy carport with four plastic chairs and a community dog bowl.

Nick Sortal

Standing In for Love

I value the friend who for me finds time on his calendar, but I cherish the friend who for me does not consult his calendar.

Robert Brault

Some people would say I had spoiled her, but my youngest child, Jenna, would not go to sleep until I had read her a story while rocking her. The rocking was for me as much as it was for her, because after she was born, I was told there could be no more babies for me. My dream of having a large family was gone, and she would be the last baby I would have the joy of rocking. So even though she was two and a half years old, her nighttime ritual included being rocked.

Jenna awoke one night screaming in pain. My husband, Joe, and I, too scared to wait until babysitting arrangements could be made, woke up our two boys, and we all rushed to the hospital. A battery of tests revealed a large tumor pressing painfully inside one of her tiny kidneys. The doctors were amazed that it had not bothered Jenna earlier. Joe and I took turns holding her, trying not to let our terror show, while emergency surgery was arranged.

For the first week that Jenna was in the hospital, I stayed with her day and night. The nurses put a rocker in her room so we could continue our nighttime routine. After she was asleep, I got what rest I could in the stiff recliner by Jenna's bed. Jenna was doing well, and Joe began to talk about how the boys needed me, too. Also, his burden of having to work full time and take care of the house and all the needs of the boys was beginning to wear him down. Reluctantly, I agreed that I should go home in the evening, have dinner with the boys, then return to the hospital until Jenna was asleep. Then I would come home for the remainder of the night.

The first time I saw the joy on my boys' faces when I tucked them into bed, I knew I had made the right decision. Still, I worried that Jenna would wake up in the middle of the night and cry for me.

Sleet began to fall one evening as I hurried home to make dinner. By the time our meal was done, the roads were treacherous. Joe stood by my elbow as I gazed out the kitchen window. "I don't want you going out in this weather," he said firmly.

"Joe," I protested, "I have to read Jenna a story and rock her. She won't be able to sleep if I don't."

"Honey," he said, "be reasonable. What if you have a wreck and get hurt . . . or worse? What if you take a chance and are never able to rock her again?"

I called the hospital, unable to keep from weeping. "It's the first time since she was born that I haven't rocked her at bedtime," I told Sallie, the middle-aged nurse with bright red hair who worked a twelve-hour shift from 7 AM to 7 PM.

"She'll be fine," Sallie said in her soothing voice. "I'll go in to see her before I leave and tell her that when she wakes up her mommy will be here."

"Thank you, Sallie," I said. "Tell her that I love her, too."

I woke up at dawn. Sometime during the night the salt trucks had been by, and although far from being clear, the roads were in much better condition. I dressed hurriedly, certain that I would find Jenna red-eyed from crying for me. Remembering Joe's admonition from the night before, I forced myself to drive slowly. I pushed open the door to Jenna's room. My feet froze to the tiles and my jaw dropped.

There, sitting in the rocker was Sallie, snoring softly as she cuddled a peacefully sleeping Jenna. *The Gingerbread Man*, one of Jenna's favorite books, was lying on the floor where it must have slipped from Sallie's hand after she fell asleep. I tiptoed over and kissed Jenna softly on the cheek, then impulsively kissed Sallie, too. Sallie's eyes flew open. She blinked at me for a moment and then smiled sheepishly.

"I didn't mean for you to catch me," she said.

"Sallie," I said, "your shift starts in an hour. How will you make it through the day?"

She smiled down at Jenna. "If I had walked away from her last night, I would have seen her little tear-streaked face all night." Sallie looked up at me, and I saw more kindness in those green eyes than I had ever seen in a human being before. "I can cope with losing a little sleep, but she wasn't coping very well with having to go to sleep without seeing her mommy. Well, I'm not her mommy, but I don't think I was a bad stand-in. We got through the routine, and both of us managed to get some sleep."

Before Jenna left the hospital I took a picture of Sallie holding her in the rocking chair. The picture is in a frame on Jenna's dresser. I tell her often about the kind nurse who couldn't leave a crying little girl, even though her own family was waiting for her. I used to hear my grand-mother say that so-and-so was a "good" person. It's an old-fashioned expression, but sometimes it is the only phrase that truly fits. Sallie is more than a good nurse, she is a good person.

Elizabeth Atwater

Maggie's Miracle

In prosperity, our friends know us; in adversity, we know our friends.

John Churton Collins

From the moment my husband and I were first introduced, our life has been one miracle after another. The most recent miracle has been the story of our Maggie. We'd been married for four years, and we often questioned if or when it was time to add to our family. Each time we thought we were ready, we put too much thought into it and talked ourselves out of it. The one time we ignored any of the "facts" and decided to trust God with a pregnancy, he wasted no time at all taking on the challenge! I was pregnant in less than a week.

Maggie was six weeks premature, and at less than four pounds and sixteen inches, she won the hearts of my coworkers at the bank. They were amazed that anything so tiny could not only survive but thrive.

And she was very healthy . . . except for a perceptible heart murmur. The doctors weren't necessarily worried, but they wanted to err on the side of caution and keep a close eye on her development.

The day she left the hospital was the same day she had her first appointment with a heart specialist. Dr. Burton was encouraging as he agreed that it was possible for Maggie to outgrow her heart murmur. All went well for Maggie's first eighteen months. She had a hearty appetite and played with enthusiasm, even though her day-care provider and I joked that Maggie was the only child in day care who actually looked forward to a nap.

At our next appointment, Dr. Burton detected a noticeable difference in her heart rhythm and was able to explain why Maggie tired so easily. Apparently, not only had the murmur become loud enough for his experienced ear to hear without a stethoscope, but also her aortic valve was not working properly.

At eighteen months, her tiny body was working overtime to keep her heart going, leaving her exhausted after a few hours of play. Maggie would need open-heart surgery—the sooner, the better.

In one single moment, all the mundane concerns of the day—what was for dinner, did we need to get milk on the way home—diminished in importance. Nothing else mattered as I held my baby to my chest. I knew this was too big for us to handle alone. I quickly breathed a simple prayer: "Lord, help us."

After the initial shock wore off, John and I were ready to make the necessary plans. The hospital was two hours away. Our oldest daughter was in school, so she would need to stay with someone for a week. We would need someone to feed the cats while we were gone. We would need to put a hold on our mail and newspapers, as well as arrange to pay any bills that were due while we were gone.

Finally, John and I would have to make arrangements

with our employers. It was only February, and both John and I would need all of our vacation and sick days to be with our little patient during surgery and recovery.

We learned that in addition to Maggie's weeklong hospital stay, her chest would take a full three weeks to heal. I was fortunate that I had two weeks of paid vacation, one week of sick pay, and some personal days left to use. John, however, had only two weeks of paid vacation available. By the time Maggie would be well enough to return to day care, and I would be able to return to work, all of our paid leave would be gone.

In the two short weeks before Maggie's surgery, my coworkers were secretly organizing a silent auction that would be held among only the bank employees. They pooled, not only their money, but their talents as well. Some donated crafts, others offered to bake a pie or cookies each month for an entire year. Another agreed to cater a party to the highest bidder. The range of donations was amazing!

Two days before Maggie's surgery, John and I were invited to a "little get-together" in the bank's breakroom after work. That's when we first learned about the silent auction. The last time I had seen so many of my fellow employees gathered in the same place at the same time was at the annual Christmas party a few months earlier. Some had driven forty-five minutes from our branch offices to be there with us. And they were all there for the same reasons—to support our family and to show how very much they cared.

John and I went home wholly encouraged, knowing that their thoughts and prayers would be with our family.

The next morning at our staff meeting, the usual announcements were made. My stomach was in knots; I'd always been more comfortable being on the giving end of a blessing rather than on the receiving end. As I sat there waiting, I knew I was surrounded by people who had completely and unabashedly opened their hearts to me and my family.

The project leader stood up. "When we started this a week and a half ago," she said, "we had a goal in mind. When we finished last night, we hadn't reached that goal yet. So this morning, I've been hitting up people for more money." As everyone laughed, I was just as embarrassed as I was amused at the thought of my coworkers being solicited around the coffee pot. As the giggles and knowing looks subsided, she continued. "Now we have met our goal!" As she walked over to me, I stood to meet her. She handed me an envelope filled with cash.

"LaRonda, here's $2,500 for your family. And," she added, "those of us who were able to have donated a total of seventeen sick days so you and your family can still have a vacation this summer."

I was overwhelmed by the enormity of what had happened. And while I was stunned by the amount of money raised in such a short time by such a small group of people, I was not surprised at the level to which they had risen. In the years that I had lived in this town and worked at this bank, I had seen the hearts of each and every employee go out, not only to each other, but to the community as well. Being there when you're needed is something our bank is committed to, and it's a commitment that is easily fulfilled when there is the support of loving, hardworking folks like those who were standing with me at this moment.

In the end, we had enough money to pay for gas, food, and housing during Maggie's hospital stay, and we were able to focus completely on her recovery without worrying about our finances. We also had enough money to compensate for John's lost wages when we visited Maggie's Grandma Bourn in Nebraska that summer.

Today, Maggie is a vibrant, loving four-year-old who no longer looks forward to naps. And each time she asks me about the thin scar that runs down the middle of her chest, I tell her the story of how God used sixty-two amazing people to answer our prayers.

LaRonda Bourn

Stocking Feet Faith

Give, and it will be given to you.

Luke 6:38

After twenty years of driving buses for the county transit system, John thought he'd seen everything. But something happened one cold December day in the early 1980s in Milwaukee, Wisconsin, that changed all that.

John was worrying about his problems just like the next guy. Wondering how he was going to pay the December gas bill. Wondering if he'd be able to buy any Christmas presents that year. Wondering if he was ever going to get ahead of the game.

On that cold, dreary gray-sky day before Christmas, the temperature was ten degrees and it was trying to snow. Every time John opened the bus door, a blast of cold air slapped him in the face.

"Lousy time of year," John grumbled. "Just plain lousy."

As usual, around 3 PM, John was driving his bus down Wisconsin Avenue. At Marquette Prep School, a private boy's high school, he picked up the usual group of students. It seemed to John that as Christmas drew closer, the high school boys grew louder and rowdier.

Pushing and shoving, they stumbled to the back of the bus. "Rich kids," John mumbled disgustedly to himself. Most of the boys from the prep school lived in the ritzier suburbs and would be transferring off his bus in a mile or so.

A few stops later, John pulled up in front of the Milwaukee County Medical Complex grounds where a woman was waiting in the bus shelter.

She looked to be about forty years old and pregnant, her dingy gray coat tattered from collar to hem. When she pulled herself up the steps of the bus, John noticed she was wearing only socks, no shoes.

"Good Lord, woman, where are your shoes?" he blurted out without thinking. "It's too cold to be out without shoes! Get on in here and off that cold sidewalk!"

The woman struggled up the steps, pulling her gray buttonless coat around her protruding belly. "Never mind my shoes. This bus goin' downtown?"

Still staring at her feet, John answered, "Well, eventually we'll get back downtown. Have to head west first, then we'll turn around."

"I don't mind the extra ride, long as I can get warm. Lordy, it's cold out there. Wind must be comin' off the lake!" she sighed as she handed John her money and sat down on the front seat.

The high school kids in the back started in. "Hey, lady, nice coat!"

"That a Saks Fifth Avenue special?"

"Doesn't she know we don't serve patrons without shoes?"

John felt like strangling every one of those kids. To distract the woman from their remarks, he continued his conversation, "Yup, it's a rough time of year all right."

The woman sat up straight in her seat and smoothed the wrinkles in her coat. "Sure is. I got eight kids. Had enough money this year to buy shoes for every one of 'em, but that was it. I got some slippers at home, but I didn't want to get 'em all wet in case it snowed."

John kept the conversation going. "Yep. It ain't easy with Christmas and all. Money's scarce. And if this weather doesn't warm up, I'm wonderin' if I'll have enough to pay the gas bill."

"Mister, you just be glad you got a place to live and a job. The good Lord will take care of you. Always has for me."

John couldn't believe that a woman who didn't have any shoes was telling him to stop worrying.

Before long, the bus was at the end of the line, time for the kids to get off and transfer to other buses that would take them to their comfortable suburban homes.

As the boys filed off, one young student named Frank, a freshman who had been sitting just a few seats behind the woman in the gray tattered coat, stopped in front of her and handed her his new leather sport shoes, saying, "Here, lady, you take these. You need 'em more than I do."

And with that, Frank, a fourteen-year-old kid, walked off the bus and into the ten degree evening in his stocking feet.

The busy Christmas season that year turned out better for John than all the other years and months put together.

And it wasn't just because when the woman tried on the shoes she let out a whoop and a holler. "Why, they fit perfect! Can you believe that? Perfect. Nice and warm, too. Bless the Lord. Mister, I told you not to worry 'bout nothin'. Don't you see? The Lord always provides. Always."

On a bus heading west, John's faith in God and in mankind was completely restored on that cold gray day in Milwaukee by a woman wearing a very expensive pair of sport shoes.

Patricia Lorenz

Never Alone

The person who removes a mountain begins by carrying away small stones.

Author Unknown

I never liked being alone. It was too quiet, disconcerting. Ever since I was a little girl, I felt uncomfortable on my own. Even as an adult I found it distressing.

One day my son was off at a friend's house, my daughter was away at her first year of college, and worst of all, my husband, Mike, was in the hospital. I was worried, and alone.

It was a minor surgical procedure. Laparoscopic. Nothing serious. He seemed to come through it fine and would be home the next day. *One more day,* I thought while getting ready for bed.

I wished my mother could be with me, but she lived hundreds of miles away, and Mike's folks were away at their summer place. It was vacation time, and all my friends were out of town. I stared at the shadowy wall all night, unable to sleep, feeling the emptiness beside me.

First thing in the morning I took a taxi to the hospital.

"How's . . . everything . . . at . . . home?" Mike asked, his voice weak and labored. I took his hand; his skin was cold and clammy. His eyes were wide. Something was wrong.

A nurse with a cheery smile popped into the room. As she bent over Mike to take his vital signs, her smile disappeared. Before I knew it, the room was full of worried doctors and nurses. I was pushed back away from his bedside, against the cold cement block wall.

"Pulse is rapid." "Blood pressure elevated," I heard the nurses say. What was going on?

Suddenly Mike was whisked out of the room. One of the nurses noticed me standing alone by the wall, my knees shaking. "Your husband is having trouble breathing. We're taking him for an MRI. We think he has blood clots in his lungs." She looked into my eyes. "I'm sorry."

I'm sorry! That's not what I wanted to hear. What about "Everything's going to be fine?" or "It's nothing serious!" Blood clots in the lungs? That was serious!

I stepped into the hall and stared. What did I do? Where was the waiting room? I didn't even know which way to go.

"You should go to the ICU waiting room," a nurse said, noticing my confusion. "Second floor."

I went there and sat with other quiet, anxious strangers. I spotted a phone on the wall, and I fished for quarters in my pocketbook. The first call was to Mike's parents. They'd come home right away, but it would take a while. I called my mother, wishing she wasn't so far away. Then I called my daughter, Kate. I didn't want to worry her. But she'd always been a rock for me. It helped a little just to hear her voice. When I hung up, however, I choked back the tears.

I started to put away my pocketbook, but I had one last call to make. I dialed the number of my church. An answering machine picked up my call. Should I leave a message? What should I say? We hadn't been attending long so I didn't know many people. Finally I just said that Mike was in the hospital and had taken a turn for the worse. Maybe they could say some prayers.

It seemed like forever sitting and wondering. I put my head in my hands and tried to hide my tears. Suddenly, a woman walked in and approached me.

"Peggy?" she asked, kneeling beside me. "I'm Lisa. I'm a social worker here at the hospital, and I also go to your church. I got a call from the pastor that you were here, so I ducked over to see if you were okay."

I looked up, surprised. She seemed so calm and gentle. Seemingly out of the blue, someone had found me and offered help. I wiped the tears from my cheek.

"If you need anything, ask someone to page me. Okay?" She put her hand on my shoulder and smiled comfortingly.

"Yes, thank you so much," I sniffed. Before long, I was allowed in to see Mike. He was hooked up to monitors, IVs, and was wearing an oxygen mask, but I was so happy to be with him again. "You're going to be fine," I said, stroking his arm. I hoped. I looked to the doctor at his bedside.

"There are multiple clots in both lungs," he said. "He's on heparin and coumadin; blood thinners. The next few days are very important."

I understood. Hopefully the blood clots would break up and dissolve. But if they didn't, or if they traveled to the brain, the results could be fatal. Blood clots were serious business. The doctor left, and Mike dozed off. I sat by his side, aching for something I could do to help him. I put my head against his hand and cried. Then it was time to leave for the evening. I returned home alone.

But as I sat there in my quiet house, eating my dinner, the phone started ringing. First, a woman from our church called; she identified herself as Sue and offered to give me rides back and forth to the hospital. She even insisted on driving three hours each way to pick up Kate at college and bring her home for the weekend. Then someone else called and said she'd stop by with a meal. I didn't even know these people! Finally, just before I went to bed, the phone rang again. It was my mom.

"I was trying to arrange to take a bus tomorrow," she said. "But my friend said, 'No way!' She's going to drive me there right now. We'll get in about 2 AM."

"She'll drive all that way in the middle of the night?" I asked, unbelieving.

"Yup. I'll see you soon. Just hang in there."

I did, thanks to the support of Lisa, Sue, and others I barely knew. Mike recovered, came home, and gradually grew stronger. And I was stronger, too. With good, caring people everywhere, ready to lend a hand, I am never really alone.

Peggy Frezon

Wheels of Kindness

We ourselves feel that what we are doing is just a drop in the ocean. But the ocean would be less because of that missing drop.

Mother Teresa

A traffic light in my hometown is thought to be the longest light in the whole, entire world. I always seem to arrive at this lengthy and spacious intersection just as the light turns yellow, thereby giving me ample time to ponder the upcoming events of my day, or perhaps, more important, put on my makeup. But one morning, during rush hour traffic, I witnessed one of the greatest acts of random human kindness I have ever seen. Two men coming from opposite directions on the sidewalk met on the corner of the busy intersection.

Nothing so unusual about them until I realize that they are both in wheelchairs. One of the men had a motorized chair with plenty of power and ease of operation simply by pushing forward on the hand control. The other gentleman, however, was not so fortunate to have such a chair. His was large and bulky, and he had to use his own manual power by turning the enormous wheels by hand.

He was the smaller of the two men, and his arms did not appear to be large enough to turn the oversized shiny wheels that propelled not only the chair's weight, but his own as well. He was breathing hard as he reached the corner of the busy intersection and seemed to welcome the break as he waited for the light to change. The man in the motorized chair filled his seat completely. He had large, muscular arms that looked like he may have been a bodybuilder at one time in his life.

These two men are in the wrong chairs, I thought to myself. The burly man in the motorized chair sat, resting comfortably, waiting for the light to change. The other smaller man in the manual chair, however, appeared to be doing stretching and breathing exercises as if he were an athlete warming up for a marathon. He was actually warming up for the long trip across the intersection, which to him probably did feel like a marathon. Even though the two men exchanged smiles, they did not appear to exchange any words, and it was apparent they had never met. It was just a coincidence that two men in wheelchairs arrived on the same corner, at the same time, and from opposite directions.

The light turned green, and they were off! The man with the motorized chair sped down the concrete ramp with great ease and had no problem reaching the top of the thirty-degree incline in the middle of the crosswalk, nor did he have any trouble ascending the steeper curb ramp on the other side of the street. The man in the manual chair, however, went down the steep, bumpy ramp much slower, as not to catapult himself onto the pavement when his wheels hit the crevice in the gutter. To gain enough momentum to navigate over the street's incline, he had to push hard on the large steel wheels of his chair. I could see his upper arm and neck muscles and blood vessels bulging under the strain. I found myself cheering him on as if I was on the sidelines of a big game. Go! . . . Go! . . . Go! The light is going to change! Push! Push! C'mon, you can do it! I actually found myself yelling.

The light turned yellow, and I could hear car engines rev, but he was only halfway across the intersection, almost to the top of the incline! I wanted to get out and push him safely to the other side, because I knew he would never make it up that ramp in time. I feared he would get run over by the impatient drivers. Then, suddenly, it was as if time stopped for a brief moment, as if everyone saw the same thing at the same time—motors decreased their rpms and it grew quiet as we sat there, stopped in our cars.

The man in the motorized chair was well on his way down the opposite sidewalk, when he stopped, paused, and after putting his head down for a short moment as if in prayer, turned his wheelchair around, revved his motor, and headed back toward the intersection with its now red light.

Without even looking if there were cars advancing into the intersection, he once again sped down the concrete ramp and up the incline, meeting the man in the manual chair in the middle of the crosswalk. With a flowing and precise maneuver, like an acrobat catching the flying trapeze in midair, he did a one-eighty in front of the man in the manual chair, then backed up so the struggling man could reach out and take the handles of the motorized wheelchair. Once more, he pushed forward hard on the hand controls, and the motorized chair began moving, a little slower this time under the added weight of the manual chair. The man in the motorized chair was pulling the man in the manual chair across the intersection and up the curb ramp, onto the safety of the sidewalk! They exchanged smiles once more, but this time with an added

READER/CUSTOMER CARE SURVEY

We care about your opinions! Please take a moment to fill out our online Reader Survey at **http://survey.hcibooks.com**.

As a **"THANK YOU"** you will receive a **VALUABLE INSTANT COUPON** towards future book purchases

as well as a **SPECIAL GIFT** available only online! Or, you may mail this card back to us.

(PLEASE PRINT IN ALL CAPS)

First Name _____ MI. _____ Last Name _____

Address _____

State _____ Zip _____ Email _____ City _____

1. Gender
- ☐ Female   ☐ Male

2. Age
- ☐ 8 or younger
- ☐ 9-12   ☐ 13-16
- ☐ 17-20   ☐ 21-30
- ☐ 31+

3. Did you receive this book as a gift?
- ☐ Yes   ☐ No

4. Annual Household Income
- ☐ under $25,000
- ☐ $25,000 - $34,999
- ☐ $35,000 - $49,999
- ☐ $50,000 - $74,999
- ☐ over $75,000

5. What are the ages of the children living in your house?
- ☐ 0 - 14   ☐ 15+

6. Marital Status
- ☐ Single
- ☐ Married
- ☐ Divorced
- ☐ Widowed

7. How did you find out about the book?
(please choose one)
- ☐ Recommendation
- ☐ Store Display
- ☐ Online
- ☐ Catalog/Mailing
- ☐ Interview/Review

8. Where do you usually buy books?
(please choose one)
- ☐ Bookstore
- ☐ Online
- ☐ Book Club/Mail Order
- ☐ Price Club (Sam's Club, Costco's, etc.)
- ☐ Retail Store (Target, Wal-Mart, etc.)

9. What subject do you enjoy reading about the most?
(please choose one)
- ☐ Parenting/Family
- ☐ Relationships
- ☐ Recovery/Addictions
- ☐ Health/Nutrition
- ☐ Christianity
- ☐ Spirituality/Inspiration
- ☐ Business Self-help
- ☐ Women's Issues
- ☐ Sports

10. What attracts you most to a book?
(please choose one)
- ☐ Title
- ☐ Cover Design
- ☐ Author
- ☐ Content

TAPE IN MIDDLE; DO NOT STAPLE

BUSINESS REPLY MAIL
FIRST-CLASS MAIL PERMIT NO 45 DEERFIELD BEACH, FL

POSTAGE WILL BE PAID BY ADDRESSEE

Chicken Soup for the Soul®
3201 SW 15th Street
Deerfield Beach FL 33442-9875

Iₐₗₗₗₗₗₗₗₗₗₗₗₗₗₗₗₗₗₗₗₗₗₗₗₗₗₗₗₗₗₗₗₗₗₗₗₗₗₗ

FOLD HERE

Do you have your own Chicken Soup story that you would like to send us? Please submit at: **www.chickensoup.com**

Comments

glimmer, the kind that comes from the satisfaction of doing a good deed. They both then went in opposite directions on the sidewalks.

I do not know how many times the light changed during all of this, but not one car moved. As the light turned green again, we just sat there in our cars, knowing we were all a little bit changed by something divinely placed as a reminder to perform our own random acts of kindness.

Patricia Cena Evans

"A hacker broke into our computer and, in an act of random kindness, organized all of our files."

Finding Blessings
Amid Destruction

The love of our neighbor in all its fullness simply means being able to say to him, "What are you going through?"

Simone Weil

I hugged a total stranger today. In fact, in the past months I've hugged a lot of strangers. Since Hurricane Katrina forced my family and me to evacuate our home just north of New Orleans, people will notice the Louisiana plates on our car, my son's LSU T-shirt, or our accents, and they want to know if we're okay, if we have a house to return to, and what they can do to help.

You can see in their faces that they mean it, too. If we told them we needed money, they'd find a way to give it to us. If we needed a place to stay, they'd put us up.

I've heard that disasters bring out the good and the bad in people. We've all seen the bad. The news media made sure of that. But not enough has been said about the good.

After the storm, communities for miles around the Gulf

Coast opened their towns, homes, schools, and hearts to us. Stores and restaurants offered discounts to anyone affected by the storm. Schools registered children with little or no records. Pharmacies filled our prescriptions, and banks cashed our checks pretty much on the honor system.

A week after the storm, my family and I were eating in a restaurant. We mentioned to the waiter that we had evacuated because of the storm, and the next thing we knew our meal was on the house. I met a woman at a church we visited, inquired where she got her hair cut, and my entire family was treated to free haircuts. My kids came home daily from their temporary school with armloads of gifts from teachers, parents, and the PTA.

Back home we found volunteers everywhere. People from Minnesota, Ohio, Georgia, Illinois, Alabama, and New York flooded into our little country town handing out food, water, ice, clothing, medicine, and their blood and sweat helping us clean up. People from all over the country got into their cars, drove down, and looked around until they found a way to help.

Our tiny church served 400 hot meals a day to whoever showed up to eat them. Church members formed chainsaw crews and scoured the countryside looking for people needing help. Those who could donated generators for families who needed them. Some days we weren't sure where the money would come from for the next day's food, or for gasoline for the chain saws and generators. Then, the next day rolled around and the money was there. One day a total stranger showed up, handed our pastor a fistful of one-hundred dollar bills, and then drove away.

Families doubled up, shared what they had, and pulled together to get the work done. With no electricity we were forced to spend time talking. Without televisions, computers, Play Stations, or phones, we rediscovered one another. Longtime family feuds dissolved. Pride melted away as some learned to give and others learned to take.

One day I spent seven hours standing in line to apply for Red Cross assistance. That might sound like a nightmare, but it was surprisingly pleasant. There we were, thousands of us—old, young, black, white, professional, and working class—crowded together, waiting in the scorching Louisiana sun. I saw people exchanging phone numbers and offers of help, pooling their resources of food, water, chairs, bug spray, sunscreen, and diapers, and even survival stories.

One lady waited in a line for three hours only to discover the help available was only for people affected by Hurricane Katrina. She was from Texas and had been wiped out by Hurricane Rita. Fighting back tears, she started gathering up her chair and purse, but before she could, men started pulling out their wallets. Women opened their purses. She tried to protest, but she left with a handful of money to see her through until she could apply for Red Cross assistance somewhere else.

It's been years since Katrina clobbered our community. The effects are like ripples on a pond, one bad consequence leading to another. Every so often, one of us thinks out loud that we can't wait for things to get back to normal, only to realize that "normal" as we knew it will probably never come again.

Yet, the things that have happened to us in these months have become a part of who we are. Strangers, friends, and family members have done wonderful things for us, and we've had the opportunity to do for them. Most of us wouldn't have missed these experiences for the world. Every day God opens our eyes to see blessings amid the devastation. I can hardly wait to see what today will hold.

Mimi Greenwood Knight

Family Ties

You can have everything in life you want, if you'll just help enough other people to get what they want!

Zig Ziglar

On tiptoes, I strained to look down the concourse to see my son Pete's waving hand for as long as possible. He, Paula, and my two-year-old grandson sped away in the crowd of travelers, eager to begin their work and studies halfway around the world. I wanted them to succeed and find joy in their work; but if I probed my heart honestly, part of me hoped they'd spend a few months in Asia and change their minds.

That didn't happen; they were excited to discover their new city and immerse themselves in a new culture. After three or four months, I congratulated myself that my yo-yo attitude rose more frequently to "I can be genuinely happy for them" than spinning near the ground at "maybe the plumbing will get to them yet."

Then, during an evening webcam session, Pete enthusiastically affirmed their colleagues and new acquaintances. "Yeah, they're just like family to us!"

My string snapped. Thank goodness our webcam's field of view relayed only half of my husband's smiling, and my stricken, face to their computer monitor. My rational self acknowledged they needed good friends in that challenging place, but—"family"? My heart objected; that's what *we* were. We'd been replaced—or at least seriously elbowed aside!

I knotted my attitude and wobbled along for nearly a year, when at twenty-nine weeks into her pregnancy, Paula's water broke and she and the family were air evacuated. Hours after we heard the news, I caught a plane to Hong Kong.

They didn't know anyone in Hong Kong, and I didn't either, except for my friend Chu Li's mother. Jet-lagged and worried for Paula and the baby, I felt scared and anxious because Pete couldn't meet me. I planned to wave Chu Li's wedding photo frantically once I reached the lobby of the Lantau Airport, hoping that Chu Lin would recognize it and see me. I was totally dependent on a near stranger.

In the clamor, I spotted Chu Lin's small waving hand holding a sign with my name. Chu Li's mother hugged me—like family—and whisked me through the airport, onto a bus, under the harbor, into a taxi, and down a quiet street where I saw Pete holding our grandson and waving to me in the night. Relief, mixed with humble gratitude, welled inside me.

And I felt those emotions over and over during the next six weeks.

I learned that Pete and Paula's colleagues had tended to my grandson, taken dinner to Pete and Paula, and packed the three small bags they were allowed to take on their flight. Others traveled to the city with additional clothing and items forgotten in their hasty exodus to Hong Kong. Another rushed into action and found an apartment we could rent for a month so we didn't have to spend $200 a night for a hotel. Yet another woman—whose husband was recovering in the same hospital as Paula and our tiny new granddaughter—brought food, cleaning supplies, and toys for our grandson.

"Friend" was too glib a word to apply to these people. They cared; they traveled; they helped despite their own lives, schedules, and needs. They practiced unselfish, sacrificial love—the kind of love a family shows to each other.

I returned home with a deep understanding and heart-felt appreciation. Now, my son's friends are like family to me, too. No more knots in my attitude. In fact, I even learned a new yo-yo trick in Hong Kong: I call it "Around the World!"

Rose M. Jackson

2

A MATTER OF ATTITUDE

When one door closes, another door opens; but we so often look so long and so regretfully upon the closed door that we do not see the ones which open for us.

Alexander Graham Bell

A Boy Ought to Have a Chance

Once we believe in ourselves, we can risk curiosity, wonder, spontaneous delight, or any experience that reveals the human spirit.

e e cummings

The little boy eyed all of the colorful items in the old fisherman's tackle box. He wanted to touch, but he didn't dare.

"You like to fish?" the fisherman asked.

"Don't know. Never have," said the boy, whose eyes never moved from the contents of the box. "You use all that stuff, Mr. Russell?"

"At one time or another. How come you never been fishing?"

"No one ever took me," the boy answered.

The fisherman studied the little boy he had known for only a few weeks. Richard was a foster child living temporarily in my home. Soon the boy would be moving again to a permanent placement.

"Never been fishing," the fisherman later repeated to me. "No one ever took him." That just didn't seem right to him. A boy ought to have the chance to go fishing. That was an important part of growing up. What kind of man would this boy grow up to be if he never went fishing, if he never patiently waited for the tug on a line?

The fisherman decided that Richard would go fishing before he moved. But going fishing wasn't enough. The boy had to catch a fish. How could he be sure that the boy would experience the joy of hooking a fish and landing it? He decided to enlist the aid of another fisherman—his older brother Ernest.

The two men discussed the problem and decided on the solution. They would take young Richard to a fishing hole on their nephew's place. The pond was overstocked with finger-size fish. Richard would get his chance to catch a fish. It might not be bragging size, but it would be a catch that Richard could delight in.

When the day arrived, the two men and the boy climbed into the pickup truck for the ride to the fishing hole. The boy watched as the men took turns getting out to open gates as they crossed one field after another. At last they stopped near a barbed-wire fence. On the other side was the fishing hole. They walked along the fence until they found the spot where the ground dipped a little. The men showed the boy how to get down and slide under the fence.

At first the boy was reluctant to move too far from the fence because of the nearby meandering cows, but the men assured him that he would be okay. They would protect him.

The men showed the boy how to bait his hook with the worms he had found earlier that day. Shortly after putting his hook into the water, the boy saw his float wiggle and then begin to bob up and down. One of the men told him to give his line a quick yank and pull it out of the water. Sure enough, dangling from the end of his line was a fish—small, very small, but a fish.

"Look, Mr. Russell! Look, Mr. Ernest! I got one!" the boy shouted.

"That is sure some fish!" one of the men responded.

"We got to get a picture of this," said the other, pulling out the camera.

The old fisherman saw the boy catch his first fish that afternoon and helped create a memory that the child could take with him wherever he went. Three days later the boy was gone.

There were other young boys and girls who came, stayed awhile, and then left the temporary foster home. There were also some local kids who needed an unofficial "grandfather." The man took the time to teach each one something. Becky learned to build a birdhouse. Jason learned to build a campfire on the first try with just one match. Beth learned to use a screwdriver and complete a project. Lisa learned to swim in a country pond, and Colby learned that someone cared enough about him to just sit and listen as he grieved over the loss of his father.

The man, who once thought it was time to retire and do his own thing, discovered there were kids who needed just what he could give them—his time.

Dorothy Hill

Hand Me Downs

Nothing makes you like other human beings so much as doing things for them.

Zora Neale Hurston

My hand-me-down wardrobe was threadbare by the time it got to me—the fourth girl out of a family of five. How I envied Ken, the only boy, for he always managed to get new clothing. No faded undershirts or pants with the knees out for him, no siree. He got brand-new. It was so unfair to be one of four girls.

The only good clothing I ever got were those that were the "ugly" clothes—the ones my siblings had received as gifts and were too awful to wear, that had been stuffed into a drawer until they were deemed too tight. That lovely yellow sweater Aunt Martha had sent Cathy, the one with the ducks on it. Pants that were wide-legged when the style was slim. These were my "new" clothes. Luckily, until I was ten, I had the fashion sense of a wart hog, and as long as it fit, I wore it. But one day, something changed.

My friend Rena lived next door. She was older than me,

pretty, and fun, and she came from a Ukrainian family. I loved the clothes she wore, full of color and tradition. One day when I was at her house learning how to make perogies, her mother brought out a bag of clothes bound for Goodwill. "Would you like to go through these first?" Mrs. B. asked. I eagerly dropped my dough and went for the bag. At the top of the pile of hand-me-downs was the most beautiful shirt I had ever seen.

It was red, bright red, and silky. There were no tears, no sweat marks, no runs, and it had seven gold buttons on the front, and one on each silky sleeve. I was in love. I crushed it to my stained T-shirt, and saying "thank you," I quickly ran home to show my mom my new shirt.

The new shirt had a magic to it. For the first time I started to look in the mirror before I left for school. I combed my hair more than once a day and brushed my teeth more than twice. Dirty clothes were put in the laundry pile before they walked there by themselves. I started to notice what other people wore and even sneaked looks at my sister's fashion magazine. I showed an interest in sewing and soon was making my own clothes out of castoffs.

They were not always successes, and some my mother wouldn't let me wear out of the house, but eventually I did learn to create a passable wardrobe for myself.

I wore the beautiful, red shirt at least three times a week. I wore it on special occasions, and to school on the days we had assembly. I polished the gold buttons to a shine, and I hung it up after every washing. At twelve, I had blossomed into a young lady with style, all because of that wonderful red shirt.

One day my mother watched as I struggled to button the shirt. I had grown, and unfortunately my shirt had not grown with me. I cried and tried to figure out a way to make it bigger without hurting it, but I could not bring myself to change it. It was perfect, and could not be altered to fit who I was becoming.

Mother had just prepared a basket of things to take over to a new family. They were Portuguese and had recently moved into our small town. They did not have much money to go round, especially after their move. The father had just begun a new job, and the mother did not know much English, so she could not find work in any of the shops. I remembered seeing their youngest girl in school with her threadbare clothes and worn shoes, mussed-up hair, and dirty face. It hurt to remember how much she looked like me two years ago, as I had sat in Rena's house.

I placed the red shirt on the top of the basket. My mom nodded and said, "Now you have grown in more ways than one." I smiled and took one last look at my favorite red shirt. It had brought me luck and I hoped it would do the same for her, too.

The next week in school, I saw the little girl, whose name was Marta. She was busy making friends and playing games. Her smile was a little brighter, her hair combed and tied with a scarlet ribbon to match her new red shirt with the shiny gold buttons that someone had handed down.

Nancy Bennett

"I was once a caterpillar like you, then I developed the
proper perspective and attitude and voila!
Look at me now!"

Nameless Faces

Human beings, by changing the inner attitudes of their minds, can change the outer aspects of their lives.

William James

I was nineteen years old the first time I saw my own true character. I wish I could say I was proud of what I saw, but that would be a lie. At least I can say that my true character changed that day. My overall outlook on people managed to take a 180-degree turn in less than ten minutes. Who would have thought that the first person to change the way I viewed humanity would be a complete stranger?

For about a year, my voyage to and from work each day included a subway ride followed by a ten-minute walk through the heart of downtown Toronto. As with most large cities, the homeless population of Toronto often congregated on downtown corners, asking pedestrians for their spare change. Like most busy citizens, I learned to ignore the nameless faces who begged me for money each day. When it came to homeless beggars, my limited life experience had led me to one assumption—you are on the streets because you choose to be, probably due to drugs or alcohol.

I remember noting how particularly cold the weather had been that season. It was mid-December, and the temperature was a chilly minus 20-degrees Celsius. I walked with my head down, desperately wishing that my office was closer to the subway stop. I passed the usual mobs of homeless beggars, ignored all of them, and continued walking. As I crossed the intersection of Queen and Yonge streets, I saw him sitting against a building, wrapped in several layers of thin cloth, holding a white cup in front of him. I heard his shaky, pathetic voice target me as I sped past him.

"Spare some change?" he asked. "I would really appreciate it."

I didn't even bother looking up at his nameless face. I briefly pictured him walking into the closest liquor store and stocking up on whiskey with whatever money he managed to conjure up that day. Or, maybe he needed another hit of cocaine. Clearly, if he had ever been married, his wife would have literally kicked him to the curb when he couldn't get his habit under control. See, like most teenagers, it took me only moments to pass judgment on his life.

"I have no money on me," I said quickly.

Looking back now, I feel as though fate had set out that day to teach me a lesson. And it succeeded. Just a few feet past him, I managed to find the only ice patch on the sidewalk. As I slipped, I tried to position myself so the impact would occur on my hip and thigh, but unfortunately my aim was about as good as my judgment of character, and I managed to land square on my right knee. The pain seared through me as I lay on the ground for several moments wondering if I had fractured my kneecap. As I tried to come to grips with the notion of actually getting up, I heard a familiar, gruff voice only inches above me.

"Are you all right?" he asked.

I knew immediately that this was the man I had just rushed past. Even in pain, I still took a quick moment to sniff for the faintest smell of alcohol on his breath. There was none. Before my eyes began to well up with tears, I saw the smooth, sympathetic look in his eyes. He wasn't drunk or high.

I held his hand as I struggled to get to my feet. He held my arm as I hobbled to the nearby bus stop and quickly sat on the bench. The pain in my leg told me that I had definitely done more than simply bruised my knee. I needed an x-ray.

"My name is Mike," he said, as I tried to find a comfortable position on the bench. "You really shouldn't try walking on that leg. That was quite a fall you took, and you really need to get it checked by a doctor," he said with deep concern.

"This bus goes past the hospital," I said quickly, pointing to the bus sign above me.

Mike paused, and a look of sudden realization crossed his face. He reached into his pocket and pulled out his small white cup. He dumped the meager amount of change into the palm of his hand and counted it. He held only money out toward me, and after a few confusing moments I looked up at him in sheer bewilderment.

"I know you don't have any change on you," he said, "but I can always give you this. I think there's just enough here for you to take the bus."

I was overwhelmed with guilt as I remembered the lie I had told him only a few short minutes earlier. I turned away from his offering hand and reached for my purse. I pulled out my wallet and dumped my own change into the palm of my hand. I felt Mike's eyes on me as I counted through the money that I had told him didn't even exist. I had at least ten dollars worth of change in my hand. I counted out enough money for me to take the bus to the hospital and then turned to Mike to offer him the rest. He held out his cup as I placed the handful of change in it. I wished I had some bills to give him, but I hadn't been to the bank yet that day.

"Thank you," he said quietly. It was by far the most sincere "thank-you" I had ever heard in my life. Just behind him, I heard the bus approaching. He held out his hand to help me stand up.

"Thank *you*," I said as the bus slowed down in front of me. "You take care of yourself," I said sheepishly. Both of us knew that five minutes earlier I couldn't have cared less what happened to him.

"I will," he said. "And you take care of that leg."

"I will."

I hobbled onto the bus and took a seat by the window. I watched Mike as he clung to his cup of change, cherishing it as if it were the first gift he had ever received. Despite his gratitude, I didn't feel absolved for my actions. A half cup of change seemed too small a gift for the man who gave a name to every nameless face I've ever seen.

Alexandera Simone

Don't Ever Give Up

For nothing will be impossible with God.

Luke 1:37

Sam Hensen was celebrating his ninth birthday at summer camp. The counselors and other kids threw him a party with cake and gifts his parents had sent along.

He wasn't a popular boy and didn't have many friends. On his eighth birthday, only one little boy showed up for his party. None of the parents allowed their children to go to Sam's party, because they were afraid he would scare their children.

Sam was mentally disabled. He couldn't speak or walk like other children. He was shunned by both kids and parents alike. But his ninth birthday party was different. At camp, he saw there were people who cared about him. One boy, in particular, befriended Sam. His name was Bobby. Bobby was eleven, and though he wasn't mentally challenged, he had a younger brother who was. Sam reminded Bobby of his brother, and they developed a friendship unlike any other.

Bobby came to Sam's cabin every morning to help him

get ready for his daily exercises and get to breakfast on time. He also helped him in sports. Sam loved baseball, and Bobby took on the challenge of trying to teach Sam to bat. They worked for hours and days, but it seemed nearly impossible that Sam would ever hit the ball. The counselors tried to teach Sam, too, but it seemed hopeless.

One night, while reading the Bible, Bobby thought of Sam and said a little prayer for him. After praying, he went over to Sam's cabin and woke him up. "C'mon Sam! Wake up! Let's go try to hit the ball!"

Sam opened his eyes. What was Bobby doing, waking him up in the middle of the night? Bobby pulled him out of bed. "It will only take a moment and we'll be right back."

Bobby and Sam sneaked by their counselors and went out to a lighted parking lot. Bobby got the bat and ball and helped Sam get into position to bat. Through sleepy eyes, Sam tried to focus on the ball. He swung several times but still couldn't hit it.

Bobby still didn't give up. He told Sam, "I'll pitch one more and I know you're going to hit this one."

Bobby pitched the ball, and for the first time ever, the ball went sailing by his head! Sam had finally hit it! They began to jump and yell excitedly.

A voice came through the parking lot, "What are you boys doing?" It was their counselor, Chris. They told Chris what had happened, and a smile crossed his face. He said, "You two could be in real trouble for sneaking out of the cabin, but I'll let this one slide. I know you have helped each other and worked hard together and I'm proud of you."

Chris put his arm around Sam and told him, "I knew you'd hit the ball one day. Aren't you glad Bobby didn't give up on you!" Sam nodded his head, yes, and all three guys headed back to the cabins arm in arm.

Sam fell asleep that night with a smile of accomplishment on his face. Bobby learned to always have faith, even in the midst of impossible circumstances. He went on to play baseball in college and was elected to his school's Hall of Fame.

Sam said, "Every time I go see Bobby play baseball, if he ever strikes out or gets mad at himself, I stand up and yell, 'Don't you dare give up!'"

Years later, Sam was asked to throw out the ceremonial ball at a professional baseball game, and he eventually returned to teach baseball at the old summer camp during their Special Olympics.

Scot Thurman

Charlie Counts

If you help someone up a hill, you're that much closer to the top yourself.

Carol Jacobsen

Charlie McCrary served with pride as my mailroom attendant. As the administrative director of a small government agency, I oversaw all the resources that the employees needed to perform their duties—office space, salary, supplies, furniture, and the mail service. Charlie was my right hand in the mailroom, fifty years old, a head-injury survivor, a gentleman, and an obstacle in the way of those rushing through life with sharper reflexes.

At times I failed to fully listen to Charlie. Then I wrestled with my conscience until I made a point to chat about his annual vacation, his volunteer work at the hospital, or his beloved University of South Carolina Gamecocks in spite of my alumni status with archrival Clemson University. Those who took the time to hear and study Charlie learned that he was a phenomenal person in spite of his physical obstacle. On a clerk's salary, he was debt-free and owned a condominium in town, a sedan, and managed a little account that enabled him to take trips to such places as Alaska, Israel, and assorted Bowl games. Having no wife or children, he had the ability to escape his menial mail tasks and follow his passion to travel. I admired his drive to be part of the world.

One morning Charlie arrived at work, smiling as usual, but complaining about his forearm. As his supervisor and friend, I asked why. Charlie often rode the bus to save money. He explained that the evening before, he had awaited the stoplight change, then stepped off the curb to approach the bus stop across the street. An impatient young man ran the red light and knocked Charlie over his hood onto the pavement.

"Charlie! Are you okay? Tell me what happened! Have you told your family?" I asked questions, expecting to hear all about the excitement and pending legal or insurance claim. As director over human resources, I also knew about Charlie's medical coverage. "Have you been to the doctor?"

"No. My wrist hurts, but it doesn't look bad. The guy stopped and we exchanged driver's licenses, but before I could write everything down, he grabbed it out of my hand and sped off. Why would he do that?"

I made him tell me everything he remembered, which was remarkably detailed—the man's name, the make and model of the car, the license tag, even that the guy was headed to a job interview and was currently unemployed.

Most people underestimated Charlie, and I suspected this driver had as well once they'd started talking. I didn't want the experience to fade away and erase what he remembered, so I gave him an assignment to write everything down for me by the end of the day. Recording it for him would have slighted his feelings.

"So what is your family doing about it?" Charlie lived alone. Sometimes his siblings knew about his daily details, and other times they, too, became busy with life's demands.

"Nothing. Since I wasn't really hurt, they said to forget about it."

"What about the authorities? Did you call them?"

"Honest, I talked to them. I walked over to the police station and told them all about it. I couldn't call them on the street corner. I don't have a cell phone. Besides, the other guy was gone. But the police wouldn't even take my report. They said there was nothing they could do."

"Charlie, go to the doctor for your wrist. It could be broken. I'll see what I can do for you."

"But what about my deductible?"

"Charlie, if you can't afford it, I'll pay the deductible. Go get some medical attention."

The next day, Charlie returned in an arm cast protecting a mild fracture. The most sympathy Charlie received from coworkers came in the form of, "good thing you weren't really hurt or even killed." I seethed that someone had run down this man and evaded responsibility. I sensed that Charlie's limitations led everyone, including the police, to take less interest in his narrow escape. I called my husband, who worked in law enforcement.

"What can we do about this? Charlie doesn't have much money for medical bills and therapy for his arm. That other guy's insurance ought to be paying for this. Instead, no one gives a damn! Not a soul."

The man I married possessed a gruff exterior but a huge heart for the underdog. "Give me the information you have, and I'll see what I can find out. Think Charlie would give us permission to represent him, since no one is listening to him?" By the end of the day, I had power-of-attorney to handle the situation for Charlie, and the momentum to support a man who no one took seriously.

The next day, my husband picked us up for lunch. We ate

in our leisure van and chatted with Charlie to make sure my husband had all the information necessary to pursue some answers. We praised him for having such keen forethought to note such clarity in detail, and we assured him we'd do everything possible to recover his medical bills. Charlie felt like a king receiving so much attention. He beamed the rest of the day just knowing someone cared. If we accomplished nothing else, we'd stroked his feelings to show he wasn't always alone.

Ten days later, after we'd held multiple conversations with the driver, the driver's mother (who owned the car), the driver's insurance company, and the company's attorney, Charlie held written promise of a $2,000 settlement. He had enough to cover his medical deductibles, loss of time for doctor visits, and a little extra for pain and suffering. The amount represented a substantial sum to him—close to two months' take-home pay.

Charlie diligently reported to work in his cast, continuing to distribute mail, open boxes, and stack supplies. He saved every dime that didn't go to doctor bills and invested the funds. He resumed his routine like nothing had happened, holding no grudge against the driver, the police, family, or friends.

I, on the other hand, rode a high for weeks knowing that a wrong had been righted. I couldn't pass Charlie without smiling, without stopping to hear about the fall prospects for his college football team, or his plans for another trip. All my errands, my deadlines, my rushing to and fro seemed frivolous in comparison to listening to the words of a man who had little audience. Never before had I realized how mere listening exemplified a simple, honorable, proper way to give back to humanity. Yes, I deduced, Charlie counts.

Cynthia Hope Clark

The Smallest Caregiver

An attitude of gratitude creates blessings.

Sir John Templeton

Our granddaughter Hannah had appointed herself Grandpa John's helper. She was too young to understand the meaning of "caregiver," but we all watched with astonishment as her heart led her to say and do things that brought comfort and hope.

We'd just returned home from an appointment with John's orthopedic surgeon. Our daughter Cathy's blue van pulled up to the curb, and moments later our vivacious, four-year-old granddaughter, Hannah, ran toward us.

"Hi!" she called out. "Grandpa, is your knee all better?"

"Not yet, Hannah. My doctor has to put me in the hospital. Then he'll make my knee like new."

Suddenly, John winced and moaned with pain. A look of compassion crossed Hannah's face.

"Grandpa, take my hand, and your knee will feel better."

John grinned for the first time all morning. "You know, I think you're right, Hannah."

Her sparkling blue eyes looked up at her granddad reassuringly as she placed her hand in his. The two of them headed for the house, her strawberry blond ponytail bouncing back and forth. Cathy and I both chuckled at the sight.

Once we were all in the house, Hannah followed me out to the kitchen and watched as I took an icepack out of the freezer. She'd seen me do this several times before.

"Grandma, can I put ice on Grandpa's knee?"

"Of course, Hannah," I replied. Her face glowed with anticipation as I handed her the icepack and paper towel.

Moments later I felt elated about the conversation I'd overheard.

"Grandpa, this will make your knee feel better. There, now can I sit on your good knee?"

I walked into the living room to find them snuggling closely together, happily reading a story.

Hannah pointed to a bike in the picture book and said, "Grandpa, if you do what the doctor tells you, you'll be able to ride your bike again."

"You know, I think you're right, Hannah."

Over the next three weeks, John had to endure the drudgery of preoperative tests.

During that time his anxiety level climbed. His hazel eyes, dulled by pain, lost their luster. Even his normally healthy bronze complexion turned a grayish color.

Finally, the day before surgery, John announced, "I just want this all behind me. Whatever it takes to feel normal again—bring on the surgery!" Even as he made this announcement, I heard an underscore of worry in his voice.

Later that afternoon, Hannah brought her coloring books over and sat down at the dining room table. "I'm going to color a picture," she announced. "Grandpa, what's your favorite color?"

"Red," John replied. Once again I watched as the two of them energetically worked on Hannah's art project.

"Grandpa," she said, placing her prize picture in her grandpa's lap, "I want you to have this picture so you won't be afraid when you get your knee fixed."

No one had ever mentioned Grandpa's being afraid. Yet Hannah's sensitive heart seemed to understand.

The night before John's surgery, Hannah came to visit. "Grandpa, Mommy said I could come see you in the hospital."

"Hannah, that makes me happy," John replied as he hugged her.

Early the next morning on our drive to the hospital, I notice a remarkable change in John's physical and emotional state of being. He looked peaceful and sounded confident. "Karen," he said, laughing, "with my new knee you won't be able to keep up with me."

"I'm glad you're so happy!"

"Thanks to my littlest angel, Hannah," John exclaimed. "Her compassion and her childlike faith and trust have been a light shining on my doubt."

I, too, felt confident. John entered the hospital smiling and making others smile. I was allowed to sit by his bedside until they took him into surgery.

A few hours later I sighed with relief as Dr. Jamison entered the waiting room and said, "John's surgery went well. He'll be in recovery for a while."

The next day Hannah and Cathy came to visit. John, heavily medicated, slept unaware of their presence. My granddaughter's eyes widened with curiosity as she looked at the IV and all the tubes hooked to her grandpa. With one hand on her hip and a little stuffed bunny under her other arm, she asked in bewilderment, "How am I supposed to get to Grandpa with all that stuff around him?"

"Grandma," she finally said, "please put this bunny in bed with Grandpa. It's my gift. I want him to know I was here." Then she blew him a kiss. Placing a brownie covered with splashes of colored candies in my hand, she whispered, "This is for Grandpa, too."

The bunny snuggled almost protectively against John's arm. Later he woke and immediately acknowledged the presence of his furry companion.

"Hannah's been here."

"Yes, your little angel has been here."

"Karen, Hannah has been good medicine for this old grandpa."

The day John came home, Hannah continued her role as nurse. "Grandpa, did you like your brownie?"

"What brownie?"

Hannah looked at me sternly.

"Your brownie is in the refrigerator," I replied. A few minutes later I gave him his treat, smashed and stale. John ate it anyway.

"Best brownie I ever ate," he announced. Hannah giggled.

Three years later, the bunny still has a place of honor in a basket next to John's recliner. Daily the little brown bunny acts as a reminder of our granddaughter's love. Hannah also maintains a place of honor . . . on her grandpa's new knee.

Hannah may be the smallest caregiver, but it's the heart that counts—and Hannah's compassionate heart is huge.

Karen Kosman

Smelling the Roses

Let us be grateful to people who make us happy; they are the charming gardeners who make our souls blossom.

Marcel Proust

Stressed out again. My car flew through the streets of my quiet town as my mind was a blur with the mental image of my to-do list for that day. Better than a Blackberry, my brain ticked off the list one by one, sending each item into a time slot on my mental schedule, slowly realizing that there was definitely going to be spillover into tomorrow. *Will my to-do list ever end?* I thought in exasperation as I turned onto a busy street lined with cookie-cutter houses. They all looked the same, except for one.

I tried to slow my car in time to get a better look, but it appeared that on the front lawn of the gray house in the middle of the block was an old man slumped in the dirt amid a breathtaking garden. I looked at the zooming cars around me as I quickly pulled over, wondering if I was the only one seeing this, the only one concerned about the old man's welfare. I threw the car into park and jumped out, running toward the old man. The words, "Sir, are you okay? Is everything all right?" escaped my lips just as I got close enough to notice that his stooping figure was, not only alive and moving, but it appeared to be pushing something into the dirt.

"I'm fine, sweetheart," he answered as he turned around at the sound of my approaching steps. He looked at me curiously. "Just a lonely old man taking care of his garden."

His eyes were deep blue, set back with pockets of soft skin surrounding them. There was a certain far away look in his eyes that caught me immediately.

He seemed to be about eighty years old and was very frail looking. His back already had a hunch, and I was immediately concerned about his bending over so much to do gardening.

"Were you worried about me for a specific reason?" he asked.

"Well, I was driving by, and from the street it looked like you had keeled over," I said without really thinking, both relieved and concerned about him all at the same time.

He chuckled in a sweet way that made the soft skin around his eyes crinkle at the corners. "Come to think of it, I can see how it would look like that," he mused. "You know, I've been out here for weeks at a time every spring for about the past ten years, and no one has ever stopped."

"Don't you have anyone to help you?" I asked, immediately regretting the question as a look of sadness passed over his gaze.

"It's just me and my flowers," he said.

My heart went out to him as I began to get a sense of what the garden meant to him. *I can push my to-do list off by an hour*, I thought. *Can't I?*

"Just you and your flowers, until now," I said to him and

smiled. "Can you ask them if they wouldn't mind my joining you guys for a while?"

Amused, he introduced himself as Mr. Jenkins and patted the tender earth next to him again and again for me to join beside him. Meanwhile, I tried to convince him to sit on the lawn chair a few feet away so that he could let me do the bending over while he rested.

He repeatedly refused, and as soon as I found myself beside him digging small furrows in the soft ground and planting marigolds, I felt terrible for not having successfully convinced him to sit down and relax. *What am I accomplishing here if he is still straining his back and neck bent over the ground?* I thought. *Some help I am.*

However, as he began to speak I realized that my purpose there was much more than just being an extra hand for planting and weeding. "My grandchildren used to play here in the garden every summer," he said. "My wife would bring out lemonade, and we would all sit together and enjoy the flowers. But then, within one year my son moved away with the grandchildren and my wife passed on," he added sadly.

"Well, don't they visit?" I asked.

"Rarely," he said. "That was a long time ago. They are older now and all off doing their own things. If anything, they come visit in the late fall or wintertime."

"And yet, you still keep the garden flourishing so perfectly. That's a huge amount of work," I noted, a hint of a question in my tone.

He smiled wistfully. "It's a small price to pay for seeing my wife still in the roses, and hearing the voices of my grandchildren amidst the bushes. The memories that it sets the stage for is worth every minute of work," he said.

"There were so many times during those summers that I would busy myself with something else in the house, would have something that needed fixing or doing, and I missed so many precious moments in the garden with them. I guess I kind of feel that, better late than never, I'm making up for lost time."

The afternoon flew by as I found myself pushing off my to-do list hour after hour to keep Mr. Jenkins company and help him make his garden beautiful. At one point, I finally convinced him to take a break, and he let me go inside and bring out lemonade. We sat on the lawn chairs together and chatted about his life for hours.

"You know," he said at one point as he slurped a few final drops from the bottom of his glass through a red-and-blue-striped straw. "I haven't had someone really listen to my stories for such a long time."

The time finally came for me to leave, and I got up to go. "Not just yet," he said softly. Suddenly, he got up from his seat and walked around the garden plucking various flowers from the earth. Roses, lilies, beautiful things whose names I didn't even know. He excitedly pulled at stalks and yanked out roots, putting them all together in a large bundle he finally handed to me with a big smile. "Thank you for helping me today," he said, "with more than you know."

I looked at my bouquet of mismatched stem lengths and colors. It was beautiful. I left that day slightly sunburned, quite tired, a to-do list completely abandoned, but realizing that by helping Mr. Jenkins, he had helped me so very much as well. He taught me about the pure joy that can come from helping others, how life is too short not to revel in the precious moments, and so much more. Most important, he taught me that no matter how busy life gets, no matter how crazy things are, one should never forget to make time to stop and smell the roses with those they love.

Beth Pollack

Little Things Do Make a Difference

Start by doing what's necessary, then what's possible, and suddenly you are doing the impossible.

Saint Francis

It tore at my daughter Laurie's heartstrings to hear the sobs of my granddaughter. This was the third time in a week there had been bullying problems at the elementary school my granddaughter attended.

Creative juices flowing, Laurie realized she had the perfect answer. It would take a lot of planning and even more time on her part, but Laurie became a woman on a mission.

After gaining the approval of the school principal, Laurie developed a program that would help the students focus on positive actions and words. She was about to inspire and motivate hundreds of children, and she realized a lot was at stake. *It has to work,* she thought. *It just has to!*

Laurie explained to the school staff that the students were to be encouraged to file reports on one another for their kind gestures, no matter how small the deed. "The interesting thing about it all," said Laurie, "is that it truly was the little things that they all began noticing." She picked up two reports at random and read them. "When I was by myself, Jeffry sat on the swing with me." "I slipped and cut myself on the ice, and Sara sat with me." Similar reports handed in by the school children eventually soared from the hundreds to well over the thousand mark.

"The children revealed a lot about what their concerns are during these early school years. I observed a noticeable pattern emerge in the reports," said Laurie. "The children spoke a lot about their appreciation for being included, their appreciation for having someone to play with, and their relief and appreciation when another student comforted them after a spill."

The response to the new program was astounding and was more than Laurie had hoped for. Participation by the students increased weekly. Subsequently, the load of volunteer work for this one parent increased by leaps and bounds. Students had filed sixty reports of kindness in one week alone.

"It became a challenge to fit everything on the bulletin board, and to keep it sparkling and colorful. The kids loved the glitter of the displays," Laurie said. She devoted hundreds of hours working both at home and at the school to prepare materials and build weekly displays to keep the children engaged.

The elementary school took on a conspicuous change. Kids were sharing lunches and opening doors for one another. Kindness thrived! Even the crossing guard at the crosswalk was reported for her acts of kindness. "The wonderful thing about this," observed Laurie, "was that the report was put in by a youngster who was so shy he had never even spoken to the crossing guard, although the guard had spoken words of encouragement to this particular child many times."

A child who held the reputation for being arrogant was

suddenly helping another clean out her desk. One lonely child reported of a classmate: "When I needed a friend to play with, she was there." The reports went up weekly, but not just as ordinary reports. Each weekend Laurie chose a theme. One week she placed the names of the youngsters on lightning bolts, and another week every report was done on teddy bears, and yet another time on little T-shirts, all hanging on a clothesline.

The bulletin board itself was always eye-catching, and crowds gathered so that soon parents, teachers, and other staff were also gathering around to view the theme and designs for the new week.

When the school year drew to a close, Laurie took each and every "good deed" report and attached them to one long continuous roll of paper. Once posted, this was to be the final reminder to all—that little things do make a difference. She chose a time when only teachers were at the school, and she and her young daughter literally wrapped the school walls with over a thousand kindness reports.

Motivated by her concern for her daughter and the other children, one parent found a way to counteract bullying and meanness—by reporting acts of kindness.

"I sincerely believed, and still do, that an act of kindness should receive ten times the attention given to a deed that came about because of wrong choices. I wanted my program to encourage both students and adults to focus on the positive, on what is appreciated, not on what is annoying or hurtful."

On the final school day that year, Laurie asked the principal if the children could leave their classrooms and walk about to view this accumulated list of their good deeds and thoughtfulness. The students were told that any reports that featured their name could be taken home as souvenirs.

Choked with emotion, Laurie felt an overwhelming

sense of satisfaction as she watched excited students gather around the reports, first reading them, then commenting and remembering. Students took great pride in how many reports bore their names and raced around the halls to retrieve the reports to take them home as mementos. In recognizing the smallest of gestures, these students made a huge difference in the lives of one another. Just wait until next year!

Ellie Braun-Haley

Courageous Giving

We are obligated to be more scrupulous in fulfilling the commandment of charity than any other positive commandment because charity is the sign of a righteous man.

Maimonides, Mishneh Torah

Keith Taylor had never forgotten his parents' lessons in generosity, evident in tithing to their church and helping others. Nor had he forgotten the helping hand his boss had given him in his youth. Keith knew he wanted to help others, but on a university professor's salary, he thought he'd never have the money to spare. Then he changed the way he thought. He decided to live on less to set aside $350 a month. Next, on a simple, homemade website that he called ModestNeeds.org, Keith offered a one-time gift to whoever needed it.

Even without any advertising or publicity, a few people found his site. One young man wrote to him, asking for $78 to fix his car so that he could get to work and pay his rent. This small, unexpected-but-necessary expense stood between the man's self-sufficiency and disaster. Keith paid the car-repair bill, and it made all the difference in that young man's life.

Keith had launched ModestNeeds.org on March 21, 2002. On May 1 of that year, he received request number 100 from a working couple with five children in Baltimore, Maryland. Madeline and her husband had been shocked to get a huge water bill from the city in December 2001. They discovered a leaking pipe under the house and had it fixed, then paid down the bill the best they could for months. But by April there just wasn't enough to feed a family of seven, pay all the bills, and pay extra on that debt. The city was about to auction this family's home to collect the balance of the water bill, which was $310.09. For a $310.09 utility bill, this family was about to become homeless.

The auction was set for Monday morning, and on Friday the balance in the ModestNeeds.org bank account was $36 short of what was needed to help this family. On his way to the post office, Keith prayed for a miracle to save the family's home. A miracle was waiting in the mail. The letter from a teacher explained that she had heard about the Modest Needs Foundation and told her students about it. The class had chosen to give up lunchtime ice cream for one day to help somebody else. The teacher had made a small donation herself and asked the school to send a check.

"The enclosed check was for forty dollars exactly—just a few dollars more than was necessary to pay off the city of Baltimore," Taylor recalls. "At eleven fifty-one PM on Sunday, May twelfth, two thousand two—nine minutes before the final deadline—the auction of this family's home was stopped, thanks to the generosity of these children and the power of their ice-cream-sandwich blockade."

As people heard about ModestNeeds.org, or found it on the website, word spread—and the good news reached the media. Keith was interviewed by newspapers and magazines, including *People* and *Reader's Digest*, and appeared on radio and television shows, including *Today* and *The Early Show*. Thousands began to visit Keith's site and to write to him. But they weren't all writing to ask for help; they were writing to offer help. They wanted to know where to send money to help others.

In March 2004, Keith literally stumbled across Jessica, a homeless twenty-year-old in New York City. She had a tin cup, which he accidentally knocked over, and a sign that read, "Homeless five more days. Still hungry. Help if you can."

Jessica had applied for a program that provided food and shelter for homeless women who demonstrated a commitment to self-sufficiency by seeking work. When she got a job, the program would help her get a home. She was accepted into the program and would have a place to stay after only five more nights on the freezing streets.

Keith searched the city until he found a clean, safe hotel that would provide a room with breakfast for five days at half price. Then he went back for Jessica. She couldn't believe that anyone would give her a place to stay, expecting nothing in return. "I explained, very simply, that we wanted to help her because we wanted her to know how much she was worth to all of us," Keith said.

Jessica was still crying when Keith left her in that hotel room. "Wait." Wiping her eyes, she took Keith's hand and emptied her tin cup into it. Closing his hand around the change, she looked up into his face and smiled. "Request number thirty-six thousand, three hundred sixty-eight 'Mom of Two Needs Help with Rent,' was funded in part by two dollars and sixty-eight cents in change donated to the Modest Needs Foundation by a person who didn't have a permanent residence, but who, thanks to this community's generosity, isn't quite homeless in the way that she was before," Keith said.

How much does it take to change a life? To the person who needs it, $100 is a lot of money—yet twenty of us giving only $5 each have the power to help keep that person self-sufficient. The Modest Needs Foundation's motto is "Small Change. A World of Difference." Today, millions of people have visited the ModestNeeds.org site. How many more can we help with the small fortune that's on our dressers, in our coat pockets, or spread in the bottoms of our purses? It takes less than we have.

As his father told him when Keith first shared his plan to give part of his income away to strangers, "If you do this, you will never want for anything the rest of your life." Dad was right.

James Robert Daniels

Playing Santa

The most vivid memories of Christmases past are usually not of gifts given or received, but of the spirit of love, the special warmth of Christmas worship, the cherished little habits of home.

Lois Rand

Every Monday night, nearly 100 students from around the world come to our free school for English as a Second Language. For seven years we've taught, befriended, and helped men and women of all ages from Bosnia, Kurdistan, Mexico, China, Vietnam, Korea, Africa, Russia, South America, Iran, Pakistan, and more.

The people have many differences in languages, customs, food, and clothing. They are excited, shy, and sometimes afraid. They are always grateful, and we are always left rejoicing in the help we can give them. We also have many similarities that blur our differences: mainly, we love our children.

Three weeks before Christmas, one of our students from Iraq approached my husband and surprised him by asking for help in creating a Christmas celebration for his children. We were surprised that a Muslim family would request this. We were curious why he would want this, but his children went to public school and were feeling left out of this exciting holiday.

The father was on disability from a job injury and the family had little. We put out the word to the other volunteers who taught, drove buses, and helped in child care for the English classes every week.

Six days before Christmas, we went to the family's apartment, loaded with a gift for each of the four children, fruit, a basket of olive oil and spices, homemade cookies, beans, and rice.

We were greeted with smiles and led to the sparsely decorated living room. While we talked with the children, their parents put together a tray of sodas and sweet bread.

We talked about how they were doing with practicing their English, how they were adjusting to America, and we joked with the children, whose eyes strayed to the wrapped packages nearby. When I couldn't stand it any longer, I asked their parents if the children could open their gifts.

Everyone helped the eighteen-month-old daughter, who was almost completely blind. Familiar with the child's problems, one of our volunteers had purchased a push button toy full of sound and bright lights. We laughed as this little girl, who had smiled very little when we came in, now laughed, and clapped her hands as she pressed the buttons of the toy with her hands, feet, and mouth.

The two-year-old daughter hurriedly unwrapped her gift, a see-through backpack full of blocks. Soon miniature buildings filled the living room. The twelve-year-old son gasped when he opened his package containing two small remote-controlled cars inside. And the fourteen-year-old daughter, her English near perfect, couldn't wait for me to cut open the plastic that held her new cassette player and headphones. Soon, like any teenager, she was nodding her head to the rhythm of her favorite music.

Their mother smiled and made us promise to come back soon for dinner. We felt like the three kings bearing gifts; my husband, daughter, and I couldn't imagine a nicer feeling. We made a new connection with this family that Christmas week.

Yes, there are many differences between us and our students. We speak different languages, eat different foods, celebrate different holidays, and see the world just a little bit differently.

But the reality is that when Muslims and Christians become simply parents, we are very similar.

Kathryn Lay

Learning to Share

Shared joy is joy doubled. Shared sorrow is sorrow halved.

Source Unknown

Sharing was an important lesson I learned at an early age. Whether it was a favorite toy, room at the dinner table for someone less fortunate, or a little extra change in the Sunday collection plate, it became part of the family consciousness to share. Even when we didn't have much, it was reinforced in me how there were others in worse situations than we were.

My grandparents, L. and Moma, were born in separate small Southern towns in the early part of the twentieth century. Because they were raised in such small communities, they had a closeness to their neighbors one could never experience in a city. And because they were raised with such a strong faith, they were always mindful of the blessings they had and were willing to help those in the community who were in need.

Even after my grandparents moved to San Diego in 1947, those small town influences were present. They permeated every aspect of my grandparents' lives. If someone was ill, off their feet, and couldn't care for themselves, Moma could be counted on to bring one of her specialty meals, capped off with a healthy slice of homemade pound cake, and help them attend to any business.

If someone needed a ride to church, my grandfather would always make time for that. "Here, take this," the rider would say while handing a few dollars to my grandparents. "Now, you put that away," Moma would say with a wave. I never saw them take anything. It just wasn't their style.

Over the years, there were many, many people my sister, Cheryl, and I made room for in the backseat of the ever-present station wagon. Each person had his or her own unique situation. Each was grateful for my grandparents' generosity. But there was one passenger who seemed always to have a reserved seat.

Carl was confined to a wheelchair. He had no means of transportation. We often noticed him wheeling himself down the street in various parts of town. There were times when all we could see was his silhouette and the reflectors on his chair as he made his way down the dark street. As usual, we would pull over and load Carl up and drop him at his destination, wherever that might be. Whether we were on our way to church or another destination, my grandfather would pull the station wagon over, place Carl's wheelchair in the back, gently place Carl in the car, and head up the road.

Carl couldn't speak very well, and it was hard for me to hide the fact that I couldn't understand what he was saying. To me his words seemed like grunts and garbled sounds. But my grandparents appeared to understand him because they would hold a conversation with him the entire time he was in the car. After riding with him more and more, I started to pick up on what he was saying. Not every word, but just enough.

Eventually, we would reach Carl's destination. Sometimes it would be church and we would all get out together. My grandfather would help Carl up the stairs and we'd all enter the sanctuary together. Sometimes it would be another destination and my grandfather would help him out of the car; we'd all bid Carl farewell and be on our way. As I got older, I helped my grandfather with the wheelchair. I wasn't aware of it at the time, but I was learning a valuable lesson without a word being said.

"Thank . . . you," Carl would say as we placed him in his chair. Every time I saw the gratefulness in his eyes, it touched something in my heart that I still remember today.

Lawrence D. Elliott

The Worth of a Soul

To touch the soul of another human being is to walk on holy ground.

Stephen Covey

By the time Helen was eighteen months old, her eyes were a bright blue, and her hair was a golden red. When her eyes changed from sky blue to sea green, I was certain that she would be a rare beauty.

The camera always adored Helen. However, Helen's personality and innate kindness would always outshine her physical beauty. Her smile reflected a loving nature that permeated every fiber of her being.

At three years old, Helen had already developed an unusual logic that made perfect sense to her. Of course, she would give away her favorite teddy bear to a child "who needed it" more than she did. In kindergarten it seemed perfectly natural for her to love the unlovable, including the teacher who struck terror within the hearts of the other students. Helen was quite certain her teacher was delighted to be with her, and by the second week of school, Helen was feeding her teacher oranges from her grimy little hands.

By second grade, Helen had become the champion of the weak, the hope of the hopeless, and she did it all with a self-less grace that was nothing short of miraculous.

When Helen reached high school, it was pretty evident that our house would always bulge with teenagers of every shape, creed, and ethnicity.

I still have the pictures from Helen's thirteenth birthday party. I can pick out the boy who needed to check in with his parole officer before the cake was cut.

Then, there is the girl who couldn't drink cola because her religion forbade it. We went running across the street for chocolate milk. In the corner was the boy whose parents had escaped from Vietnam when he was a baby, and the girl whose father was a Taiwanese diplomat.

African American, Irish, Filipino, and Caucasian faces stare cheerfully out at me. It was an incredible feat just to round up all the kids for a one-of-a-kind picture. It took three snapshots to complete the photograph. What an unforgettable sea of grinning faces peer out from those pictures, as though the United Nations had dropped off all its teenagers for a day of ice cream and cake.

In the fall of her sophomore year, Helen and I were shopping the malls for school clothes. I was doing some creative arithmetic, trying to make our budget stretch into something that would delight and still be affordable.

At one point, I noticed a man and young girl moving straight toward us. The man was dressed in work clothes, and he seemed to be encouraging the overweight youngster closer to us. I could identify with the girl. I looked back upon my teenage years with horror. These two seemed to be disagreeing and were almost upon us.

Helen had just finished exchanging greetings with one of her countless squealing friends, and as she turned around, she came face-to-face with the reluctant teenager. Faster than the speed of light, Helen's eyes sparkled with recognition. Her face broke into a brilliant smile, and she shrieked with joy!

"Cindy!" she squealed as she threw her arms around the chubby girl's neck. Cindy's face broke into a beautiful smile, and she squealed right back at Helen. Then they both did a hand-holding, happy dance while grinning and shrieking with delight. Cindy was transformed from a rather sad, "just-like-I-was" kid into the vivacious young girl she truly was meant to be. Cindy and Helen chattered away, totally oblivious to Cindy's father and me as we stood amazed.

Who was this unconsciously generous, loving daughter of mine? How had God graced my life with someone so bright and beautiful? How different my life might have been had there been a Helen to accept and love me when I was a teenager. When I turned back to Cindy's father, I saw his face transformed from frustration and sadness to joy.

Cindy had seen Helen, he confided, long before Helen spotted her. She had identified Helen as "one of the popular girls." As Cindy's father encouraged her to speak to Helen, Cindy had refused. Why would a somebody, she reasoned, want to talk to a nothing?

Cindy's father had felt helpless to make his daughter believe how precious she truly was. Helen, in one unpretentious act, had given Cindy and her father a priceless gift of unconditional acceptance and love.

Cindy's dad's eyes shined with pride and gratitude, but no more than the gratitude that filled my heart for the gift that was Helen. I learned a great lesson that day. I learned that true friendship does not measure another with speculation. Fourteen-year-old Helen taught me that the worth of a soul is not in the eye of the beholder. It's in the heart.

Jaye Lewis

Looks Can Be Deceiving

Great opportunities to help others seldom come,
but small ones surround us every day.

Sally Koch

I woke up at 7 AM on the ninth day of my hospital stay and saw the night nurse writing the day's shift information on the chalkboard across from my bed.

Tracy would be the nurses' assistant for the day. I looked to see who would be my nurse and saw the name, Lady Di. *Great. Just what I need,* I thought. *Probably some Queen Latifah wannabe with more ego than actual nursing experience.*

I was definitely not in a good mood. Recovery from emergency abdominal surgery had been a nightmare in itself. The daily injections to keep my blood from clotting and the twice-daily finger pricks to keep a check on what looked suspiciously like an acute diabetic condition had me at the very end of my rope.

I was a bit frustrated with the fact that years of constant complaining to doctors about abdominal pain had been casually dismissed as "nothing to worry about." Now here

I was in a hospital bed trying to come to terms with the reality of how this surgery and my condition would affect the rest of my life. The surgeon had explained it as a congenital defect. After 30 percent of my colon and small intestine were removed, I was told I was very lucky to have even survived. I tried my best to hold on to grateful thoughts as the pain seared through me.

I had not eaten since days before the surgery, not had so much as a sip of water. With tubes in every orifice of my body, I looked like death warmed over. My lips were dry and cracking from lack of moisture, and my hair—well let's just say the matted mess was in dire need of a Clairol makeover.

The only good thing I could deduce from this dilemma was that I had lost ten pounds, and even that didn't seem to make much difference, not with the six-inch scar running up the middle of my body. Every day was a stifling repeat of the one before, but at least this day I had something to look forward to—I was curious to meet the royal RN dubbed Lady Di.

Tracy, my aide, came in to get me ready for my morning bath. She helped me to sit up in the bedside chair, placed the tray table in front of me with all the necessary toiletries, and then left to help the nurse with a patient in the next room.

I may as well have had both my hands tied together, with the tube down my nose and IVs in both hands. I sat there wondering how I was supposed to manage to soap up without getting myself tangled up in a mess of tubes and cords that were now an external part of me. The water in my wash basin was nearly ice cold when an elderly woman poked her head in to see how I was doing. She took one look and correctly guessed that I was in desperate need of an extra pair of hands. She ran fresh, hot water and began the chore of helping me clean up.

I was having a hard time placing this friendly woman. She didn't wear the customary smock of the nursing assistants. She certainly wasn't dressed like a nurse. Her scruffy shoes, baggy clothes, and tousled hair had me guessing cleaning lady, but they, too, wore identifying uniforms.

She took a bottle of shampoo from her pants pocket and began to lather my messy mane. The shampoo's scent resembled floral paradise. Out of the other pocket she produced body lotion, smoothing it onto my skin until I felt like silk from head to toe. I still looked more than a little under the weather, but now my inner spirit was beginning to shine. I felt more human and alive than I had in a long time.

She made my bed, cleared everything away, and set up my bedside table so all my essentials were within easy reach. She told me she'd be back in a little while to check on me. That was the first day that I truly felt like smiling since my medical ordeal began. No amount of flowers or fancy gifts could have given me what this kind and caring woman did. I didn't feel like I was drowning in a mountain of medical problems. I was seeing a light at the end of the tunnel.

I looked in the mirror and almost recognized myself again, knowing I owed it all to this mystery woman who whipped me into a better frame of mind with a little TLC.

Tracy returned, apologizing for being gone so long. She immediately noticed I was all coiffed and chipper. I tried my best to describe the wingless angel who had hovered around me like a mother hen, giving me a much needed lift with her loving touch of human kindness. Tracy knew right away who I was talking about. "Oh, that's Diane, she's always helping out whenever she has the chance," Tracy declared matter-of-factly. That's when I found out that this kind and gentle woman was Lady Di, the nurse on duty that day. I also found out it was the nursing staff who gave her the nickname, Lady Di.

I often think of her, especially when I'm tempted to judge someone solely on looks. Thanks to her, I now know better. I never did find out why the hospital staff nicknamed her Lady Di, but if you ask me, I think it just may be because she treats her patients like royalty, going beyond the call of duty to make a difference in the lives of the patients who cross her path.

There are nurses who do their job with professional expertise, and then there are some who go above and beyond the job description. They have a special gift and have perfected the art of treating their patients with down-to-earth compassion and care. They are the angels among us who are a blessing in disguise.

Kathy Whirity

Eight-Penny Blessing

When you rise in the morning, form a resolution to make the day a happy one for a fellow creature.

Sydney Smith

I had nearly two hours to burn in the Detroit airport, a layover on my way to Seattle. I'd flown through Detroit a number of times by then, and I'd become familiar with the airport. I made some phone calls, finished writing a letter and tossed it into the mailbox, and bought some fries at McDonald's.

Then I was thirsty. I'd already downed one bottle of water, but airports seem to dry me out. Besides, I wanted some water for the plane. I stopped by a shop, took a bottle of water from the refrigerated case, and waited my turn in line.

The lady in front of me had several items, and her total rang up to some odd dollars and eight cents.

"Do you have the eight cents?" the clerk asked, after the woman handed him a twenty-dollar bill.

"I'm sure I do," she said, as she dug around in her

wallet. I waited patiently behind her—I was in no hurry, having an hour until my plane left—holding my two dollar bills for my $1.99 water. The dollars had been in my back pocket, change from my french fries, put there so I wouldn't have to dig for my wallet in my carry-on bag.

Finally the woman gave up, saying that she had no change at all. The cashier made a face, showing that he did not want to have to count ninety-two cents in change.

"I have eight cents," I said. I knew I had at least eight pennies. My wallet is always full of pennies. It meant that I had to dig out my wallet, exactly what I tried to avoid doing, and I silently cursed myself for this sudden burst of altruism.

"Okay," the sales clerk shrugged, counting out the change in paper money, then looking expectantly at me while I stuck my hand into the bowels of my suitcase's front pocket. As long as he got his eight cents, he didn't care where it came from.

The woman, however, turned to me, her eyes examining me up and down. "You'll pay the eight cents?" she asked, skeptically.

"Sure, why not. It's only a few pennies, and I have them." By now the wallet was in my hand, and I counted the copper coins as I pulled them out with the tip of my finger.

"You're serious?" she said incredulously. "I've never had anyone do anything so kind for me for no reason." She put her hand on my shoulder. "May God bless you, dear. God will bless you for your kindness." She hurried away to make her flight, while I counted the change for the clerk before he rang up my bottle of water. I was pleased that I made her so happy, but it was nothing except one of those tiny windows where you get the chance to do someone else a favor. I kept coming back to the monetary value of the deed. Eight cents. Why on earth would anyone get excited over that?

I had forgotten about the woman by the time I was on the plane, and I doubt I would have remembered her again if it hadn't been for another incident that happened during my visit in Seattle.

My friend and I drove through the city, planning to attend a lecture. It was a spur-of-the-moment decision, and my friend wasn't quite sure of the exact location. After driving the same four-block area a couple of times, we pulled into a gas station. My friend hopped out of the car, and I thought she was going inside to ask a clerk for directions. Instead, she walked over to a woman and young boy sitting on a curb. I watched them talking, then my friend crouched down and leaned over the boy. She held up her hand, indicating they should wait just a moment, and she came back to the car, took a bill out of her wallet and a business card from her purse. "I'll be right back," she said. She went back to the couple, leaning over the boy again. This time I noticed he had a book on his lap.

When my friend came back to the car, I asked her if she got directions. She shrugged. I wondered if they had insisted on being paid for helping her, and I was about to offer to pay her back if that was the case. This lecture was my idea, after all.

"Oh, here it is," she said as we finally found the building we'd been looking for. She pulled into the parking lot, and we got out of the car. "They had just come here from Texas," my friend said, "so they weren't exactly sure if this was the right building. The boy was having trouble with his math. He's fallen behind. The money," she said, "was to help them buy some food. The business card was so they could contact me for more math help."

"What a good person you are," I said. I thought her act was selfless, but she waved me off. "You'd do the same thing," she replied. And I remembered the eight cents.

"People don't expect kindness from strangers," my

friend said after I told her the story. "You might think it was only eight cents, but to that lady, it was a sign that there are good people in the world. Don't be surprised if good things happen to you now from that one little deed."

My friend had it wrong. Good things happened to me before my one little deed. God has blessed me in many ways, including having the extra pennies in my wallet so I could help someone else.

Now I dump a lot more spare change into the fund-raising tin on the counter of my favorite coffee shop. I regularly offer to pay the odd cents of someone's bill. It may not sound like much, but it gives me the chance to share God's good blessings, eight cents at a time.

Sue Marquette Poremba

The Wall

The first step towards the solution of any problem is optimism.

John Baines

It was a sunny day at the beach. Young children were scattered about, playing in the sand. Different races. Different backgrounds. Different lifestyles. They didn't know one another before that afternoon. Not until they became involved with the Wall. As I sat on the beach, I watched the drama unfold.

Somewhere out at sea, a storm gathered. The waves tossed high, gaining power. Too treacherous for swimming. Beachgoers were allowed at the water's edge, but no farther. Children were cautioned to stay out of the dangerous currents that could pull at their small feet and young bodies and drag them into deeper waters.

One of the children began to build a sand wall. It was his intention to keep this mighty ocean away from the castle he had built by himself. He had worked on it all afternoon, and now it was being threatened by an ocean out of control. So he began working on the wall. He had very small hands and very heavy sand to carry back and forth to the wall he intended to build in front of his castle. He rushed across the beach, up and down to the water's edge, bringing the supply of wet sand that would fortify his protective wall. For those who watched, it was clear that it was a futile enterprise that would take much longer than one person could possibly manage in a day. His castle could not survive for many more minutes with the stormy waves headed in its direction.

Another child standing nearby sensed the emergency and decided to help. The two began working together, carrying, lifting, and racing against the incoming tide. A third boy who had been watching the two joined with them, piling the wet sand on the wall, mixing it with dry to make the protective barrier stronger. A few girls passing by surveyed the castle, the growing wall, which was stretching now as many feet as there were children, and they joined in the construction. In a short time, the wall grew higher. And wider.

The working crew also expanded. More children were attracted to the wall and to the battle to preserve the castle, even though it wasn't their castle. Though they were strangers to one another, they had a common goal, to hold back the ocean. It became the irresistible challenge.

The children laughed as they piled the sand higher and gave one another instructions. Discussions arose as to how high and how thick the wall should be and which sand was best, the wet or the dry, and how much time they had to complete their task. The waves refused to accept defeat as they beat against the barricade, adding cracks as quickly as they were mended, taking sand away as quickly as it was added.

Now it became a battle of wits and endurance between the sand-gatherers and the incoming tide. The wall symbolized something that only those involved could understand. Parents called to them that it was time to go home. "In a minute," one answered. "Not yet," said another. Their faces took on looks of determination. They had worked too hard for too long to give up now. Even though the whitecaps taunted them, slapping their construction around roughly, the wall held strong. Each time a wave failed to diminish its exterior, the group shouted in victory. Again and again, without mercy, the waves pounded, but the wall stood firm.

Eventually the children went their separate ways. But the wall remained upright for hours, protecting the castle, with its endurance amazing those who remained. It had come to represent much more than a pile of sand. Many children had joined together, and in that moment on the beach, I watched the impossible become possible.

Harriet May Savitz

Measuring Miracles by Leaps and Bounds

It's the constant and determined effort that breaks down all resistance and sweeps away all obstacles.

Claude M. Bristol

I am no stranger to being different and challenged. It took a while, but I finally got used to people asking, "So, how did you lose your arm?"

Losing my arm to cancer when I was only eleven was a hard way to learn what it means to be handicapped. Doctors discovered a tumor the size of an apple when I broke my left arm in three places. It cost me my arm and shoulder, and because I lost my shoulder, I can't wear a prosthesis. Trying to join in sports was an exercise in frustration for me: I was always picked last, or not at all. So my first challenge was adjusting to life as the "one-armed" kid. When I got over the shock, I determined to be the best I could be at everything I tried. This cancer wouldn't stop me!

I discovered vaulting at Cal-Poly when I was working on a degree in animal science. Vaulting is gymnastics on a moving horse, sort of like Cossack horsemen or circus performers. It is definitely a two-armed sport. The more I watched the Cal-Poly team, the more I knew I wanted to vault. Quite an ambition for a young man with one arm. The school said, "You can't vault . . . you only have one arm." Well, telling me "can't" is like guaranteeing my success. As the first disabled competitive vaulter, I became a bronze medalist. I was even part of a special demonstration at the 1984 Olympics.

After college I got a job as a vaulting coach working with the handicapped in a therapeutic program. That's where I met my wife, Virginia. Just when things were going well, the nonhandicapped program was discontinued, but I was not going to give up my dream of creating the first team of handicapped and nonhandicapped vaulters who would compete in mainstream competition. Virginia and I took the vaulters who wanted to continue in the program, and with more determination than money, we formed Valley View Vaulters. Virginia became the manager and longeur (the person who controls the horse by holding the lunge line, which is attached to the bridle of the horse as it moves in a circle), and I coached the vaulters of all ages and abilities.

We were so broke we couldn't even afford one horse. We set up a practice barrel in Virginia's backyard for our integrated team of seven (one-third handicapped and two-thirds nonhandicapped), and as we entered competitions, people who believed in what we were doing would lend us their horses.

We knew that our fledgling team would raise the bar for the handicapped, achieve success, and share in the joy of one another's accomplishments. Since 1980 I've coached thousands of kids and young adults. In 1993 we began winning competitions, and in 2002 we captured the Trot Team National Championship, a remarkable accomplishment,

considering our overall team remained one-third handicapped and all of our competitive teams included members with handicaps. Our team was winning time after
time without any special considerations.

We have helped kids who have cerebral palsy, autism,
Down syndrome, spinal bifida, schizophrenia, ADD,
vision or hearing loss, acute arthritis, and more have a better quality of life. They believe and they achieve. When
they look at me doing what I do with one arm, they figure,
if I can do it, they can, too.

At the 1996 Nationals, the American Vaulting Association
acknowledged our program's amazing successes, and for
the first time in their history, a demonstration class for disabled vaulters was included. Thirty-three-year-old Jeffrey,
who only four years earlier had been confined to a wheelchair, performed in a special exhibition class for more
severely handicapped vaulters. He was one of five partic-
ipating Valley View Vaulters whose disabilities ranged
from cerebral palsy to autism. Raising himself up from a
chair in the arena, Jeffrey walked without help to our big
white horse and mounted, assisted only by me giving him
a leg up. His face glowed with achievement as he stood
upright on the horse's back and flawlessly executed a
series of intricate compulsory exercises before facing back-
ward and dismounting by swinging off the horse. He
walked back to his chair unassisted. Thunderous applause
from teary-eyed spectators filled the arena. There is no
way to place a value on his accomplishment.

After Jeffrey's performance, his father reminded us,
"When Jeff started, he could barely get his legs apart.
Remember, Rick? It took four men to lift him onto the
horse. You not only helped him physically . . . you helped
his socialization. Now he wants hugs from everyone. You
and Virginia gave him that kind of freedom."

As Virginia often says, some of our kids don't do well in

school. They are not in the top of their classes—for the most part, they are really struggling and don't feel good about themselves. With vaulting they get in touch with life, go forward, and gain self-esteem.

Our profits can't be tracked on a balance sheet, because we are always struggling to stay out of the red, but they are greater than most would ever hope for. Since raising enough money to fund the team is a constant struggle, we measure our profits in achievements of the students and the loving support network that has been formed by all of the vaulters and their families.

I don't know who gets more out of the programs—those with disabilities or those without. The kids who don't have physical or psychological problems learn what it means to care and be sensitive to those who do. But they don't see the difference as a curiosity; it just means their friend and teammate needs a little more help or time. It gives them wonderful values.

When we watch determined youngsters with challenges successfully accomplish what should be impossible, those are our riches. No one could ever hope for more.

Rick Hawthorne
as told to Morgan St. James

I'm Somebody!

In order to succeed we must first believe that we can.

Michael Korda

Tommy was quick-tempered and passionate, yet there was something special about him that touched my heart. He had the sharpest sense of humor I've ever seen in an eight-year-old child. He was my daughter Jenny's best friend in second grade.

"This is my friend, Tommy," Jenny said, as she pulled him toward me for the introduction. He kicked an imaginary clod of dirt, and his eyes would not meet mine.

"Well, well, Tommy," I smiled. "That big clod of dirt you just kicked sure is attracting your attention, isn't it?" I teased. Suddenly, his twinkling dark eyes met mine, and he kicked the floor again.

"Take that, you old clod!" he cried, his face breaking into an irresistible grin.

I kicked the floor and cried, "Yeah! You old clod!" Tommy and Jenny cracked up just as the teacher walked up to introduce herself. She smiled at me, then gave Tommy a cold look.

"No nonsense today, young man," the teacher scolded. Tommy's face fell and his shoulders drooped as he walked away. Placing his hands in his pockets, he turned and met my eyes. I'll never forget that look. It was a look of total hopelessness.

The woman thanked me kindly when I offered to become "room mother" to her class. It was one of the best decisions I ever made. I baked cookies, taught crafts, went on every field trip, and I became attached to Tommy. If ever there was a prophecy of failure, it was Tommy. He was a marked child from the day he took his first step into kindergarten. I couldn't understand it. How can a life be marked for failure in second grade? I found him to be bright and endearing, but my heart was completely won over when I saw the pattern of failure written on his life.

I remembered painfully what it felt like to be eight years old and to have my father turn on me one day, with his face twisting, and scream in my face, "You will *never* amount to anything!" I could feel shock waves of ice water streaking through my veins.

I saw a similar pattern in Tommy's life, and I swore I would do everything in my power to make certain that the disaster that had infected my early life wouldn't happen to him. I became his champion. I helped him with his lessons every day. I laughed and I dreamed with him.

"Oh, I'll be nothing," he would say. "My dad's nothing. My granddad's nothing. I'll be nothing, too. I'd like to keep that in the family." Then he'd laugh. I chuckled, but I didn't think it was funny. It was all too real.

The first field trip I chaperoned was very illuminating. Before we left the school, and once on the bus, the teacher warned Tommy, "No pranks, now. The first time that you step out of line, the field trip will be over for you!"

I heard Tommy mumble, "Well, there goes my trip to the planetarium! I'm doomed."

"No, Tommy, you're not doomed," I whispered. "You'll see the planetarium! I'll be right there with you!" He turned away and stared at the fields racing by. When we stopped for lunch, Tommy received his third warning. I tried to lighten the mood by saying, "That's okay, I'll stay with Tommy." I laughed nervously as Tommy looked away stone-faced. He ate in silence, sitting next to one of the other second grade boys.

Then I saw it. I was right across the table. The boy next to Tommy wiped ketchup on Tommy's brand-new shirt. Lightning flashed in Tommy's eyes as he shoved the boy off the bench and onto the grass.

"*Tommy!*" the teacher cried. "*I warned you, young man!* You are banned from the planetarium! You will wait in the lobby until everyone else goes through!" A secret smile slipped across the perpetrator's face.

"Wait. *Wait!*" I cried. "It wasn't Tommy's fault. This other boy wiped ketchup on his shirt. Tommy shouldn't be punished! This other boy is at fault. Tommy needs to see the planetarium!" I needed for Tommy to see the planetarium.

Hard blue eyes looked at Tommy. "*No!*" she said. "Tommy knows better. There will be no fighting! He *must* learn!" I felt just awful. What could I do?

As we loaded onto the bus and continued our journey, I sought the woman out. I begged and pleaded. Please. Please! *Please!* Any kind of punishment but failure. Nothing worked. Her mind was made up. She explained how Tommy's "bad record" went back to kindergarten! He was a bad seed. He'd never do anything. Or be anything. My blood ran cold, remembering my father's prophecy.

I had no idea how to remedy this situation. I volunteered to stay in the lobby of the planetarium. The teacher urged me to join the children, and she would stay with Tommy. No, I assured her. I wanted to stay with Tommy, and after all, the other children would have so many questions for her to answer. I didn't tell her, but I needed to stay with Tommy.

Tommy and I sat on a bench in the lobby for a long time, not speaking. Then, he began to talk. "I don't remember ever doing anything right in my whole life, Miss Jaye."

I put my arm around him, and I said, "I know how that feels." Tommy looked up at me with adoring eyes. Except for my children, this was a new experience for me. "Tommy, I was just like you, honey. Just like you. I never succeeded at anything. But my life is different now." I paused, looking into his eyes, with deep conviction.

"What changed, Miss Jaye?" he asked.

"Well, Tommy," I began, "it's pretty simple, really." He gave me a look that told me he was hanging on to every word. "I couldn't change the people around me. Not my teachers. Not my classmates. Not my parents. Not anyone else. So, I changed me."

Tommy's eyes looked puzzled, and then the dawn of understanding burst forth! I've never seen such sudden awareness in the eyes of anyone so young. We continued to talk, and I told Tommy all about that day when I became nothing, and I told him what a lie it was. I told him that I knew I was somebody, because a wonderful God says that I am wonderfully made. I told him that many adults say terrible things that come from their own fear of failure. I told him that this day could be the turning point in his life. I told him that he was a wonderful, somebody special with the power to change his own life. Oh, I told Tommy a lot that day, perhaps more than I had ever told anyone and Tommy believed me. Every word.

The next day I went to the school counseling office and spoke to the social worker assigned to the school. He turned out to have a powerful influence on Tommy's future. Tommy was removed from his second grade class and put into a special education class. The second grade teacher told me, "I'm not surprised. He just couldn't last in a normal class." It sickened me, yet I was elated at Tommy's new possibilities.

I heard a few whispers that Tommy was "remarkably, making A's," that he was accepted into the gifted and talented program, and "what was our educational system coming to?" I'd smile and say I hadn't a clue. I saw Tommy only once after this.

When Jenny was in the middle of third grade, I left my abusive husband and fled with my children to a women's shelter. What had I done with my life? Perhaps my dad was right. Was I nothing? I felt trepidation about the future, yet I knew I would fight any dragon just to keep my children safe.

Months later we were safe. I returned to the elementary school for copies of my children's transcripts and as I walked down the hallway I heard footsteps behind me. Before I could turn around, a pair of small arms encircled me, squeezing me tight. I heard Tommy's voice cry out, "Miss Jaye! Miss Jaye!" As I turned, he threw himself into my arms. He had grown so tall! His eyes were shining, and he was laughing. He once again met my eyes with the same adoring look! "Miss Jaye!" he cried. "You were right! I can change myself! And I did! I'm happy now. I'm *somebody!*"

Tears sprang to my eyes and fell upon Tommy's brown hair. I brushed them off as I squatted to study his face. "Yes, Tommy, you are somebody! You have always been somebody!" I hugged him to me, and my eyes locked with the man in the office behind him. That same wonderful counselor, overqualified and underpaid, smiled at me, and gave me two thumbs up!

"Gotta go, Miss Jaye! See you soon!" Tommy gave me one last hug and turned to go. He stopped midstride and looked back at me. "I love you, Miss Jaye!"

"I love you, too, Tommy!" I choked, my eyes blind with tears. Then he turned and ran out of my life. Twenty-five years later, I am still amazed at the impact that young boy had upon me, and how he changed my view of myself.

As I walked out of the school, carrying my children's records, I stepped into the bright sunshine of a new life. In spite of my personal struggles ahead, I felt hope for the future. Every day since, I have felt Tommy's words echo within my own heart.

"I'm somebody! *I'm somebody!*"

Jaye Lewis

3

CHARACTER AND COURAGE

Dream lofty dreams, and as you dream, so shall you become. Your vision is the promise of what you shall one day be; your ideal is the prophecy of what you shall at last unveil.

James Allen

A Box of Missing People

Have courage for the great sorrows of life and patience for the small ones; and when you have laboriously accomplished your daily task, go to sleep in peace. God is awake.

Victor Hugo

My younger sister, Marney, and I had planned to celebrate the last few days of the summer of 2001 in New York, painting our toenails and eating good meals, before she returned for her senior year at Stanford. Instead, we sat horrified, watching television, bearing witness to the tragedy unfolding nearby on September 11.

Feeling a need to do something, we headed to a large sports facility at Chelsea Piers where CNN reported volunteers were setting up a family crisis center. A woman with a clipboard took our names and telephone numbers and then sent us home, asking us to return early the next morning to relieve the volunteers who would be there all night.

The next morning, Marney and I woke early and walked the three blocks back to the Piers. We stood on a basketball court full of volunteers divided by skill: doctors and nurses sat at one end, construction teams at another, and the rest of us stood at half-court waiting for our assignments.

I escorted anxious parents and ex-wives and cousins clutching photographs and flyers to an indoor soccer court. From the door of the Chelsea Piers basketball court to the entrance of the soccer court, I learned the parents' names, the name of the son they couldn't find, and their first language.

Marney sat behind a sign that read "English & Spanish." She filled out a handwritten form for the parents of a son who was missing. He was 6'1", weighed 180 pounds, wore a gold Rolex on his left wrist, worked on the seventy-eighth floor of Tower 1, and had brown hair and blue eyes. He had spoken with them on his cell phone after the first plane hit. Marney wrote down all of these details, including his Social Security number and his parents' telephone numbers. She handed them a photocopy of a list of hospitals and other emergency contacts. She pointed them to counselors and religious leaders who were sitting at round tables in the middle of the room, speaking softly. And then she placed the paper full of information about their missing son in a cardboard box—on top of hundreds of other forms.

In the afternoon I left my post at the door and joined my sister at the long tables in the soccer court. I observed her with awe. She acted so kindly and calmly, with compassion and authority in her steady voice. She answered questions and gave fearless advice.

I met two men from South Africa who were missing a friend, and they explained that they thought he was at a hospital in New Jersey. They asked me where the hospital was and how they could get there. I didn't know.

I met a wife. She had heard about a list of victims the

hospitals had compiled. She asked me if I had that list. I didn't. A brother-in-law asked me where they were taking the bodies. He said he heard they were in the ice rink. I didn't know. I placed the sheets of missing people in the same cardboard box.

My sister created the missing persons database on September 12. At 6 PM technicians began to set up donated computers in a small office. Marney helped to design a Microsoft Excel document to input all of the missing people listed on the forms in the cardboard box. She had watched the pile of forms in the box grow all day, and she tried to make it stop.

We had arrived at Chelsea Piers around 7 AM and lost track of time inside. It was dark by the time we started typing. We were a typing team. We switched tasks on and off; one read the details of the handwritten sheets while the other typed on the laptop. About ten people occupied the small room: some typing, some reading, and technicians working with cables and wires. Over the course of the evening, someone figured out that we held important information regarding people's identities, so a guard was posted outside the door.

The basic pattern of the database soon emerged: specific companies on upper level floors were mentioned frequently. But what transformed the names into people were their details. Gold watches, scars, shamrock tattoos, wedding bands, and birthmarks. We stopped to list our own personal details. "Remember my scar on my right knee and the mole on my lower back." We thought of tattoos that would be good identifiers.

We cried at a wedding picture with a red circle around the bride. We burst into giggles at a headshot of a man with crooked teeth. And I began to shake when I saw the photo of a classmate's girlfriend. I was confused about what we were supposed to feel, and how we should express ourselves.

Gatorade and cookies fueled our dramatically fluctuating energy levels. We were peppy or sluggish, depending on the moment. The ten of us typing were each treated to a session with a volunteer masseuse. She massaged my cramped muscles and my fragile skin; I cried into the headrest.

After we had worked through the forms in the cardboard box, we were handed a set of folders full of more missing person flyers that had been collected at hospitals around the city. Some of the faces were familiar; families had traveled from one trauma center to the next, distributing their missing person papers, and looking for hope.

As we neared the end of the flyers, Marney hit a wall. "I have to go home. I can't do this anymore." She apologized unnecessarily and gave me a large hug with weak arms. When she left the little room, I lost momentum. Ugly scenarios ran through my head, and I needed desperately to be by her side. I finished typing the pile of flyers, saved the data to a disk, and handed it off to a man escorted by policemen. I shut down the computer, rubbed my eyes, and shook hands with the other typists. I shivered with cold exhaustion. And in the quiet dark night I ran home to my sister.

Corey Binns

Mudfish and Pythons

Man can live for about forty days without food, and about three days without water, about eight minutes without air . . . but only for one second without hope.

                                                                Hal Lindsey

The trailhead of San Elijo Lagoon, nearly invisible in the foliage, is a door into San Diego County's largest coastal wetlands. I've hiked it with many people, but my hiking partner today knows more about survival in the wild than any of them.

Benson Deng, now twenty-five, was seven years old when he fled a thousand miles barefoot across Africa, keeping his two five-year-old companions, a brother and a cousin, alive. They ran into the night to escape death when their villages in southern Sudan were attacked.

Camera around my neck, I grab water bottles from the car. Before setting out, we read the posted information about rattlesnakes and mountain lions. When crossing Sudan, Benson witnessed boys killed by lions. "Our lions are not true lions," I explain. "They are part of the cougar family and weigh less than you. Not six hundred pounds like the African lions."

Benson seems unphased and forges ahead. The eucalyptus trees canopying the trail sway in the ocean breeze, playing a soft percussion to the caterwaul vocals of ubiquitous crows. Walled-in by snarled undergrowth, the first quarter mile is a jungle. Breaks in the foliage reveal mounds of dead pampas grass that resemble villages of queer thatched huts. When my son, Cliff, was a preschooler, we'd come here to "troll village." With a plumed felt pirate hat and plastic cutlass in hand, he'd slash and stab the grassy huts, driving imaginary enemies from their hiding places.

No hat or sword for Benson, just the longest pair of legs I've seen on anyone his height. I'm lathered in sunscreen and swaddled in long sleeves, but Benson is bare-armed in a tank top, his ebony melanin a superior sunblock to any cream or lotion. He's told me that on their trek, they walked mostly at night. Nevertheless, I imagine their sun exposure was extreme. Benson had shorts, or underwear as he calls them, but his cousin and brother had nothing. Like Benson, they, too, are blessed with skin that can withstand the equatorial sun. In that situation, I wouldn't fare better than a naked mole rat.

The trail narrows to single file, and we catch our first glimpse of the Pacific Ocean. I'm in the rear, trying to keep up, much like a hippo keeping pace with a gazelle. We come to cattails soaring over our heads and Benson stops. "We have this grass in Sudan." He yanks out several green reeds, plops onto a nearby log, whips off a shoe and sock, and loops the reeds around his big toe. His nimble fingers braid expertly. Slipping the finished rope through a loop, he hands it to me. "If night comes, you can tie up your goat."

I give the cord a hard tug. "The goat's there for the night with this."

Proceeding on, the sun warms our backs and the ocean fills our nostrils. Mist huddles in low areas, trying to escape the rising sun, while snowy egrets lift their feet like ballerinas, and blue herons, still as statues, deceive their prey below. Benson strays off trail. "Mudfish like to live here."

"What does a mudfish look like?"

"Like an eel. To catch one you must know the sound they make to call their mates."

"What sound is that?"

Benson puffs his cheeks. "Hooph, hooph." The sound is like an owl with a lisp.

"Did you ever catch one?"

"Many times. The spear is best, or you can push a grass stalk down their hole. When they bite the stalk, you pull it out." He jabs with a stick. "They like this type of mud." Like Smilla knew snow, Benson knows mud. As he pokes around, I envision him as a seven-year-old on that terrible exodus, at times drinking his own urine and eating mud to survive. "But you must be careful catching the mudfish with your hand. If it bites it won't let go until it dies."

"Spear method sounds better."

"Yes, but in muddy water you could hit a python or crocodile."

"Oh." Spear the wrong beast and you could end up wearing it or missing a leg.

"Pythons are dangerous. One ate my dog. A good dog. He'd go with me all day. I didn't have to bring food, he was so fast he could catch gazelle."

"Then how did the python catch your dog?"

"My dog chased a squirrel into his hole and the python grabbed him." His voice drops. "A very good dog."

Farther ahead, he points out plants, describing how his mother would utilize them as food, medicine, or tools.

Even though I helped Benson, his brother, Alepho, and

their cousin, Benjamin, structure their memoir, *They Poured Fire on Us from the Sky: The True Story of Three Lost Boys of Sudan*, it still remains unfathomable to me how little boys endured such extreme hardship. When I hear of their ingenuity, smearing urine on their bodies to repel fire ants while picking mangos, or harvesting and roasting termites, the more impressed I become at their heroic survival and recollection of detail.

"You were so young. How did you learn and remember so much?"

"I helped my mother."

As Benson's mentor through the International Rescue Committee, I'm usually leading him through the bus system, applying to college, or filling out medical insurance forms. If you can imagine growing up in a remote village, five years of fleeing a war, followed by nine years in a refugee camp without running water or electricity, then you can begin to understand what it takes to adapt to life here. You won't starve or be eaten, but even though you speak the language, few understand your accent, social customs seem illogical, a missed bill and your credit is ruined forever, and cars can imperil your life as easily as a feisty lion.

The adjustment is overwhelming, but Benson is the champion of adaptability. Here only four years, he runs the computer and digital photography system at a large company, instructs me on the esoteric features of Microsoft Word, and shows me how to use my new picture phone. I enjoy these role reversals, especially today when he's teaching me how to survive in his world. Even visiting with park docents, I didn't learn as much about my surroundings—or at least it didn't stick with me like mudfishing, tying up my goat, and avoiding pythons will.

We make one more stop at a huge twisted eucalyptus that reigns over the wetlands. Benson drags large dead branches into a pile. Naturalists frequent this preserve with clipboards, recording the minutest movements of nature. I hope none will bust us for this most unnatural accumulation of wood.

"Take a picture, please. If this were Kenya, I would be a very rich man." In the refugee camp, food was scarce but firewood even more so. Those willing to risk their lives collecting outside the camp could sell it for a premium. I raise the camera. Standing before me in the sunshine, his wiry arms full of the sun-bleached branches, with that sparkling smile in his eyes, Benson looks wealthier than anyone I know.

Judy A. Bernstein

Entertaining Angels

Do not neglect hospitality for through it some have unknowingly entertained angels.

Hebrews 13:2

RITA—Relentless! Intense! Terrible! Awful! Words used to describe the Category 5 hurricane that bore down ruthlessly on the Texas coast in late September 2005. It was headed for Houston, and the projected path predicted her blowing right through my hometown of College Station.

As the evacuation of more than 2.5 million people from the Houston area began, horror stories from the massive gridlock poured in from people confined for hours in vehicles that ran out of gas and overheated. Evacuees turned off the air conditioning to conserve gas and then sweltered in over 100 degree heat. Not only was gas unavailable, but also many necessities. A journey normally taking two hours now required twenty-two, and Rita kept coming, moving steadily, faster than the traffic in the gridlock.

My church was designated as an evacuee shelter, and I became caught up in the innumerable preparations required for such an undertaking. Evacuees streamed in, each with a heartbreaking story: hours on the road, nowhere to go, sick with worry over their homes and their livelihoods. We had anticipated housing 225 people, but in less than a day, we had opened our doors to more than 370. And still they came. We faced the unthinkable task of turning some away.

When I arrived at our church refuge shortly before noon of the second day, hauling in blankets and electric cords, the harsh sound of a horn brought me up short.

"Are you still taking evacuees?" A handsome Hispanic woman leaned out of the window of her car.

"I don't know. I just got here." I walked closer and saw a woman reaching the end of her rope.

"Where do you go to find out?" Her voice was steady, but her eyes were welling with unshed tears. She was trying very hard to hold on.

I gave her directions and then encouraged, "I'll meet you there."

"Thank you so much." A beautiful smile crossed her fatigued face. "I'm worried about my aunt. She had a stroke a year ago and is on a walker. I left my family in the parking lot of Motel 6 while I try to find shelter. We've been on the road for twenty-six hours. We went to Brenham, but all the shelters were full, the motels, too. They sent us here, but I can't find anyplace that will take us."

"Let's go see."

I made my way through the madhouse of confusion and looked for her at the registration table, but she was not to be found. Then, I saw another worker leading her to the area.

"There you are," I called out. Once again I was graced with that beautiful smile.

"I couldn't find you," she responded and grabbed me into a tight bear hug, her eyes once again glistening with tears about to brim over.

I took her to the registration table, only to see her shoulders slump as they informed her we were full. Graciously, they told her where she might go, where there might be room for her. I faded into the background and went about delivering my supplies, haunted by the look in her eyes. I could not forget how she clung to me.

When I walked back through the intake area, she was still there getting directions to a special needs shelter where she might find a place for her aunt. Our eyes met and I knew, without a doubt, what I had to do.

"Never mind, Eleanor," I said to the registration volunteer. "She's coming home with me." I put my arm around her and felt the relief pass through her body. "Let's go get your aunt."

Walking to our cars, she said, "I can't believe this. You're so wonderful." Then she stopped short and looked me directly in the eye. "There are five of us, you know."

No, I didn't know. She had said her family was waiting but had mentioned only her aunt. "We'll manage," I replied, surprising myself with my confidence. I was committed to this course, and with God's grace I would complete it. I had adopted Naomi and her family who I was about to meet.

Forging our way through heavy traffic, we finally reached the hot, tired, hungry family consisting of her son, Fabian, a handsome young man of about thirty, whose smile was to die for; Aunt Eugenia, four feet tall and a former mariachi singer; sister, Sylvia, thin and willowy, who later revealed to me that she was seventy-one; and friend James, an oil rig worker with long hair and turned around baseball cap, who volunteered to come along to help drive.

Three jammed-full vehicles fell in line behind me as I zigzagged home, avoiding further traffic. I no sooner got my adoptees home than I had to go back to church to fulfill my commitments there, so I said, "Here's my home. Welcome. See you later."

I returned several hours later to a delightful surprise. It seems when they left they had cleaned out their freezer, knowing the contents would spoil if there was no electricity. They packed it all in ice chests and threw in a portable barbeque pit. I arrived home to the marvelous aroma of grilling chicken and to a smiling family gathered around my picnic table. For the first time since Rita threatened, I found myself relaxing.

Silvia spoke up. "I was thinking I would have to shower at a car wash." We all broke into laughter at this visualization. Slowly, I began to learn about my new family.

Naomi was a pipefitter, working in various refineries. A former law enforcement officer, this woman could handle herself. She loved motorcycles and didn't mind at all if her luxurious, long black hair was tangled beyond combing. Her goal was to own her own Harley. Watching her laugh, I realized where Fabian got his killer smile.

Naomi described her son, Fabian, as quiet, but he had a depth to him that might not be apparent at first. He worked for ten long years to get his college degree and was unassumingly proud of the accomplishment.

Aunt Gina not only was a mariachi singer but also she had her own radio show for a while. The first thing she did when she arrived at my home was to pull out her Bible, lay it on the hood of the car, and pray. "I always pray when I come to a new place." Sometime during the course of that first day, she pulled out her drivers' license and showed me. "This is who I really am." Pictured was a striking woman with long black hair.

"You're the only person I know who has a good-looking driver's license picture," I said.

"I used to wear spike heels," she proudly claims. "I even had house slippers with high heels."

"She's the only woman I know that dresses for bed. She even fixes her hair before going to bed," chimed in Sylvia.

"I want to look good. I might die," was her response.

Aunt Gina wore a brace on her right leg, and she had little use of her right arm. She used a walker most places, but not in my house. One of the rubber tips was missing and she would not take the chance of scratching my floor.

Sylvia loved the Dallas Cowboys and television, especially the soaps. She also loved the outdoors and spent as much time as she could in the wooded area around my house. Naomi liked my little piece of heaven, too. In fact one of her first comments was, "I think I've come home to heaven."

James's muscle shirt showed off the pecs he gained in his profession. We talked sports as he barbequed. This big hunk of a man was gentle with Aunt Gina and never failed to respond to me with a "ma'am." He was respectful of me and my belongings, even asking if it was okay to get a glass of water. In a quiet moment when only the two of us were in the den, he shyly said he would like to leave his cash as a thank-you to me.

"Nonsense," I reply. "But I tell you what you can do for me."

"What?" His eyes light up. He's ready.

"When you have the opportunity, pass this on. Pass on a kindness." Understanding, he made the connection.

My guests remained for three days and two nights. Mostly we were glued to the television, seeking information on the status of their hometown and the traffic, but we shared a lot of conversation, too. The capricious storm turned. It was going to miss us. A cheer went up. Later, when we learned my granddaughter lost the roof on her home, they commiserated with me.

On Saturday evening I went to Mass, leaving my new family to relax. Relax, my foot. Naomi cooked up a feast, while Sylvia took my radio on the deck and, in her words, "danced with the broom." In my words, she swept every bit of the debris off the deck.

Sunday, my orphans decided it was safe to go home. While we all wanted our lives back to normal, I was surprised at the sadness I felt at their leaving. In a flurry we exchanged addresses and phone numbers, promising to keep in touch.

"Promise me you'll call when you get home. I want to know you're safe."

"I will, I will," vowed Naomi.

"Let's pray before you go." So we stood in a circle and I offered a prayer in thanksgiving for their presence in my home, for their safe journey, and for the security of their homes. "In Jesus' name," I concluded. But there was more.

"And for this lady who took us in when she didn't have to. Bless her always." It was James who offered the prayer for me.

"Not everyone would do this," he said.

"Well, I'm a little crazy." I laughed.

"And, we're so glad you are," Sylvia joked.

My new family arrived home safely. All was well. I know this because Naomi kept her promise to call.

I shall not forget Rita and the opportunity God gave me to take strangers into my home, the opportunity to be God's hands. I think I may have entertained angels named Naomi, Fabian, Sylvia, Eugenia, and James.

Nancy Baker

A Safe Haven

*No love, no friendship can cross the path of our
destiny without leaving some mark on it forever.*

Francois Mauriac

Two weeks after my husband and I moved into our new
house in Oklahoma, he was deployed to Iraq. As I
unpacked boxes, hung pictures, and tried hard to make
our house feel like a home, I wondered how I would get
through the coming months without him.

Our three-year-old son cried himself to sleep each
night, asking me if Daddy was ever coming home.
"Mommy, I miss my Daddy," Cameron would say as tears
streamed down his cheeks. I did my best to console him
by singing silly songs, reading his favorite book, *The Big
Red Barn*, over and over, and giving him countless hugs.

"Daddy will be home before you know it," I'd say, smiling, trying to look convincing.

Most nights he ended up in bed with me, snuggled
tightly at my side, tossing and turning, and mumbling
"Daddy" until the wee hours of the morning. Often I
would feel his tiny hand gently patting my face, making

sure Mommy was still there. Our four-month-old baby, Colby, was the only one sleeping soundly, but he barely had a chance to bond with his father before he went off to war.

Even though my parents lived only thirty miles away, I felt like a single mom and utterly alone. I missed living on a military base where I experienced the only real community I'd ever known. I'd met a few neighbors in our new neighborhood, but everyone was busy with careers and driving children to baseball games and ballet. We barely even spoke.

One morning I glanced out the window and noticed something strange. I walked outside and saw a green tinge to the sky that made my hair stand on end. The sound of the phone ringing jarred me from my thoughts.

"Hello."

"Hi, Mom."

"There is the possibility of tornadoes tonight," she said, sounding a bit nervous. "I'll be over later this afternoon. I don't want you and the boys to be alone. Your dad is working late."

When I hung up the phone, I felt a sense of relief sweep over me knowing that I had Mom to count on. We ordered a pizza, and she and Cameron went to pick it up. While they were gone, the tornado sirens jolted me from my chair. I turned on the news to learn of a tornado forming above our town.

I called Mom on her cell phone and told her to get back here fast. Soon after she arrived home the tornado warning expired. Our scare was over—for the moment.

"I'm going to head back home for the night. I think everything is going to be okay," she said as she hugged me, and kissed the boys good-bye.

"Call me when you get there," I said.

Later that evening, I turned on the ten o'clock news.

Tornadoes were popping up all over the state. Feeling fearful, I called my mother. "Sirens are going off here," she said, her voice shaking. "I have to go."

Just then the tornado sirens sounded again. I turned the volume up on the television as the weatherman made an announcement.

"Do not panic. Get into your storm shelters immediately. If you don't have one, go into a middle closet or bathroom of your house."

I bolted to the baby's room, scooping him from his crib and ran to wake Cameron.

"We need to get into the bathtub," I told him. "There is a big storm outside, and we'll be safe in here," I said, trying to sound brave.

I tried hard to pull a mattress over us but it wouldn't stay. The baby was crying inconsolably. The dog was barking. I could hear the wind howling in a violent rage outside. Fear gripped me like never before. I felt queasy and completely alone as the tornado sirens blared in the distance.

"I'm scared, Mommy."

"It's okay, little man. Let's say a prayer and ask God to help us."

"God," I prayed out loud, "please keep Cameron, baby brother, and Mommy safe," I said, trembling. With that, the doorbell rang. It was our neighbor Tim from across the street.

"Karen and I are leaving. You and the boys are coming with us."

For a second I hesitated. Where in the world were they going? If they were getting into their car, I think we'd be better off here.

Without thinking further, I ran out the door with the baby in my arms and Cameron at my side.

"Go ahead and grab the baby a blanket," said Tim.

I couldn't budge. I stood like a statue there on the porch in absolute fear, afraid to even move. Tim grabbed the baby and threw his jacket over him to protect him from the heavy rain.

"Cameron, let's play a game," he said, smiling, and grabbed his hand. "Let's run through the rain. Isn't this fun?"

Stinging rain pelted us and lightning crackled and snapped all around us as we ran down the darkened street through deep puddles toward the neighbor's house.

"Kristen and Mike have a storm shelter in their garage."

Tim knocked on the garage door and it instantly flew open. Karen and several other neighbors were gathered around a radio. "The tornado is on the ground at Fifteenth and Kelley," said the weatherman. "Be in your shelters."

That was only two city blocks from our neighborhood. We huddled in the storm shelter for what seemed like an eternity. Then it was all over.

We had minimal damage. Only power lines were knocked down on the nearby highway. I called Mom. She cried when she heard my voice. Her town had suffered little damage, also. I thanked God that we were all okay.

When my husband returned from the Middle East, I had a list of things for him to do. Number one was to have someone install a storm shelter.

"I have something that I need to do first," he said as he grabbed Cameron and headed toward the front door. I watched him from the window as he shook hands with Tim.

Several years have passed since that stormy spring night. The unexpected kindness my neighbors have shown to me and my family is something we cannot repay, but we've been able to cook dinner for one neighbor who had a new baby. We've sent words of encouragement to the family two doors down who lost a loved one.

We've become a real community who really cares for one another.

Each time my husband is away and my car won't start or I see dark clouds roll in, I know now that I'm not alone. Friends are nearby. All I have to do is head to the neighbor's house. Any one of them.

Kim Rogers

Passing the Torch of Love

If instead of a gem, or even a flower, we should cast the gift of a loving thought into the heart of a friend, that would be giving as the angels give.

George MacDonald

Tears filled the eyes of our breakfast waitress in our hotel when she learned why we had come all the way from Littleton, Colorado, to Erfurt, Germany.

"We are a group of surviving students and victims' family members from the Columbine school shooting," I explained, "here to offer support to your community."

"We know what you are going through," I said, referring to their recent school massacre at the Johann Gutenberg School. A nineteen-year-old former student sneaked in with a nine-millimeter pistol, dressed in all black and a ski mask, and fatally shot thirteen teachers, two teenage students, a police officer, and then killed himself. Just days before our visit, tens of thousands of mourners had filled the town square on the steps of the ancient medieval cathedral to grieve this unprecedented act of violence that had ravaged their lives forever.

"My niece, Inga, witnessed that angry student when he shot her teacher to death at school that day. She still cannot eat or sleep well," our waitress said in a soft voice, wiping tears with her brown calico apron. The lines on her forehead and her disheveled auburn hair revealed her own stress and anxiety.

"Please tell her that friends from the Columbine school tragedy have traveled from America to meet her. We understand what she is going through. If she wants to talk, she and any of her friends are welcome to come to our hotel here tonight."

We had no way to get the names or phone numbers of these traumatized young people. We had simply flown in faith to their quaint medieval city where Martin Luther once preached in 1501, believing that we would be directed to them some way. I was gratified and amazed at how quickly this divine connection came about within just an hour of our arrival.

Our waitress excused herself to regain her composure and then call her niece. That one phone call, and a front-page article in their local paper about our "mission of mercy" caused teens reeling in grief from this fresh tragedy to come out of the woodwork to find us.

Word spread quickly to these traumatized high-school students and teachers that a group had come from Colorado to express sympathy and compassion. We placed two six-foot-wide floral wreathes of gorgeous gold and purple flowers on the steps of the Gutenberg school. The burning candles and clumps of bouquets were reminiscent of the Columbine memorial displays. The white satin sash draped across these giant floral symbols of sympathy read, *Mit Liebe Aus Littleton, Colorado*, "With Love From Littleton, Colorado."

Officials would not sanction a school meeting, believing these young people needed no outside help. However, the students knew what they needed and came by the dozens to seek us out late at night in our modest hotel.

"Are you sent by some American business or government corporation?" Friedrich asked, representing a group of six somewhat reluctant teens standing behind him.

"No. We all paid our own way with the help of some of our friends in America," I told them, startled by their suspicion. Friedrich translated for those who did not understand English as well. Their eyes widened. "Thank you . . . we don't know what to say," several replied.

Visibly shaken, two blond girls with nose and lip piercings embraced and began to cry. "Please, sit, and let's learn each other's names," my husband began, trying to make them feel comfortable. The conversations began. . . .

"My favorite art teacher was gunned down at my feet," mumbled Marta, squirming in her chair. "She was one of my best friends."

"I looked out in the hall and saw my history teacher lying there on the ground. I thought he was just playing dead as a joke, until I bent down to talk to him and saw the blood," remarked Hans, catatonically.

"We were hiding for hours in our classroom, all huddled together, listening to the screams and gunshots just outside our doors, . . ." Heidi, a younger girl, cried, reliving the horrific moments.

"I've been on the faculty here for twenty years," an attractive petite short-haired teacher reflected, "and I lost a dozen of my closest colleagues in one day. I've been to twelve funerals." Her voice broke. "Why am I still alive?"

We listened to them. We wept with them. They did not need to be muzzled by shame or wear a tough facade to mask their terror. It was all right to cry. Then they asked to hear our stories.

Beth and Dana shared the horrendous experience of losing their precious daughter and sister, seventeen-year-old

Rachel Scott, who was the first to be shot down by one of the murderers at Columbine. Students on our team tearfully opened their hearts to relive nightmares of hiding under library tables while their friends beside them were slaughtered before their eyes. Sobs followed by silence punctuated our time together. A holy exchange of "knowing" one another's suffering bound us together as one.

The natural questions followed.

How did you get through the pain, the nightmares?

How long did it take you to want to live again?

I feel guilty that I am alive. Did you feel that way, too?

The natural answers (or nonanswers in some cases) shared in this sacred meeting of open, wounded hearts came flowing out with tenderness and sensitivity. "It was our relationship with Jesus that got us through and still gets us through the heartache. Without Him we could not have made it. He carried us through every step and stage of our grief," Rachel's mother, Beth, shared in her soft and compassionate way, passing around a picture of Rachel for everyone to see. The sincerity of her mother's heart and words penetrated deeply.

By the end of our week, we had become friends in affliction, acquainted through grief, and healed with compassion. We had issued invitations to the community to a public expression of solidarity on our last evening. We gathered in the very old ornate high school auditorium with dark paneled walls and stained glass windows. Students and families and people from the community began to arrive.

A middle-aged gentleman shyly approached me, very reverent in his demeanor. "I am William Brown. My wife, Helga, was one of the teachers who was murdered. I have written a song in her memory. May I have the honor of playing it for you?" he asked, his eyes markedly red from crying.

"I am very sorry for your loss," I offered, "and it would

be a great honor for us, and to her, for you to play your composition for us." We welcomed our guests and then signaled to William. He slowly walked to the piano and introduced the song written for and dedicated to his late wife.

"My wife loved teaching because she was passionate about her students. We will never forget her," he said with sincere admiration.

A blonde girl, maybe thirteen-years-old, clung to him, keeping her hand on his shoulder as he tried to compose himself before starting. "That's his daughter," a student next to me whispered into my ear. William's haunting and beautiful composition to Helga filled the room and moved everyone deeply.

The lighting of the Memorial Torch, an Olympic-size gold torch engraved with all the names of the victims at Columbine High School, was the climax of the evening.

This very torch, with its brilliant flame, had been gripped by hundreds of thousands of youth around the world, pledging to counteract violence with love and compassion. Now the invitation to lay a hand on and "take up this torch of love" was offered to the most recent victims of the cruel pain inflicted by hate and violence.

I watched, deeply moved, as the entire front of the auditorium filled with students and families responding to this call. We passed the glowing torch carefully from hand to trembling hand.

In the end, no one wanted to leave. We lingered long in the afterglow of love, and I witnessed a new look in many eyes: hope.

When it was time for us to return home, we had breakfast once more in our hotel restaurant. The auburn waitress we now knew as Ingrid was working and rushed over to us, much more like an American friend than the reserved German woman we had met that first day.

"My niece is eating and sleeping now! Her heart is so much better," she reported enthusiastically. "We are so very grateful—," her voice broke as emotion welled up and tears wet her cheeks, "—that you came to us."

And so were we.

Claudia Porter

Without a Thought

If the creator had a purpose in equipping us with a neck, he surely meant us to stick it out.

Arthur Koestler

Rolling my car window down was not enough to keep me awake at five o'clock on a cold and dark winter morning. I had just ended my night shift at a local mail processing plant and was starting my fifteen-mile journey to pick up my four-month-old daughter.

I swooped my braids to the back, then pulled my skullcap down over my ears. I blasted the radio. I sang loud and off-key to the music and through commercial breaks. I needed to stay alert.

I guided my car onto Cedar Avenue, a long road that runs miles from downtown Cleveland to the eastern suburbs. Streetwalkers and drug dealers inhabit the first few blocks on Cedar Avenue, so I proceeded with caution—doors locked, windows up, and sitting upright.

Despite my efforts, I found myself asleep at a green light and with a set of headlights beaming in my car from the rear. I didn't want to be the lead car so I slowly eased my way through the light. Even with the right lane clear of traffic, the vehicle behind me did the same.

To my left were a few condemned textile factories and dilapidated homes. To my right was an open field and a lady dressed in a pair of slacks and a long thick coat and standing at a pole marked "Bus Stop." The vehicle behind me quickly switched to the right lane and abruptly stopped in front of the woman. She walked away. The vehicle backed up toward her. She picked up her pace in the other direction. The vehicle crept forward.

I proceeded to the next light, watching in my rearview mirror the headlights of the other car steadily creep along. My unease turned to concern; that woman was in danger. I turned around, headed back in her direction, and pulled up close to the car that was now up on the sidewalk near the bus stop. The lady frantically walked toward the open field. Out of fear for her, I put as much bass in my voice as a woman possibly could.

"Leave her alone!" I demanded, my skullcap pulled down to my eyebrows and over my ears. I hoped I would pass for a man.

"Mind your own business!" a man shouted from the other car.

I didn't know what to do next. Without thinking I drove over the curb, into the open field, over gravel, broken glass, and debris. The man jumped out of his car to pursue the lady on foot.

"Help me!" she frantically screamed.

"Leave her alone!" I demanded, still trying to sound like a man.

"Mind your own damn business!" the man shouted again, picking up his pace behind her.

I pulled alongside the woman, "Look, I don't know you and you don't know me, but you better get in this car now!" I swung open my passenger door. She jumped in, the man leaping after her. I sped off before she had a chance to close the door, causing him to loose his balance and fall onto the gravel.

I drove a couple of blocks. What had just occurred began to sink in. Relieved to have gotten away safely, the woman held her hand to her heart and thanked me. Between breaths, she managed to tell me her destination and how much she appreciated my bravery. Minutes later, I dropped her off at a well-lit bus terminal. I watched her walk away, pause, and turn back as she mouthed the words *thank you*.

I sat in my car alone. My hands trembled on the steering wheel. It frightened me to think I had risked my life to save someone I did not know. It hurt me to realize that my baby would have been without a mother. Suddenly, I was no longer cold or sleepy, and there wasn't a song on the radio I cared to sing. Instead, nervous and scared, I gave thanks and prayed out loud.

Vickie Williams-Morris

The Compassionate Enemy

War educates the senses, calls into action the will, perfects the physical constitution, brings men into such swift and close collision in critical moments that man measures man.

Ralph Waldo Emerson

The first time I saw the enemy, he was pointing a machine gun at us. It was early spring of 1945, and my grandparents and I had just emerged from a bunker, where we had spent a terror-filled night.

I was nine years old and lived in Hungary. World War II was playing havoc with our lives. My grandparents, who were raising me, and I had been on the road in our horse-drawn wagon for many months, searching for safety. We had left behind the village of our birth in the Bacska region because Tito and his Communist partisans were closing in on the region.

By day we moved swiftly, ready to jump out and take cover in a ditch if warplanes approached. By night we camped with other refugees along the roadside. I usually lay bundled up in my featherbed in the back of the wagon, cradling my cat. War was almost all I had known during my nine years of life.

After Christmas of 1944, when we were almost killed in a city bombing, Grandfather decided that a rural area would be safer, so we moved and settled in a small house that had an old cemetery as its neighbor. Here Grandfather, with the help of some neighbors, built a bunker in a flat area behind the house. And on that early spring day in 1945, we spent the entire night in the bunker. Warplanes buzzed, tanks thundered, bombs exploded over our heads all night, but finally at dawn everything grew deathly still.

Grandfather decided it would be safe to go back to our house. Cautiously we crept out into the light of early dawn and headed toward the house. The brush crackled under our feet as we walked past the cemetery. The markers looked lonely, separated by tall, dry weeds. I shivered, holding on to my orange tabby cat tightly. He had spent the night in the bunker with us. Without warning there was a rustle in the bushes just ahead. Two men jumped out and pointed machine guns directly at us.

"*Stoi!*" one of the men shouted. Since we were from an area where both Serbian and Hungarian was spoken, we knew the word meant "Stop!"

"Russians!" Grandfather whispered. "Stand very still, and keep quiet." But I was already running after my cat. He had leaped out of my arms when the soldier shouted, so I darted between the soldiers and scooped him up.

The younger of the two soldiers, tall and dark-haired, approached me. I cringed, holding the cat against my chest. The soldier reached out and petted him. "I have a little girl about your age back in Russia, and she has a cat just like this one," he said, gently tugging one of my blond braids. "And she has long braids, too, just like you."

I looked up into a pair of kind brown eyes and my fear

subsided. Grandfather and Grandmother sighed with relief. Both soldiers came back to the house with us and shared in our meager breakfast. We found out that the Soviet occupation of Hungary was in progress. Many atrocities occurred in our area, as well as throughout our country in the following months, but because the young Russian soldier took a liking to me, we were spared.

He came to visit often, bringing little treats, and always talked longingly of his own little girl. I loved his visits, yet I was terrified of the Russians in general. Then one day, almost a year later, he had some sad news. "I've been transferred to another area, *malka*, little one, so I won't be able to come and visit anymore. But I have a gift for you," he said, taking something out of his pocket. It was a necklace with a beautiful turquoise Russian Orthodox cross on it. He placed it around my neck.

"You wear this at all times, *malka*. God will protect you from harm." I hugged him tight and then watched him drive away, tears welling in my eyes.

World War II was over, but for the people of Hungary a life of bondage was at hand. Many men, like Grandfather, who had been involved in politics, or deemed undesirable, were being rounded up by the secret police, never to be seen again. Not long after the end of the war, the dreaded knock on the door came. The police had come to take my grandfather away. Fortunately, Grandfather managed to flee and went into hiding. Then it was just Grandma and I, trying to survive as best we could. Fear became our constant companion, and prayer our solace. Sometimes I would finger the cross the soldier had given me and wonder where he was. Was he back home with his own daughter? Did he even remember me?

Time passed in a haze of anxiety and depression. Then in the fall of 1947, a man came to get us in the middle of the night. He said he would take us to the Austrian border, and we'd be reunited with my grandfather. We traveled all night to a place where the ethnic Germans of Hungary were being loaded into transport trucks and deported from Hungary. The man gave us counterfeit papers so we could cross the border to freedom. When we arrived at dawn, a weary-looking man with a thick, scraggly beard and a knit cap pulled low over his forehead was waiting for us.

"Grandpa!" I cried out, rushing into his arms. It was so wonderful to see him again. Then we walked toward the transport truck loaded with dozens of people and got on, fake papers in hand. I knew if we were found out, it would mean Grandpa would get hauled off to prison and, worse yet, he might even be executed. I glanced toward the Russian soldiers who were coming closer to inspect the papers. Fear gripped my heart. Then I looked up as a guard boarded our truck. I caught my breath.

"Grandpa," I whispered. "Look, it's my soldier, Ivan! He is checking this truck." I wanted to leap up and run to him, but Grandpa shushed me cautiously.

"Maybe he won't recognize us," he whispered, pulling the knit hat farther down his forehead. He seemed afraid of Ivan! Then the Russian stood before us. My grandfather handed over our papers without looking up. I leaned closer to Grandfather and put my hand protectively on his shoulder, peering cautiously at Ivan, hoping to see the familiar kind sparkle in his eyes. But he was intent upon the papers, his expression grave. I didn't dare to breathe. Finally, he handed the papers back to Grandpa.

"Everything is in order in this vehicle," he said. Then winking at me, he walked away and got down. The next instant the truck began to move on. I looked over my shoulder and caught his eye.

"Thank you," I mouthed, holding up the cross hanging around my neck. He nodded discretely, then quickly turned and walked away. And as we crossed the border to freedom, we all sighed with relief. Although we had suffered much sadness during the war, one blessing will always stay with me: the memory of a kind soldier who turned my fear into faith, and showed me that compassion can be found anywhere, even in the eyes of an enemy.

Renie Szilak Burghardt

Diana's Christmas

We can do no great things—only small things with great love.

Mother Teresa

It was December in the Ozarks, and a skiff of snow was on the ground. I was busily baking cookies and shaking some Christmas-colored sprinkles on top of them when I heard the sound of the school bus pulling away on the gravel road in front of the house. My nine-year-old daughter, Julie, came bounding through the front door, and as usual, she was hungry. There's something about being in school all day that works up a good appetite. I handed her a couple of cookies and poured her a glass of milk.

Her preschool sister and brother joined her for a snack, and as we sat around the table, Julie eyed her Christmas cookie, examining each side of it. Then she said, matter-of-factly, "Diana isn't having Christmas."

"Who is Diana?" I asked.

"She rides the school bus and sits by me sometimes, and when I asked her what she wanted for Christmas, she said she wasn't having any Christmas."

She continued. "Diana has pretty red hair, but I think she forgets to brush her hair, and the other kids don't sit by her. I think it's because she's different."

I questioned my daughter about Diana and her family and where she lived, but Julie didn't know very much. She only knew there were other children in the family and that they got off the bus along the road where there wasn't a house.

All evening I was plagued by thoughts of a little red-headed girl who "forgets to brush her hair and wasn't having Christmas," as Julie had described her.

The next morning after Julie had left for school, Diana was still on my mind. We had lived in the area for only a short time, but I knew that the grade-school principal knew everyone in the community, so I picked up the phone and called the school. I asked him if he knew of a little red-headed girl named Diana who rode Julie's bus. "Yes, she's one of the Martin kids, lives off the main road a little ways. Why, is there a problem?" he asked.

I explained to him what Julie had said and asked him if he thought they might be a family who needed some help this Christmas. The principal told me that the Martin family probably did need assistance, and he seemed glad that someone had thought of it. I told him that our family would personally do something and I would also give their name to the Christian mission in town that always helped others at Christmas time.

I found a big box, and later that night we all discussed what should go into the box for the Martin family. Christmas was only a few days away, so we began to wrap gifts and fill the box. Jeanna chose some age-appropriate toys and games along with a cuddly, stuffed teddy bear for one of the younger children. Even Jeremy, who was just a toddler, watched what was going on, then ran to his own little box of toys and began throwing some of them into the box. I began cooking and baking what I could in advance to go in a separate box of food items that would make up a traditional Christmas dinner. I asked Julie if she would like to add something special for Diana to the box.

"Can we get her a pretty hat with gloves to match?" Julie asked. "We could get green like Diana's eyes!"

"Green it is!"

That night I put the finishing touches on the box by including a children's Bible with the story of the birth of Jesus marked with a bookmark.

The next day was Christmas Eve, and after work my husband, Mike, loaded the boxes into our van. We had directions from the principal and we were all putting our coats on to leave when Julie said, "Mommy, I don't want to go."

"Well, why not?" I asked. "Don't you want to take the gifts to Diana?"

"Maybe Diana might hide her face," Julie said, a worried look clouding her face.

I knew what Julie was feeling. She was concerned that because Diana knew her, she might somehow be shy or uncomfortable knowing that Julie had "told" about there not being any Christmas for Diana. Although I didn't think it would be a problem, I told Julie she didn't have to go along.

We drove up an old dirt road and found a little house in a clearing in the woods. Mike got out and went to the door while I stayed in the van with the baby. A couple of very friendly dogs met him as he got out, then a man came to the door. As Mr. Martin stood at the door, a small child peeked around the doorjamb and waved at me. Mike talked a moment and then handed him the packages. When Mike turned to leave, Mr. Martin said something else and shook Mike's hand.

We enjoyed Christmas a little more than usual that year

and learned that it is truly more blessed to give than to receive.

When school started again after Christmas break, I heard the familiar sound of the bus outside once more as Julie came bursting through the door, a huge smile on her face. She stopped right in front of me and said, "Mommy, Diana knows!"

"Knows what?"

"She knows I told. Mommy, Diana was wearing the green hat and gloves today. When I got on the bus she hugged me and then she said, 'Julie, we did have Christmas!'"

Pamela R. Blaine

The Accident

*We are each of us angels with only one wing,
and we can only fly by embracing one another.*

Luciano de Crescenzo

The accident should have been fatal.

It would have been, too, if not for a series of serendipitous events that, together, saved my life.

It had been a long day, longer than most. I was up at 5 AM, an hour-and-a-half commute into Manhattan's financial district, a busy schedule of meetings and interviews, and then the same grueling commute home. Nothing unusual, except this time, my day was far from over.

No time for dinner. My teenage sister, ten years my junior, had been unable to take the bus to a youth retreat, and she was waiting for me to drive her three hours to the retreat center. I left a note for my husband, grabbed the car keys, hopped into the car, and swung by my parents' home to pick her up.

We drove straight through, arriving a little after nine. She took her suitcase and waved good-bye with barely a look back as she followed one of the camp counselors who had met us as we pulled up. Turning down an offer of refreshment, I started up the car, eager to get back on the road. The sooner I started the three-hour drive home, the sooner I would arrive.

The drive back seemed interminable, my fatigue compounded by sniffling and sneezing. Allergy season was at its height. The highway stretched out before me, a dark ribbon hypnotically set against an even darker horizon. It was after midnight on the Friday before Labor Day, and few cars were on the road. Time seemed to stand still. I was exhausted, and the long day was finally taking its toll.

I didn't notice any other vehicles as I was driving in the right lane. Light poles along the side of the road cast a limited glow, straining to pierce the blanket of darkness that engulfed my car. Twenty minutes from home it all caught up with me. Shortly before the highway traveled under an overpass, I ran off the road at fifty miles per hour, plowing through weeds and shrubs until the car plunged down a slope. Shrubs and undergrowth closed in around the car as it collided, head-on, with the embankment wall.

The car was hidden from the view of any driver who might be on the road. To make matters worse, I had not worn a seat belt. The doctors later determined my face had hit the steering wheel, smashing the bridge of my nose, causing broken bones and substantial bleeding.

The driver behind me witnessed what happened, stopped his car, and lit flares to attract help. According to the police report, he extricated me from my vehicle—which now resembled an accordion—and waited with me until a state trooper arrived. Then he disappeared. There is no record of his name or license plate number in the report. The state trooper could not explain why he didn't follow procedures and obtain my rescuer's identification. Although we later tried to track him down to thank him, it was as if he never existed.

Had the Good Samaritan not stopped, I would have bled to death overnight, unnoticed because of the camouflage of trees and shrubbery that hid my car.

The ambulance rushed me to the nearest hospital's emergency room. Medical personnel bustled around me. In spite of their purposeful activity, I was scared and confused. I wanted to go home. I wanted to be in my own bed, far away from this nightmare. I decided that if a doctor was necessary, I would see my own physician the next day.

My husband soon arrived and, along with the medical staff, convinced me to stay. Neither he, nor the doctors, allowed me to view my face. If they had, the shock would have been more than my conscious state could have processed.

The ER doctor took one look at my smashed nose, with fractured bones sticking out perpendicular to my face, and fearing she would leave severe scarring, declared to my husband that she would not attempt to repair the broken bones. Instead, she called a surgeon specializing in reconstructive surgery. The surgeon arrived within the hour—a Jewish doctor called out on Yom Kippur (Day of Atonement), the highest holy day of the Jewish calendar. He performed the surgery at 3 AM. Within two days I was released from the hospital.

One week later, I saw the surgeon for the first of several follow-up visits, over the next six months. It was a few weeks before I could look at my face in the mirror without breaking into tears.

A week after my final visit, I returned to his office to thank him and his staff, only to find the doctor gone. He had left his practice for a sabbatical—but he didn't return. Our efforts to locate him ended in failure.

These two men, my rescuer and my surgeon, seemed to come out of nowhere and disappeared just as mysteriously. I think of them as my guardian angels—to whom I will be forever grateful.

Ava Pennington

A Walk in My Shoes

You can easily judge the character of a man by how he treats those who can do nothing for him.

James D. Miles

My father has suffered from Parkinson's disease since his late thirties. For the most part, he could do everything it took to work his full-time job, raise five kids, and keep my very busy, stay-at-home Mom happy. But when he hit his early sixties, he woke up one morning unable to move his legs.

Within three months, he lost his job and spent all of his time going to doctors to find the right combination of medicine that would allow him to lead the life he had before that dreadful morning. But it seemed no matter how the doctors increased or decreased his medicine dose, life as he knew it had permanently changed. Slowly but surely, medical equipment began to fill his home, including a wheelchair.

Life has not been easy for him. But every so often something happens that reminds him that the world is still good. While at a hotel in Delaware, Mom was pushing Dad in his wheelchair. He needed to use the restroom, but with Mom weighing only half of what he did, it was very hard for her to lift him out of his chair. They needed help and searched the lobby for someone who looked as if they had a big enough physique, and heart, to come to their rescue.

Before long, a gentleman approached them and asked if they needed assistance. My mother explained that Dad needed to use the restroom but she didn't think she could get him out of the chair. Although he wasn't a large man, he swooped my dad out of the chair and got him in a stall. He called Mom into the bathroom and guarded the door while my parents were in there. When Mom needed help to get him back in the chair, the good Samaritan reappeared and, with very little effort, hoisted his arms under my dad's and sat him back in his seat.

After receiving very appreciative thanks from my parents, he turned and walked away. It was only then that Dad noticed the most remarkable thing about this man. He was a double-amputee with two prosthetic legs.

Cheryl M. Kremer

Ten Feet and Still Rising

Knowing which way to turn gives you self-confidence. Taking a chance and going the opposite way gives you a chance to see what you are made of.

Bob Perks

BOOM! The skies lit up, and the rain continued to fall. The deafening noise sounded as if bombs were falling, but it was only a natural rainstorm. I wondered what could have so upset the gods, but then I realized that it was just a freak of nature.

Tropical storm Allison kept the rain falling in Houston, Texas, as the TV weathermen cautioned that the storm had stalled, dumping record amounts of rainfall on our city.

Houston is home to the world's largest medical center, and the hospitals were directly in the path of the storm. Would the gods spare the hospitals?

Unfortunately, the answer for most of the hospitals was no. The worst hit was Memorial Hermann Hospital, which has approximately 600 beds. Furthermore, the hospital serves as one of only two Level 1 trauma centers and is the only facility in the city that has Life Flight air ambulance helicopter service.

Houston has many bayous, natural and man-made. Their function is to prevent flooding during torrential downpours; however, this storm didn't relent, and the bayous near the medical center rose to dangerously high levels. The underground storm control systems were being severely overloaded. It was only a question of time before the hospitals would be forced to evacuate the patients.

For Memorial Hermann Hospital, that time arrived too quickly. We began evacuating the patients as soon as the water infiltrated the hospital and power was lost. Even the backup generators began to fail after a short period of time. Staff, doctors, emergency medical staff, patients' families, and volunteers worked together to safely evacuate the hospital.

Many unsung heroes rose to the challenge during that weekend in early June. Many critically ill patients had to be kept alive without electricity to power their ventilators. Nurses, technicians, doctors, staff, and anyone with an extra hand automatically joined the team to keep those patients alive. Workers relentlessly puffed and deflated the ventilators by hand and diligently kept every patient alive.

Evacuation of the hospital continued without power, lights, or elevators. Everyone from the CEO to the cleaning staff who were either already at the hospital or could make it there through the flood carried patients down the stairs to ambulances, or up the stairs to the Life Flight helicopters waiting to transport patients to other hospitals. Many patients were taken to sister hospitals in the system that were not affected so severely by the flood. Still others were taken to hospitals outside the system, some as far away as Austin. These hospitals, in and out of the system, saved our patients' lives.

Evenually, the rain stopped, and employees who were not at the hospital gradually made their way to the medical center through the drenched streets that only a few hours before had seemed like natural lakes.

As the last patient left for one of the other hospitals, I realized how grim the situation actually was when I saw the baby grand piano, which had been located in the "basement" atrium, floating in the water that was approaching the first floor level.

I was speechless and began to weep. I noticed others crying, also. Before, when we had patients who needed to be evacuated, we were all focused on that vital goal. However, now, we saw just how bad the hospital actually was damaged and we were devastated.

At first, the staff thought the hospital would be closed for no more than a few days, but the engineers uncovered more damage than had initially been thought. Those few days turned into a few weeks, and those few weeks turned into more than a month.

More than 1,500 contractors worked on the hospital twenty-four hours a day, seven days a week, while many of the staff simultaneously assisted at the community hospitals where our patients had been transferred. Everyone was awaiting the day when Memorial Hermann would reopen.

On Tuesday, July 17, 2001, that day arrived. At 9 AM on the helipad, a glorious, meaningful ceremony with many speakers reopened the hospital. It was truly a celebration.

Prior to the flood, Memorial Hermann Hospital was "home" to many, and on that bright sunny day in July we were back. I truly understood what Dorothy from *The Wonderful Wizard of Oz* meant: "There's no place like home."

Michael Jordan Segal

Heroes on Lake George

Courage is the first of human qualities, because it is the quality which guarantees all others.

Winston Churchill

I stood on the shores of Lake George, a sparkling thirty-two-mile body of water in the heart of New York's Adirondack Mountains. The sky was clear and blue, the lake a sheet of glass reflecting the red and yellow foliage of the surrounding hillside. I came to visit this lake often, and it was always special. On blistering summer days, the waters cooled me. On crisp autumn afternoons, its serene calmness lulled me with a feeling of security. Yet a year ago, this lake was anything but serene. And, as I lost myself in the reflection of the lake I loved so much, I wondered how to make sense of it.

In summer Lake George is a bustling resort town, but when the cooler weather arrives, the little village is quiet and still. Only a few boats splash across the expansive waters. Last October, the *Ethan Allen* slowly chugged along the shoreline.

The *Ethan Allen* was a simple forty-foot open-sided

white fiberglass vessel with dark green trim and a modest canopy. Forty-eight passengers, mostly senior citizens, sat on rough wooden benches, wrapped in their sweaters and long pants, cameras slung over their shoulders, excited about their leaf-peeping tour.

The water was calm. It couldn't have been a more picture-perfect day. There was nothing to warn of the impending danger, but suddenly the unthinkable happened. As the boat began to make a gradual turn in a cove near Cramer's Point, one side dipped lower into the water and the green hull began to rise. Something was wrong! Panicked passengers slid across the boat, falling into one another's laps. Then, just like that, the boat flipped. People were thrown over the sides and tossed out the windows into the frigid water. Weighted down by their fall clothing and wearing no lifejackets, they struggled to stay afloat.

In seconds, the peace of the idyllic little lake was shattered. Clouds of black smoke billowed from the sinking boat as the acrid smell of diesel fuel spread across the water. Desperate cries for help pierced the autumn air. At first, it seemed only a few people were around to respond; most of the vacationers had gone home. But Lake George wasn't as sleepy as it appeared.

Residents clustered nearby, perhaps out of sight but nonetheless alert. At home, at work, or just out enjoying the last rays of sunshine, they heard the cries for help. Moments later, ordinary citizens were thrust into the startling role of rescuers.

Joyce Cloutier and her husband, Larry Steinhart, were out for a boat ride and had just passed the *Ethan Allen* when they witnessed the capsizing. Joyce frantically called 911 on her cell while Larry tossed over life jackets, then lowered the craft's swimming platform. The husband-and-wife team pulled survivors aboard. "You're okay now," Joyce soothed.

Brian Hart was also passing nearby, taking his daughter

and nieces for an afternoon canoe ride. He stared in shock at what he was witnessing. Knowing that he couldn't be much help with only a small canoe, he called his brother Eric, who sped to the rescue with a larger boat. They tossed out anything that could float, then dove into the icy water and pulled victims to safety.

On shore, others heard the cries for help. Gisella Root and her husband ran a nearby hotel and noticed the commotion. They jumped into their speedboat and rushed to the scene. The two dove into the water and pulled eight people onto their boat. A local jewelry shop owner and his wife dashed to their boat and rescued six more people.

Nearby, a local scuba class was underway. No better time to use their new skills. The students hurriedly swam to the *Ethan Allen* and plunged underwater to search the sunken boat for victims.

A triage area was formed on the shore. The shivering, frightened seniors were given warm blankets and emergency first aid, then rushed to nearby hospitals. All together, twenty-seven passengers and the captain survived. Of course, I knew the horrible truth. Not everyone was as lucky.

So a year later, I stood on the shore and kicked at the pebbles. I knew that a beautiful autumn day could be deceiving, that innocent, pleasant afternoon boat rides could result in catastrophic tragedies. I frowned and wondered why. How could such a horrible accident happen? As I struggled with that question, I finally accepted that there was no making sense of it. Sometimes, horrible things happen. But there was something hopeful to hold on to. When something bad happens, good people are everywhere, people like Brian and Joyce and the others, people who risk their lives for strangers.

And one brisk autumn day on a peaceful mountain lake, they became heroes.

Peggy Frezon

You're on God's Team Now

Be a life long or short, its completeness depends on what it was lived for.

David Starr Jordan

I slid into my desk in my World History class, dropped my book bag, and heaved a large sigh. Corey whipped his head around to face me. "You don't understand anything we just covered in physics, do you?"

I smiled faintly and shook my head. Corey just laughed.

"I'll be at your house after football practice to tutor you," he said, smiling.

This had become a pretty regular occurrence. I despised physics. Corey aced every test. After football practice, he would always walk to my house and spend as much time as was necessary (and this often involved a lot of time) to make sure I understood the material for our upcoming physics test.

"So, how is your team, Coach Corey?" I asked, eager to change the subject of physics.

"Oh, they are great! They are even playing in their championship game this Thursday night," he answered enthusiastically. Corey's younger brother played peewee football, and Corey had signed on to coach the team. He adored his younger brother and his teammates just as much as he adored football.

Being captain of my high school's cheerleading squad, one of my duties was to make sure a large banner was painted before each game. As the band played, the players ran through it, making their grand entrance onto the football field.

"You know," I said, leaning toward Corey, "I could probably use some of the paper leftover from last week's game and make your team a banner to run through before their game." I watched as Corey's face lit up like a small child's on Christmas morning.

"Really? Wow, the kids would be so excited, Jami. Do you really have time?" he asked.

"Consider it done," I said happily. "This will be my thank-you to you for all your help in physics," I said, laughing. I knew how important these young boys had become to Corey and how hard he worked as their coach.

The night of their football game, Corey's peewee team ran through their first football banner. Our high school band even showed up to play our school's fight song. My friends and I yelled cheers and inserted the peewee team's mascot into the cheers as Corey's proud mother filmed the entire game. Of course, the team went on to win their peewee championship game. Despite his own athletic accomplishments, and all his A's in physics, that championship peewee football game was Corey's proudest moment. He loved coaching the kids so much that the next day he signed up to coach their baseball team.

With Corey's help, I ended up getting a B in physics, and we both graduated that spring. We also both were accepted to Louisiana State University. Corey received a scholarship, and he would be the first in his family to go to college. He planned on being a chemical engineer, and the pride in his parents' faces when they talked about Corey going off to college was obvious. His love for the young boys he coached, however, never dwindled. Corey drove home two evenings every week to continue to coach his team.

Being in college brought new experiences to both Corey and me. Though neither of us, nor any of our friends, drank much in high school, suddenly alcohol, parties, and fake IDs were very much a part of our weekly activities. We rationalized our actions: partying was what college students were supposed to do, right? Who hadn't ever used a fake ID to purchase alcohol? Our grades were good and we weren't hurting anyone. This was college and we were having fun! We told ourselves no real harm was being done, and we continued to drink and party.

"How are things going, kid?" Corey asked, late one afternoon.

I gave my usual exasperated sigh. "I failed my algebra test."

"Jami, I have an A in calculus right now. You know I'm a good math student, I could have helped you," he scolded me. "Promise me that you will call me to help you before your next exam."

I promised that I would.

"Some things never change." He laughed. "Anyway, some friends of mine are coming over to hang out later; I want you to come, too."

I plopped down on my unmade bed. "I can't," I pouted. "I have to be at my nine o'clock history class tomorrow. If I'm going to fail algebra, I at least need an A in history!"

"Okay . . . I guess that is an acceptable excuse, but you aren't going to fail algebra, because I am going to help you before your next test."

With Corey's help, I thought, I might actually pass algebra.

The next day, I made it to my history class on time and plopped down into a desk toward the back of the room. As I did every day, I made sure my cell phone was switched to vibrate mode, then I strategically placed it on top of my bag so the clock was still visible and I could watch the minutes drag by until the lecture was over.

My professor wasn't too far into his lecture on the Great Depression when I realized my mother was calling me. I smiled to myself, she was probably checking to make sure I was in my class, and this time I would be able to call her back and tell I had been! Minutes later, my phone vibrated again. This time it was my father. This was strange; he never called me in the morning. The third call was my mother again. I began to feel nervous. Something had to be wrong.

As soon as my class was dismissed, I hurriedly dialed my parents' phone number. When she picked up, I heard the tension in my mother's voice.

"Jami," she spoke quietly, "honey, Corey passed away last night. It was some sort of drinking accident. I'm so sorry. "

I stopped in the middle of the hallway, unable to breath. Students flooded out classroom doors all around me. I felt like I had been punched in the stomach and I couldn't move. I gasped for breath.

"You must have made some mistake," I exclaimed. "It can't be Corey. It has to be someone else." I felt my throat tighten and then the tears began. I felt the other students' eyes burning into me as I stood in the hallway crying for what seemed an eternity. I couldn't move.

My father was on his way to pick me up, and by the time he arrived, he had learned the details of Corey's death. After drinking entirely too much, Corey felt sick and eventually passed out on his bathroom floor. When Corey was discovered lying there gasping for breath, someone called the paramedics but it was too late. Corey died that morning of alcohol poisoning.

In complete disbelief, my mind raced. This can't be happening, not to Corey. He can't die this way. Why couldn't someone have saved him? I stared out the window for the entire two-hour ride home and let the tears roll down my cheeks, never trying to wipe them away. I tried desperately to make sense of my friend's death.

That evening, the owner of our local funeral parlor, who was also a family friend, called my father and explained Corey's family was not only dealing with an enormous loss but also the financial burden of Corey's funeral. I couldn't sleep. Corey had helped so many people throughout his life. I was his friend. I had to help him.

The next morning I dug out my high school yearbook and began calling everyone we graduated with to ask for a donation for Corey's family. *Even if I only collect a few hundred dollars,* I thought, *it can still make a difference.*

It was no surprise everyone wanted to help. Each person had a special memory of Corey they shared with me. I spent two days driving around our small town picking up cards, letters, pictures, and donations. At one point, a lady approached me in the grocery store. I immediately recognized her as the mother of one of the younger boys on our football team. Her eye's misted over as she spoke softly, "I heard about what you are doing. I don't have much money, but I want to donate this." She handed me ten dollars.

Most of my graduating class members could not spare much after going off to college, paying for new apartments, tuition, and cars. But each one of them graciously gave what they could. Some families even overwhelmed me with hundreds of dollars. By the second day, people I hadn't even contacted called me to say they wanted to help. By the morning of Corey's funeral, I had collected

$3,000. With an additional donation from Corey's church, it was enough to cover the cost of his service.

That morning, I sprayed a small box gold and adorned it with black ribbons—our high school colors. I added Corey's football number to the side; then I filled the box with all the letters, cards, pictures, and money I had collected. I told myself to be strong for Corey's family, and I left my house to tell my friend good-bye for the last time.

When I arrived at the funeral parlor, I approached Corey's mother and father. My words came out in a faint whisper as I fumbled over what I was trying to say. "I . . . I know funerals can be expensive, and well, I just know how much everyone loved Corey . . . how much everyone wanted to help. I thrust the small box into Corey's mother's hands. "It's from all the people in the community," I said quietly.

With that, his mother fell into my arms, and his father embraced me. The rule about being strong was forgotten, and all three of us began to cry. After a long moment, his mother released me and softly cupped my face into her palms as she stared into my eyes.

"My son loved you a lot. He knew how special you were, and now we see why." I knew this beautiful, yet heartbreaking moment would remain with me for the rest of my life.

About this time a small boy clutching a baseball entered the funeral parlor and walked past us. He had written a message on the baseball: "Coach Corey, you're on God's team now. I'll miss you." The young boy bravely walked up to the casket and placed the ball next to his beloved coach. For the first time since I had received the news of Corey's death, I felt peace.

Corey *was* on God's team now, and his family, friends, and the members of his community would all remain his loyal fans.

Jami Smith

Flight for Freedom

Man's most precious possession, second only to life itself, is freedom.

Col. Ben Purcell, former P.O.W.

Barely twenty years old in 1945, I was a new Air Force pilot serving in Europe when orders came for me to fly into Yugoslavia—behind enemy lines—and rescue a group of twenty-six displaced persons. People of several nationalities, including some Americans, had been hiding for months—in basements, in barns, in the woods. They were now in the custody of a few friendly German officers who somehow had contacted our security, requesting help.

Orders further stated that there would be no airport available. And, of course, it was necessary that I fly in undetected or I might be shot down. For those reasons, I was to take the absolutely smallest plane that would do the job.

The day of the mission, I reached the target area and landed on the designated tiny plot of pasture, only to be greeted by not twenty-six refugees but forty desperate souls of all ages, few speaking English.

A quick prayer went up. "Lord, what to do?" I simply did not have space for forty. Yet, they faced almost certain death from starvation and untreated health problems, or from the Nazi forces, should they be discovered. I couldn't bear to leave even one behind.

I told our crew, "Estimate the weight of each person and add them up. We'll factor in the weight of our remaining fuel and determine if our aircraft can get off the ground if we take them all." The fact that the refugees were undernourished and very thin worked to their advantage. We pushed the limit. I had them sit in the aisle, three abreast, with orders, "Do not move."

Finally loaded, we rolled down the short, grassy makeshift airstrip, straining mightily to gain the optimum 100 knots for takeoff.

"Forty knots, sir," my copilot called out. "Fifty knots." "Sixty knots." Trees at the end of the runway loomed dead ahead. At eighty knots, I dropped the quarter flap and forced the plane up, my landing gear brushing the tops of the trees.

When we reached 6,000 feet, I went back to tell our passengers, "We're out!"

A sea of faces smiled broadly. Tears rolled down cheeks. Prayers of gratitude went up.

But not one person moved.

During the following years in my military career, I experienced many hair-raising missions—combat flights in Europe and Korea, tight flights for the Berlin Airlift, unique flights to the South Pole—missions that required, and received, help from a Higher Power. Yet, that memorable moment aboard the little packed plane remains one of the most satisfying. I still can see those forty expressions—expressions that proclaimed louder than words the absolute joy of freedom.

Oscar T. Cassity, Maj. USAF (Ret.),
as told to Gloria Cassity Stargel

Road Angels

When you get to the end of your rope, tie a knot, and hang on.

Franklin D. Roosevelt

Thump! Thump! Thump! The sound I heard from the rear was not encouraging. At first, I thought it came from the rubber risers embedded in the center stripes. I ignored the drumming noise, but it got louder and nearer. As a precaution, I pulled onto the shoulder of the road. I got out and inspected the car. Yep, a flat tire. Grrrr. Sometimes life seems to be one flat tire after another. All I wanted to do was get home—from Phoenix, Arizona, to Pahrump, Nevada. Should be simple, right? What a terrible way to spoil a beautiful Fourth of July.

Simple. Only a flat tire. Unfortunately, I am mechanically challenged. When I was in high school, I took a Navy aptitude test, scoring thirty-five percent on the mechanical portion. Not a good sign. I had never changed a tire on my 2000 Echo and didn't know whether I had all the tools— any tools—in the trunk.

Although the car was on the shoulder, the Echo was still

close to traffic. As cars whipped by, the little Toyota trembled. Could such vibrations whip the car from its jack stand as I worked? Another accident waiting to happen. I paced around the car, contemplating my options. I could call AAA, but it was Sunday, a holiday weekend, and the road service response time would be slow.

I could call my brother Tom at his auto shop, but that would interrupt his day. I could replace the tire myself, and after three hours, if I hadn't been crushed by a cruising car, and if I hadn't gotten the spare on, I could martyr out and call AAA. But at least, I had to try.

I pulled the tools from the trunk and had started to pry off the plastic cover that shielded the lug nuts when a black semi pulled up behind me. I saw Arkansas plates. Two guys jumped out wearing faded, wrinkled jeans and short-sleeve shirts. One guy had a stubble, the other a beard. The one with the beard had tattoos, and frankly, people with tattoos make me nervous. Of the two things I couldn't stand—snakes and tattoos—I only had to worry about one of them, and that wasn't bad.

The tattooed guy spoke first. "Need help?"

"Yes, please," I said.

"Name's Gene. He's Jerry. We'll get this fixed in no time." Without a word, the two men had the spare on in five minutes. Gene loosened the lugs; Jerry got out the spare and the jack. Gene jacked up the car; Jerry pulled off the flat and popped on the donut. Gene replaced the lugs and lowered the car. Not even the Arizona heat and the waves of traffic could phase these guys. The Good Samaritans worked so fast you'd think it was something they did regularly to prepare for Olympic competition. "Representing the United States, Gene and Jerry in the lug nut event."

"Where ya headed?" asked Jerry.

"Las Vegas," I said. Most people didn't know where Pahrump was.

"Us, too. There's a used tire place just up the road. We'll follow you there."

"Great," I replied. Now I had "road angels" to protect me.

"Had some trouble ourselves," Gene volunteered. "Comin' into Texas, we lost an axle, and the friggin' rig flipped over. Goin' out of Texas, we had a blowout. Lost two days."

"Best get movin'. We're burnin' daylight," reminded Jerry.

We got into our vehicles.

Because the donut was smaller than the regular tire, the Echo tilted. I was nervous about how well the car would ride, so I drove under the speed limit. Looking into the rearview mirror, I saw the blessed black rig, chugging at a respectful distance. Comforted by their presence, I plugged on, hoping to see the tire shop very soon. One mile. Two miles. Three miles. And more. The Echo was steady. The donut was holding.

The tire shop was invisible; a figment of an angel's imagination?

Panicky, I kept looking at the odometer. I was approaching the point of no return. It was just as far to drive back to Sun City as it was to continue driving to Wickenburg. Wickenburg would have a retail tire store, and at least Wickenburg was in the direction of home. The flat tire reminded me how much I hated traveling. I wanted to spend the Fourth of July in front of my television, not on the side of U.S. 60.

Hastily, I darted into a rest area to mull this over. When I got out of the car to stretch, I noticed the semi had pulled off, too, about a hundred yards behind me. That black beast stared at me, its diesel heart thumping, waiting for me to move. One of the men slid out the passenger door. When I ducked into my car, he jumped into the truck. It was north or nothing, and the big rig trotted behind.

North I plodded, mile marker by mile marker. I counted familiar landmarks, each friendly sight inching me closer to Wickenburg. Forty miles. The turnoff for Interstate 17 to Flagstaff. Twenty-five miles. A billboard for AmericInn Wickenburg. Ten miles. A sign for the "14th Annual Fiesta Septiembre." A marker over the Hassayamper River, a dry riverbed. "McDonald's—five miles ahead." One mile. The speed limit slowed and the divided highway ended.

The semi with my road angels kept pace, yet kept its distance, as though we were merely pilgrims who happened to venture on the same path on the same day. The road curved to the right and uphill. Around a bend, I saw the sign for Big O Tire, and I immediately bolted into its parking lot. Ah, sanctuary. I knew now that I would safely make it home.

As I made my turn, the semi picked up speed as if on another scent. The driver honked twice as the rig sped by. "Glad you made it. See you again sometime," the blasts seemed to say.

If you were to ask me if Jerry and Gene made up their lost time, I'd say probably not. Down the road, somewhere in the Nevada desert, there'd be a black rig parked on the side of the road helping some stranded motorist. From the experience, I guess I learned two things: there but for the grace of God and the kindness of strangers go I, and sometimes angels wear tattoos.

Paul J. DiLella

4

MOVING FORWARD

Gratitude unlocks the fullness of life. It turns what we have into enough, and more. It turns denial into acceptance, chaos to order, confusion to clarity. It can turn a meal into a feast, a house into a home, a stranger into a friend. Gratitude makes sense of our past, brings peace for today, and creates a vision for tomorrow.

Melody Beattie

Jim the Boat Captain

Sometimes our light goes out but is blown into flame by an encounter with another human being. Each of us owes the deepest thanks to those who have rekindled this inner light.

Albert Schweitzer

It was early Tuesday morning when I sat in my bedroom and stared at the cream-colored box that held the cremated remains of my father. It wasn't a large box or a fancy one. It was a plain cardboard box with a sticker on the top that identified its contents. The box had been sitting on the floor of my bedroom, under a window, for almost two weeks.

My father died suddenly, unexpectedly. He was young, healthy—a vibrant man. My sister and I were also young, in our early twenties. As I sat staring at the box, she slept in the room across the hall, in the bed she had scarcely left since he had died.

Dad wanted to be cremated and have his ashes scattered in the ocean he loved so much. We would often meet for coffee or lunch and have philosophical conversations, and one day the topic of creamation came up. It was just conversation; I don't think he knew he'd die so young. I knew we had to honor his wishes, but I didn't know how. So the box sat in my bedroom until that Tuesday morning, when I knew it was time.

I got up from the bed and trundled across the hall to my sister's bedroom door. I knocked loud, louder and finally pushed it open. Sarah was buried under a pile of blankets and quilts, her head covered. The room was dark and smelled of stale coffee. Kneeling by the bed, I tried to wake her as gently as possible. She growled at me and shifted position, nestling her head deeper into the pillows.

"Come on, get up. We're going to Cape May to scatter Dad's ashes." She didn't respond. I shoved her and she groaned.

"Get up! We're going today. We need to do this."

Her head poked out of the blankets and she asked, "How?"

"I don't know. We'll figure it out. Now get up so we can get going."

We packed up my little red car with snacks and sodas and maps. I had on a big, wool striped sweater to protect me from the wind and cold of the coastline this time of year. I'd never been to the beach in the winter, and it was overcast as we left our little Pennsylvania town. Sarah and I were quiet for most of the three-hour drive. When we weren't quiet, we argued. Since Dad's death, we had both become quite irritable.

Dad didn't have any life insurance and hadn't been employed for the last year of his life. We had to call on relatives to help with the cremation costs and told his landlord to keep the security deposit to cover the last month's rent he hadn't paid. Sarah and I were both trying to pay our ways through college by working at the mall. We had almost $100 to fund this trip to carry out our father's last wishes.

At a rest station, we picked up a tourist brochure that listed fishing boats available for charter. Then, sitting in a familiar Cape May diner, we had coffee and looked through the listings. It felt weird to be sitting in the diner without Dad. Neither of us had ever been here without him.

We selected the charter boat with the best name and called to inquire about the price for a brief excursion on the *Hot Potato*. I was startled when a man's gruff voice answered. I tried to explain our situation as tactfully as I could. I knew it was an odd request, but he didn't seem put off, and said to meet him at the marina at two o'clock. After accounting for the coffee, gas, and tolls to get back home, I figured we'd have seventy dollars to spend on the boat, and I knew that was a slim budget for a private run. I asked about his fee, but he told me we'd talk about it later.

Sarah and I were relieved to have a boat. The cost was still a worry in the back of our minds, but we decided not to think about it and to take Dad for one last walk on the beach while we waited for the hours to pass. We put our snacks, sodas, and "the box of Dad" into a backpack and trudged out onto the beach. The sun had come out and it was getting quite warm for the season. We walked for a long time, quiet, just gazing out on the ocean. The salty air tickled our noses. We were the only people on the beach. After walking for a while, we sat down on the sand and set the box gently between us. We shared a soda and nibbled granola bars, looking over the crashing water.

"You know, I always knew we would do this. I just never thought we'd have to do it so soon."

I looked over at my sister and felt her words in my heart. I always knew it, too. Only I thought it would be more joyous, more of a celebration of my dad's life. I thought I'd be here with Sarah and my kids and her kids, and we'd laugh and talk about all the good times we'd all had here in Cape May with Dad.

When two o'clock came, the boat captain was waiting for us at the marina. He was a rough-looking Irish man, about my dad's age, with sandy, silver-colored hair. The sun had creased his face and his blue eyes crinkled around the edges. He was a sturdy man and looked strong from years of wrestling large deep-sea fishing equipment. He gave us a warm smile and introduced himself as Jim.

As Jim led us to the boat, I asked again about the fee. He waved off my question and helped us aboard. The *Hot Potato* chugged out to sea, and I nervously suggested we didn't have to go far, didn't have to be out too long, mindful of hourly charges. Jim simply offered us something to drink and told us he'd make sure we'd have the perfect spot.

We made small talk, and Jim told us jokes for almost an hour before he slowed the boat to a stop. He asked us if the spot was okay, and when we nodded, he ducked into the cabin to give us some privacy.

"You girls take as long as you need. And remember to toss with the wind, not into it, or you'll get a faceful," he joked and made us smile.

Sarah and I each whispered private things to our father before we opened the box to scatter his ashes into the sea. As we watched the ashes swirl in the water, the salty breeze blended perfectly with our tears. The memory of my father swelled in my chest, and I felt a smile tugging at the corners of my mouth.

"He would have loved this, you know." I glanced sideways at Sarah. She smiled and touched my hand. "He is loving this, right now." I looked into her teary eyes, shining with love for our dad, then up into the crisp November sky.

We stayed like that for a while, standing together at the

railing, our hearts drinking in the moment, the ocean, the sky, and our father's spirit.

Eventually, Jim poked his head out of the cabin, smiling tentatively, and we nodded. It was done. He turned the boat around and we chugged back to shore.

We were out for almost three hours, and as we approached the marina I grew nervous, sweating and shaking, as he pulled the boat into the dock. We had never agreed on a fee for this service, and I was terrified of not having enough money. My mind raced. Maybe he would agree to a payment plan, and Sarah and I could take turns sending him checks until it was covered.

Jim helped us off the boat and I immediately thrust the envelope that held all of our money toward him. I blurted, "I know we didn't talk about a price, but we only have seventy dollars, and I hope that's enough. If it's not, then I can take your address and we can send you a little every couple weeks or so. I'm really sorry, because our dad didn't have any life insurance and we're both pretty broke, but I promise we'll send you the money because you were so nice, and this was really important for us to do for our dad."

Jim smiled and pushed the envelope away. He told me to "quiet down" and put his arm around my shoulders. "I can't take any money from you girls. It wouldn't be right. I'm just glad I could help. What you did was real nice for your dad, and I know you must love him very much. I bet he's real proud of both of you."

I tried to protest and wanted to give him at least enough money to cover the gas for the boat, but he shushed me. He wouldn't take anything, not one dime. We thanked him profusely, and Jim gave us each a hug and told us to have a safe trip home.

I started crying as I climbed into the car. Sarah did, too.

I sniffed and said, "Well, I guess we could use the money

to pay Dad's last phone bill and electric bill when they come in."

Sarah looked over at me and suddenly smiled. "No, let's go have dinner at the Lobster House."

The Lobster House is one of Cape May's best restaurants, and Dad always talked about taking us there someday when he had enough money. That Tuesday we had a wonderful meal at the Lobster House. We sat for a long time and just talked about Dad. We shared happy memories and funny stories. It felt so very good.

On the first anniversary of our father's death, we wrote a beautiful "Thank You" card for Jim and took it to the marina, but the manager said he didn't dock there anymore. We sent the card to Jim's last known address and hoped it would reach him. We wanted Jim to know that he gave our dad the opportunity to have a very special dinner with us, one that he could never afford when he was living.

Jim's generosity started a tradition that we hold dear to this day: the tradition of honoring our father, celebrating his life, and sharing cherished memories each November when we go to the Lobster House and have a special dinner with our dad.

Colleen Tillger

God's Squad

The language of friendship is not words but meanings.

Henry David Thoreau

At fourteen, in the summer of 1956, when my parents lost their full-time babysitter, I took over the responsibility of watching my younger brothers and sister. Like most teenagers, I embraced summer vacation with zest and that summer started out happy enough. On weekends my girlfriends and I went to movies, played miniature golf, and dreamed of dating boys—none of us had been on our first date. Even during the weekdays when I babysat my brothers and sister, I embraced life with total trust, taking them to the beach on the bus all by myself.

One afternoon, I noticed a police officer directing traffic from the nearby horse races and felt compelled to take him an ice-cold glass of juice. His name was Bill, and his warm smile made me feel like I'd known him for a lifetime. I learned he was married and had two children. Number three was on the way.

Visiting with Bill became a part of my daily routine. I

soon realized that no one in the surrounding shops was a stranger to Bill. He'd wave and greet people by their names as they passed.

He loved to tease me, and after a few repeat visits, he told me, "You know, Karen, heated discussions have broken out at the police department. Officers are fighting over whose turn it is to be stationed on this corner where a pretty young teenager serves cold drinks with a smile." A hot crimson flush crept over my face. Finally, the day arrived when Bill's assignment came to an end. I really missed our chats.

A few weeks later, a stranger came to our door, posing as a contractor. He had personal information that convinced me he had been hired by my dad, and I allowed him into the house. But when he got me alone, he grabbed me from behind. I felt a knife blade against my throat as he said, "Don't scream, or I'll kill you." A ripple of terror shot through my whole body. The rapist stole my innocence and left behind a shadow of fear that seemed to attach itself to my soul.

After he left, I escaped to a neighbor's, with my sister and brothers at my side. She called my parents, and they called the police. That afternoon, I longed to be my daddy's little girl once more, to have him hold me and tell me that I'd be all right. But when he learned I'd been raped, he turned and walked away from me. The foundation of my world crumbled. When the police questioned me, I felt more like a criminal than a victim. In the fifties no rape crisis centers or support groups were available for victims and their families. My parents had their own pain and were unable to meet my needs. I felt alone and abandoned.

The day Mom called me to talk with two detectives, I had reached the bottom of my despair. Suicidal thoughts plagued me. It was with a reluctant heart I entered the

room where two men waited for me. My head was lowered as I sat on a dining-room chair. My hands were
clasped so tightly they ached. Inside I screamed, *Don't they
know each time I repeat my story, it's like being tortured?* My
thoughts were interrupted when I heard a familiar voice.
"Karen, don't you remember me?"

As I looked up at the detective sitting in the chair opposite mine, I found myself looking into the blue eyes of the
police officer who had befriended me earlier that summer.
With relief, I smiled and said, "Bill!" His warm blue eyes
smiled back at me.

Since we'd last met, he had been promoted to detective
and had been assigned to my case. That afternoon, Bill's
words felt like a healing balm touching my soul.

"Karen," Bill said, "this terrible thing is not your fault."
He stood, walked over to me, and pulled me close. "It's
okay to cry," he added. At those words a floodgate of emotions burst open—tears flowed.

For the first time, I realized that the shame inflicted on
me had not been my fault. I understood that God wanted
me to choose life and the freedom that came with that
incredible choice.

On his off-duty time, Bill would stop by at my house
and sit at our kitchen table, talking with Mom and me. I
didn't understand, but Bill realized I needed my hope
restored, and he'd started a campaign to help me. We
drove to the grocery store and around the surrounding
neighborhood.

"Watch for anyone that looks like him," Bill said. "Karen,
it takes time, but eventually he'll mess up, get careless,
and we'll arrest him."

Bill became a surrogate dad to me. His friendship
brought hope back into my life. He introduced me to his
wife, Helen, who welcomed me, and their home became a
safe place for me where love embraced me.

Bill's confidence that justice would be carried out gave me new strength. And his prediction came true. Finally, one morning in November, Mom walked into the kitchen with the newspaper in her hand and said, "Karen, look at this composite police picture and see if the man resembles your rapist." My hands shook as I looked at the familiar face. "Yes. It's him!"

After my rapist was caught and sentenced, my friendship with Bill and Helen continued. We've shared graduations, weddings, births, funerals, and a blended mixture of tears and laughter. Our friendship has endured fifty-one years.

I know how blessed I was to have met a policeman whose warm, compassionate heart became a key that unlocked my prison of fear. Over the years, I have tried to instill the gift of helping others in the hearts of my children and grandchildren, for what would the world be like if every individual reached out to help one hurting soul—like Bill did for me?

Karen Kosman

A Bride for Jimmy

Do all the good you can ... in all the ways you can ... as long as ever you can.

John Wesley

I was often the unwilling copilot on my father's delivery runs across the broad green plains of the prairies. In the prairies every grain elevator had a town or village attached, and we would wind our way through the miles slowly. The "milkstop" run it was called, and with good reason: we stopped at every milkstop on the way. But when we reached the town with the three elevators, I grew more attentive, for here is where we'd stop for lunch at Jimmy's cafe.

The paint on the outside frame, white with a green border, was weathered by the winds that blew across the dusty miles. Wind chimes, Chinese dragons, and pagodas hung outside, and they would sing to me of faraway places. This was Jimmy's, and I always got the best at Jimmy's.

Jimmy owned one of those wonderful Chinese restaurants that dotted the prairie landscapes. Dad would pull into the diagonal parking spot and turn off the engine. I'd hold his hand, which was covered with oil and dirt, and skip as we strode along the wooden walk. Jimmy's chimes would sing a warm welcome, and I would stand outside listening until I was hustled in.

"Blocking the entrance is bad for Jimmy's business," Father would grumble.

Jimmy would come out of the kitchen, white apron tied around his small frame. Jimmy had the fastest hands I had ever seen and could put Matt Dillon on *Gunsmoke* out of a job—this much I knew. When it wasn't too busy, Jimmy used to let me sit in the back and watch him make filled dumplings, or spin Chinese noodles. They were better than pasta or the homemade egg noodles my grandmother made.

Dad and I would take our usual spot on the round counter seats. They were red and slick, with a marbled thread of black running through, stuck on a silvery platform. I sat next to Jimmy's goldfish tank. "Good luck fish," he would say. I would swirl around and around on my seat until a stern look from Father would stop my dizzying dance.

As Jimmy and Father discussed the local grain situation, I was given an ice-cream soda in a tall silver flask. It was piled high with whipped cream and topped with a perfect cherry from a glass jar. Jimmy would smile at me and call me young lady, the first man ever to do so. While Father read the paper, Jimmy would show me his Chinese abacus and pictures from home when he was a boy. We talked about teachers and how I should always try to be polite, but not afraid to ask questions. "How else you going to learn?" Jimmy would say, and Father would moan quietly from his corner.

When Jimmy reached forty, something was in the air. He had been corresponding with a family member who knew a girl who might be interested in him. When we traveled to Jimmy's, he would show us letters exchanged formally with the young lady, and although they were in Chinese and I couldn't make them out quite right, Jimmy translated her words to me softly. I could tell he was falling in love.

But he was shy about approaching this young lady. He didn't know her. What did she like? What didn't she like? Would she find the winters in Canada too cold? Would she be content in the small prairie town he had grown to call home? How would he raise the money for the passage? I felt like I was going to cry for Jimmy.

Father saved me by changing the subject back to the matter at hand. "Ask the girl questions, Jimmy!" he declared. "How else are you going to learn if you don't ask questions?"

Married men offered their advice on how to court a lady, and Jimmy wrote it down. Farmer's wives took pictures of Jimmy in his best suit, showing the beauty of the prairies in all the seasons. Jimmy sent them on. Finally, he got up the nerve to ask her to marry him through an honored family go-between.

Months went by without an answer, and I began to add Jimmy to my prayers. "Please, let things work out for Jimmy," I implored. "He is so lonely."

I was there that rainy afternoon when Jimmy finally received word from China. She would come to Canada as his wife. But Jimmy had a problem. He had saved his money to buy his new bride a passage, but he had nothing to spare for the wedding he had dreamed of giving her.

"Have faith, Jimmy," the farm wives told him. But Jimmy knew there was no one to borrow money from. Crops had been poor that year, and money was in short supply, just like the rain.

The farm wives got together and schemed. Quietly, for

months, the folk who lived in the area collected for Jimmy's wedding. Father had been put into service; while on milkstop run, he took the enamel pickle jar and got his customers to contribute.

Everyone knew Jimmy, his friendly face, and the wonderful food from his restaurant, and everyone wanted to help out.

On a fine summer day, dressed in traditional clothing, Jimmy and his wife walked down the aisle in the country church, surrounded by friends they didn't know they had. The money was enough to give his bride a wedding she would never forget, and although she was scared so far away from home, she soon felt welcomed as a part of our country community.

I often think of Jimmy and his wife from far away. I know a lot of the small whistle stops of my childhood have since disappeared, but somewhere an old Chinese restaurant stands, the paint a little worn and Chinese lanterns dancing in the prairie wind. Good luck gold fish swim inside a green glass tank. This is Jimmy's, and at Jimmy's you always get the best.

Nancy Bennett

Angels on My Doorstep

*The best solution for little problems is to help
people with big problems.*

Rabbi Kalman Packouz

Today, I watch the fluffy flakes of snow drift lazily to the
ground, adding to the whiteness that ushers in the beginning of winter. The waters of Torch Lake, still fluid and
unfrozen, are a brilliant blue. I look out my window and
drink in the beauty. It was this view and the beauty of the
region that was instrumental in our decision to build our
retirement home here. But I do not know if I shall see the
lake freeze over or watch the blossoms of spring burst
forth. I have been diagnosed with the "wet" form of macular degeneration, a disease that is the leading cause of
blindness in people over the age of fifty.

My life is already changing. Grocery shopping is
becoming more difficult because labels are harder to read.
My steps are more uncertain as I loose my depth percep-
tion. I have frequent trips to the retinal doctor, where a
new drug, Macugen, is injected into each eye every six
weeks or so, in an effort to slow the progression of my

vision loss. If the treatment is not successful, the doctor has told me that I will be legally blind within a few months to a year.

As my vision dims, I have experienced an overwhelming outpouring of love and support. Friends' offer, "If you need a ride to the doctor or the store, just let me know." Notes of encouragement arrive from mere acquaintances, and a multitude of prayers are being sent my way. My twenty-three-year-old grandson tells me that he prays for me each night before going to bed.

Another grandson working on contract as a firefighter near Mosul, Iraq, wants to come home and bring my great-granddaughter for a visit. He wants me to be able to see her "once more," just in case I won't be able to in the future.

A delivery truck turns up my drive and I wonder, "What on earth have I have ordered?" Upon opening the box, I discover a magnifying makeup mirror with full spectrum light, a gift from a childhood friend I have known for over fifty years. She lives month to month, on a small disability income. She has multiple sclerosis and is battling breast cancer, yet she thinks of me!

I answer a neighbor's knock on my door and she hands me a bouquet of helium-filled balloons in all the colors of the rainbow. She wants me to "Enjoy all the colors and remember what they look like!" Another neighbor, a retired high school English teacher, tells me that if I want to dictate any of my stories, she will be happy to type them for me.

On a bleak afternoon, after just learning that the Macugen appears not to be working, there is once again a knock at my door. A dear friend stands with flowers in hand. As we settle down for a cup of tea, she hands me a small brocade purse. "This was Mama's," she says. "I made it for her many years ago. I want you to have it." How delighted I am to receive something she had made. As I take the purse in my hands, I feel something inside. When I unzip it, I find an antique, magnifying glass with a lovely porcelain handle.

A recent visit to the doctor shows that the loss of vision in my right eye has slowed and appears to be in remission for now. The vision in my left eye has not responded and continues to deteriorate, but a new, off-label drug that has been showing some favorable results is now being tried.

I do not fear the future, for I am blessed with a feeling of peace and comfort on this journey into darkness. I know that whatever happens, I have angels on my doorstep!

Priscilla Miller

The Boy in the Green Wheelchair

In any moment of decision, the best thing you can do is the right thing. The worst thing you can do is nothing.

Theodore Roosevelt

After I taught my classes in urban planning at Arizona State University, I drove slowly down an unfamiliar Mesa street. Stomach knotted, I was looking for an old converted motel that was now used as a homeless shelter. My tan and white terrier on the seat beside me sensed my nervousness and comfortingly nosed my leg. "Luke, I *hate* this," I muttered to him. "I don't know why I let Debbie talk me into it." Becoming a therapy team with my dog, as my friend Debbie had with her dog, was one thing, but the other side of that coin—volunteering at a homeless shelter for at-risk kids—was another. Finally, I spotted the shelter adjacent to a secondhand store.

One look at those two old buildings and I was right back on the poverty row of my eighteen years as a foster child—I'd been abandoned in infancy without adoption permission. I'd worked hard to ditch that welfare life I'd hated! That's why I gave money regularly to similar causes but had never gotten *personally* involved. I'd even attempted suicide as a teen to get free of that life. After that failure, with the help of a kind teacher and a young group-home leader, I'd concentrated on education as my escape tool. It worked. I won scholarships all the way through a doctorate at Harvard—me, the little black girl who'd flunked first grade and was thought mentally disabled. I'd studied like mad and made it. But here I was, back in that hopeless situation.

I parked, and with Luke on his leash, I stepped inside the door amid a sea of unkempt kids who surrounded the after-school snack table. In those kids, I faced myself as a child: their uncombed hair, their faded, mismatched clothes, and their listless, lonely eyes. I pushed those thoughts away and tried to concentrate on what I was supposed to do. "They're five to twelve years old," Debbie had said of the shelter kids. "But what we have right now are mostly five to eight. Use puzzles to teach them hand-to-eye coordination, or play checkers with them. Or help them with homework. Or just listen. Remember, your dog is the one who gains the kids' trust because they haven't always found adults trustworthy." I decided to glue myself to Debbie, who was getting out blue and pink Play-Doh in a far corner.

But no such luck. Several youngsters moved over to me because Luke was wagging his tail and inviting them with dancing brown eyes.

The sight of a frail, little boy in a green wheelchair, his arms moving almost spastically, caught my eye. I realized he was the youngster Debbie said had been a normal baby until beaten by his mother's boyfriend. It brought a lump to my throat. I wanted to bolt out the door, but I wouldn't let myself.

The next few days I played checkers with the kids,

worked Play-Doh into figures with them, and helped with homework. But nothing drew the boy in the green wheel-chair into any group.

He refused to join in, even when Debbie and I started a story-composing time, which became popular with the other kids. We'd start a story about Luke, throwing out a beginning, and the children made up the terrier's adventures from there.

While we worked on making up stories, I watched our nonjoiner. Loren was different from the others. His blue eyes were shiny, and he wore a sweet smile. His sandy hair was neatly combed, his clothes were pressed and clean. He was close to eight but so thin he seemed six. The beating had damaged the motor area of his brain. He could scramble out of the wheelchair. But when he got to the floor, he could only use his arms to crawl and dragged his useless legs behind. But crawl he did! *Maybe he avoids the groups for fear he can't keep up. Could I help him gain confidence?*

He rarely spoke, and when he did, his words were garbled. I tried to get him to talk to me, but often without response. He was used to pointing to things he wanted. He'd point to a fruit drink, but I'd make him ask for it before handing it to him. And when I asked how his school day was, I wouldn't accept "fine" for an answer. It became our game, and his eyes would shine when he said a word, however garbled.

I found myself spontaneously hugging him, something I'd rarely done with anyone, since I was never hugged as a child. But he still shied away from joining a group. Only after I'd worked with him several weeks on letter recognition, tracing the letters with his hand, and making those letters' sounds did I get him to join my group one day.

I was working with a small circle of youngsters who were taking turns playing with Luke. When it came Loren's turn with the dog, I said, "Tell me what you want to do, Loren."

Suddenly, eyes dancing, Loren said, "I want to pet Luke!" A whole sentence said clearly! Tears crowding my eyes, I brought my terrier to him, and Luke nuzzled the boy's head. Gently massaging the dog's soft tan fur between his fingers, the little boy smiled rapturously. I dropped to one knee in front of the green wheelchair and hugged the boy and dog.

From that moment on, I knew these kids and I were in sync. I also realized with an aching heart how much I'd miss Loren and each of the others when they left the shelter. But I knew more children who needed me would take their place.

How thankful I am that Debbie got me personally involved. I have worked with at-risk kids in the homeless shelter for several years now, and the hours I teach them and work and play with them are most rewarding. The experience has even helped to heal my own difficult childhood.

Theresa Cameron as told to Jeanne Hill

"I got your tests back and they show you have an enlarged heart, but don't be concerned. That's to make room for the love, compassion, empathy, and courage you have in your heart."

Reprinted by permission of Aaron Bacall. © 2007 Aaron Bacall.

Sharing Luck

If one is lucky, a solitary fantasy can totally transform one million realities.

Maya Angelou

With his thin-soled sandals, Ramon plodded several miles from his village of Maunabo, Puerto Rico, to a sugar cane plantation. He carried a large basket of pastries on his head to sell to the *macheteros*, men who wielded their razor-sharp machetes in the fields. Ramon was a delicate boy whose knobby kneed legs looked like tree twigs and who stood six inches shorter than other boys his age. He often rested under a large African palm, rubbing his neck and forearms, tired after clutching a heavy load atop his head. Ramon had a dream—a preposterous dream that everyone agreed could never come true. He knew it was beyond reason, but he followed his heart.

Ramon was the fifteenth child in his family. His mother was forty-six when he was born in 1925 and nearly died giving birth. To help support his large family, Ramon started working for the local baker when he was just seven. Shortly thereafter, Ramon developed a horrific toothache, possibly from sampling too many pastries. Rubbing his swollen cheek to dull the incessant throb, he trudged to the outskirts of his village to a free dental clinic. "Young man," the dentist calmly explained, "I will help you. Just relax." The elderly dentist squeezed Ramon's shoulder and affectionately tousled his hair before turning to prepare a syringe of Novocain.

Shutting his eyes tight, Ramon clamped the sides of the chair like a vice. Several moments passed, and he felt complete relief after the dentist gently pried his tooth loose. *Someday, I would like to help people like that, to make their pain go away,* Ramon thought.

Ramon ran home, floating on air with his newfound wish. He could not wait to share the news with his family: "I want to become a dentist!"

Years later, when Ramon was nineteen years old, he still held on to his dream, but coming from a poor family, he did not have the finances to attend college. His brothers had talked about the lottery since he was a young boy. A small portion of a ticket cost twenty-five cents, and a complete ticket cost six dollars, about as much as it cost to feed a family for a week, maybe two. However, a complete ticket improved the odds of winning a much larger prize. Ramon fantasized about winning the lottery and even envisioned a number: 14,000.

One morning in November, Ramon was working in a small store in which his mother, Doña Chepa, was the proprietor. A lottery salesman happened to stroll in. "Caimito," Ramon said to the salesman, "I would like to buy a complete ticket, but it should be a number in the fourteen thousands."

"Actually, I have one, fourteen thousand, one hundred sixty-five," Caimito replied.

Ramon had saved eight dollars over several years, as Doña Chepa occasionally gave him a few coins for working in the store. Buying a complete ticket was a financial sacrifice. With his hand shaking, Ramon bought the ticket.

Days later, Ramon took three buses to San Juan to buy merchandise for his mother's store and to see the winning lottery number. He began his errands at the shirt factory and asked the owner if he knew the winning number. "I think fourteen thousand and something," the man replied, shrugging his shoulders. Ramon gasped. With a sweaty palm, he reached into his pocket to feel his ticket.

Did the man actually say 14,000? With butterflies in his stomach, he raced to a small shop where the winning number was displayed in the window. A crowd hovered in front; Ramon stood on his tiptoes and stretched his neck to see over their heads.

There it was: 14,165.

He had won!

Despite his premonitions, Ramon could hardly believe his eyes. The hairs on his arms stood up straight. The blood pounded in his temples. In a flash, he sprinted across a wide, bustling avenue and excitedly told an elderly couple his news.

"Young man, bravo! Be careful who you talk to," the older gentleman whispered. "Someone may knock you over to steal your ticket!"

His heart pounding, Ramon raced to another shop where he trusted the owner, Hermann Gomez, to tell him the news. Hermann gave Ramon a ride to the lottery office to collect the first prize: $18,000, tax free. Hermann called Banco Publico and asked them to stay open for Ramon's large deposit. He then ushered Ramon through the large glass and metal doors and assisted him in opening his first account.

With all the excitement, Ramon lost track of time and missed the last bus to Maunabo. He sent his mother a telegram and spent his first night away from home in a hotel. Ramon could not sleep that night. Possibilities for his future swirled in his head as he lay in bed staring at the ceiling, thinking about this turn in his life.

When he arrived home the following day, Thanksgiving 1944, Ramon stepped from the bus into a dazzling reception. Dozens of townspeople waited in the plaza to congratulate him. His friends and family embraced him, throwing flower petals in the air to celebrate his good fortune. Ramon felt like a king.

Before he left the island for the first time in his life, Ramon helped his family by giving his brothers and sister $300 each. He had just enough leftover to finance his education.

Ramon sought advice from the one man in town who had attended college in the States, Antonio Navarro. "Ramon," Antonio told him, "you gotta go to Michigan State. I loved it and you will, too!" Because Antonio was fluent in English, he called Michigan State University for an application and helped Ramon complete it.

The first six months of college overwhelmed Ramon. He barely spoke English. With his Spanish-English dictionary, he sat in the front row of each class, asking his professors to "Repeat, repeat, repeat." Knowing he was a foreigner, several teachers remained after class to tutor Ramon in English. Finally, Ramon started to become accustomed to the sounds of his new language. Still, he had times when he was dismayed and wanted to return home, but realizing God had given him a gift, he was determined not to waste it.

Ramon persevered and earned his degree in dentistry in 1955.

He returned to Puerto Rico to work for the Public Health Department, where he provided free dental services. Fondly remembering the dentist who inspired his dream years before, he wanted to return the favor.

Ramon decided to visit the elderly dentist, wondering if he was still alive. Diploma in hand, he took the same route of two decades earlier to share his news with his old friend. The small wood cottage was barely visible, enveloped by vines and thickets. Ramon was close to tears; the old healer was gone.

Ramon's dental practice thrived for thirty-two years. He helped generations of families with the gifts God gave him. When he retired, his patients cried. He raised a family and sent his three daughters to college; none had to win the lottery to finance their education, and all three have successful careers.

As his youngest daughter, I have learned much from my father, who had the wisdom to take advantage of his good fortune, and the tenacity to see his dream through. Though small in stature, he accomplished the feats of a giant.

Celeste Leon

Christmas Blessings from Grandma to Grandma

The courage to imagine the otherwise is our greatest resource, adding color and suspense to all our lives.

David Boorstin

While conducting a Christmas program at the Salvation Army's Homeless Women's Shelter, I was moved with compassion for the women and children living there. I met Margaret, a grandmother raising her two grandchildren. Margaret seemed much like me, except much older, and recovering from a back injury, which left her unable to keep a permanent job.

Sara, Margaret's granddaughter, was eleven years old. Like most girls her age, she was excited about Christmas, but wondering if Santa was going to come to her home, which was now at the shelter. Billy, her grandson, was six years old. He was full of energy but seemed to be unconcerned or even aware of his surroundings. Sara was suffering the most from the loss of her mother, who was battling drug addition. Though Sara was beloved by her grandmother, her world was much harder than carefree Billy's.

As I walked into the very small room that this family called home, I could hardly hold back the tears. The room had two twin beds, which they shared, and a bathroom they shared with another family. I listened as Margaret told me her sad story, and about her pain over her lost daughter. Finally, she showed me the one pair of shoes that Sara and Billy each had. She had no money to provide a Christmas for them. Margaret was at an age when her daughter should have been caring for her, yet her eyes became moist with tears as she thought about Christmas and how little she could do for her own grandchildren.

I'm a single working mother and grandmother, and I knew firsthand of Margaret's most difficult and nearly impossible task. My heart was moved with compassion, and God began to speak to my heart about this dear family. It was through my own mother's words that I heard the message that moved my compassion into action. My dear mother used to always say, "There but by the grace of God go I." And for me, just one step removed from this sadness, I knew it was true.

My finances were limited also, but I knew I had to do something. I sneaked a look at the shoe sizes Sara and Billy wore, then I was on the move. First to the Family Dollar Store to buy toys and gifts. I loaded up! Then to the Payless Shoe Store, for not two, but three pairs of shoes; one pair each for Sara and Billy and one pair for Margaret. Of course, I had one last purchase: wrapping paper and bows.

I hurried home and wrapped the gifts. I was so excited! I called the shelter and invited Margaret, Sara, and Billy to have Christmas lunch, and to spend Christmas day in my home.

On Christmas morning, I drove to the women's shelter

and picked them up. Anticipation mounted as I drew near to my home. Margaret, Sara, and Billy enjoyed a Christmas feast of smoked turkey and ham, chicken and dumplings, pecan pies, sweet potato casserole, and lots of goodies! Little Sara began to relax into the feeling of belonging that she had not had for so long. Billy just ate!

After lunch, we all gathered around the Christmas tree. I began to place each of their gifts at their feet. Margaret began to cry. Sara and Billy eagerly tore into the boxes. Sara and Billy both had a new pair of tennis shoes and some toys. Margaret also had a pair of new shoes and a lovely gift of fifty dollars. No words could describe the scene. Sharing that day with them was my gift, but whether it was a greater gift to them or to me, I can't say. I do know that this was the best Christmas I have ever had.

Carolyn Brooks

One More Tomorrow

When the heart grieves over what it has lost, the spirit rejoices over what it has left.

Sufi epigram

She was my "buddy pal"—a pet name coined by my daughter decades ago—a second mom to my kids, my should-have-been sister, my friend.

Relationships like this are not remarkable for women. We're pretty blessed with the ability to identify good friends, nurture them, and keep them close to our hearts. Our friendships are going to last a lifetime. Isn't that the rule?

So, during all those quick cups of decaf at the French Bakery, or through that whirlwind overnight to New York City when we promised ourselves over a bottle of lunchtime chardonnay that we would be back, or during those myriad late-night phone chats between us when nothing much of significance was ever exchanged, JoAnn and I always trusted we had more tomorrows.

JoAnn and I met at Chestnut Hill Academy on the first day of pre-first for our sons, Bryan and Eric, who are today grown men. I was in my customarily worn-out exercise tights and baggy T-shirt; she was dressed, and I mean dressed. Not overdone, just picture perfect in her smart Talbots suit with just the proper scarf, her hair and makeup flawless, and it was barely 8 AM. The little guys connected, and our friendship soon followed.

Through the years, JoAnn and I shared absolutely everything.

Cooking tricks—Jo taught me to roll parboiled noodles around the ricotta filling and lay the bundles side by side for lasagna. I taught her to whip a couple of egg whites into her mashed sweet potatoes and bake them in the oven.

Kid advice—when our children balked about attending church, Jo taught me to say, "If God gives us seven days, we can give him back one hour." I taught her to substitute "honor bright" instead of "swear to God."

Secrets—one of us had never tried pot, the other had.

Stuff—we shared her black lace shawl, my grandmother's earrings, her packable travel coat, my Hermes scarf. Was that glitzy glitter bag hers, or mine? Who could remember? Who cared?

We shared our January birth month, and together we crossed over to our forties and into our fifties. She with a smile, and me not quite so thrilled. We lived through her son's first speeding ticket and my son's school demerits; we celebrated her twenty-fifth wedding anniversary, and together we shed tears during my divorce.

And then it came out of the blue. The tests, the diagnosis, the radiation, the chemotherapy, the surgeries. For over two years of extensive cancer treatments, JoAnn continued her job as assistant to the president of our local bank.

During her chemotherapy treatments that often lasted several hours, I sat on a stool by her side, sometimes holding her hand as she dozed, other times turning the pages of the endless magazines we skimmed as I bantered about this new makeup or that new accessory.

Even when enduring the worst of the radiation and chemotherapy side effects, Jo would never forget to call and remind me to have the kids wear their slickers when rain was predicted. When she should have been asleep, the phone would ring late at night—just to remind me to sign the permission slip for the next day's school trip. I guess we were taking care of each other for all our tomorrows.

The day JoAnn was rushed to the hospital for emergency surgery, I took her doctor aside and pleaded to be allowed to spend the night in her room. He reluctantly agreed. After her husband and kids kissed her good-bye, it was just the two of us. The horrific pain she had endured for many months was gone, so she had a brief respite from her suffering. That night we talked until sunrise, my best friend and me. No, we weren't at a party, or at the theater, or out to dinner. We didn't have our hair blown out, or faces made-up, or nails polished. I wasn't in my little black "Audrey" dress, and she wasn't in her favorite sapphire silk suit. We were just best friends who were treasuring the moment and, maybe, just maybe, for the first time we weren't thinking about tomorrow.

A few short weeks later, JoAnn slipped into a coma and passed away. Hours after she died, I found myself in church at the St. Martin-in-the-Fields family service. As I sat alone in the pew, my mind swirled with memories.

I wasn't concentrating on the sermon, or the prayers, and I don't even remember seeing the collection plate pass by. All I could think about was that my best friend had died and I would never, ever feel connected with her again. If only I could feel her near me one last time. I closed my eyes and prayed hard for a signal.

"Please, God," I prayed, "send me a sign, any sign that

will prove to me that JoAnn will always be with me."

Then just, as I opened my eyes, I heard the opening chords of the communion hymn: "You who dwell in the shelter of the Lord." While I had been praying for a signal from Jo, out of the hundreds of possible hymns, the choir began to sing her absolutely most favorite hymn in the whole world.

I looked up at the altar and listened to every syllable of *On Eagle's Wings*. As the familiar chorus, "And he will raise you up on eagle's wings," echoed throughout the church, I couldn't stop my tears. God had heard me and had answered my prayer.

JoAnn was truly with me. I felt her presence, just as if she had been sitting next to me. Then, out of nowhere, a hand rested on my shoulder. I turned to my left and saw that a stranger had slid across the pew and had put her arm around me to comfort me.

It was exactly what JoAnn would have done.

We sat in silence until the choir sang the final refrain.

When it was our turn to receive communion, this stranger guided me down the church's center aisle, her arm still around my shoulder. We knelt side by side at the communion rail as we received the bread and wine for communion.

Outside the church, after the service, in the crisp November breeze, we introduced ourselves. I explained to her that my best friend had died hours before, and that just as I had been praying for a sign, her hand had touched my shoulder. I told her what had affected me the most was that her act of comfort was exactly what JoAnn would have done. And for those brief moments, I had felt JoAnn had truly been with me and God had answered my prayer.

This stranger simply smiled and told me she was happy to have been sitting next to me in church this morning. We hugged and said good-bye—this new friend and I.

As I was driving home to face the first day without JoAnn in my life, the first thing that came to mind was the embroidered pillow I had given her many birthdays ago that she kept on her bed: "A friend is a gift you give yourself." Indeed, JoAnn had been a gift to me, as was this stranger this morning in church.

It's been over a year of tomorrows since JoAnn died. I still find myself stopping my car from automatically turning onto the street where she lived, or picking up the phone for one of our late night chats.

And, when these moments overwhelm me, I remember that Sunday morning in church. And then I am comforted in knowing that JoAnn's spirit is only a prayer away and that she is truly with me through all my tomorrows.

LindaCarol Cherken

Save the Best for Last

We are not put on this earth for ourselves, but are placed here for each other. If you are there always for others, then in time of need, someone will be there for you.

Jeff Warner

My dad spoke softly into the phone. "Are you sure about this?" he asked.

"Yes, Dad," I answered. "We *really* want you to move in with us. We all do."

As I said those words, I flashed back in time to when I was fifteen. I had overheard a similar conversation when my parents invited Nana to live with us. But I was a typical teen—self-centered, self-indulgent, and often just plain cranky. It didn't matter much to me that Nana became a fixture in the spare bedroom, passing the days sewing a smock or polishing her nails. Her presence didn't bother me, but to spend hours chatting with her wasn't high on my list.

I got the impression she felt the same. After all, she never inquired about boyfriends, recitals, or college plans. She never asked why I came to dinner with a tear-stained face, or if I ever resolved the ear-piercing issue with Mom. We simply had nothing in common. Nana passed away at the age of ninety-one. I cried by her grave as I reflected on the few good times we shared when I was a little girl. On her velvet couch, she taught me how to shuffle cards like a pro. In a kitchen that smelled like cinnamon with a hint of musty linen on the side, she served oven-fresh cookies on delicate china. I decided to keep those miniature memories close to my heart whenever I thought of Nana, but why didn't I have any recent wonderful memories of her? We had lived under the same roof for almost ten years.

I wondered if my children would end up with good memories of a live-in grandparent. Their granddad was eighty-four years old and in failing health. How would they respond to him? How would he respond to us? Would he notice our accomplishments, problems, and daily activities? It wasn't long before I realized Dad had no intention of hiding in a bedroom. A self-taught man and a communications junkie, he set up his computer in the family office and worked on websites, stayed in touch with friends through e-mail, and absorbed the latest trends on the Internet.

"You should know how your computer operates," he told me. "Let me show you."

I explained I knew nothing about my car's engine and that didn't keep me from using it. We giggled as we recalled that day long ago when he flipped open the hood of my first vehicle and tried to explain to me how that engine worked. Then Dad shuffled me to a computer chair and instructed me on the inner workings of my hard drive. Dad exchanged home improvement ideas with my husband, talked about tax increases with the neighbors, and often started discussions at the dinner table about the conflict overseas. "We're heading for another world war," he stated, and a lively debate over the pros and cons of involvement began.

Every family member from ages nine to twenty stayed long after dessert to hear this lieutenant colonel's personal war stories built from twenty-six years of Army service. "It all started way back in 1492 . . . ," Dad teased. We had our own living, breathing version of the History Channel, and even better yet, this historian came with a sense of humor.

On quiet evenings, Dad sat shoulder to shoulder with my college student and shared late-night snacks. "What job will you have after graduation?" he wanted to know. "Will you make enough to support a family?" I was amazed to hear my son open up and discuss his dreams with someone four times his age.

Dad subtly put in his two cents about another son's hairstyle and lifestyle. "Want a ride to the barber?" he asked, and he wouldn't take no for an answer. "Why do you watch that junk on television? Watch the news. Keep up with what's happening in the world." If I approached my son about these things, I'd get a flippant answer. This octogenarian got compliance without the attitude.

He photographed my daughter's leaps and twirls with his newly purchased digital camera. "You're a beautiful ballerina," he said, eyes glowing with love. Later, he figured out how to e-mail the pictures to her so she could forward them to friends. In a note he copied to me he said, "I'm so proud of your accomplishments. Be proud of yourself."

Dad and I talked about my youngest child's lack of self-control. He saw me struggle with her inattentiveness but never interfered except to say, "Her problems may run deeper than you think." He dabbed my tears and planted kisses on my forehead. I was instantly transformed into a little girl who had been empowered by her father's tenderness.

Dad offered sage advice or mild criticism, a hug, or an

ear for venting problems. We didn't always agree, but that was irrelevant. What was important was that he chose his words wisely and spoke in nonthreatening tones that commanded attention. So we listened. We responded. It was easy to do. It was Dad's choice to share our dreams and troubles. He made his concern for us known. He was a participant, not an observer like my Nana.

I'm grateful that history did not repeat itself, even though he was Nana's son. My children do not yet realize how they've benefited from Dad's presence in our home. He has been with us only two years, but I know our lives have been enriched. And I'm certain the memories they'll have of this man will turn into lessons for their children one day.

Now Dad's words are few but always caring and meaningful. As I bring him meals, and he struggles to sit, drink, and even lift a fork, he turns his once bright blue eyes to me and says, "How are *you* today?" I kiss his dimpled cheek and tell him about the fender bender I had earlier. He chuckles and asks, "You want driving lessons?" Forty years in the future, I may need to live with a daughter or son. I hope I can return their kindness by staying part of their lives, as my father did, and keep life rolling along until the end of the road.

Nancy Viau

In Good Hands

Hope is faith holding out its hand in the dark.

George Iles

"My name is Judie, and I'm an alcoholic," I hear her say. From the minute I walk into the room, it's easy to see where this group is anchored. The first table on the left, that's where she sits every Tuesday and Thursday morning.

With her hands wrapped around a steaming cup of coffee, she says, "You gotta get honest and you gotta get God. I didn't get this program right away. First, I lost my husband, then, my child, and my last drink took my mind. Now I'm bipolar and on medication. But by the grace of God, I'm sober today."

That's what she tells the newcomers, and anyone else fortunate enough to be sitting there. She tells us what we have to do and how we have to do it. It's not always polite, but it's honest. "Bull! You're a liar," she'll spit. And you know it's true. But she loves us back to health, sometimes to our families, usually to our jobs, and mostly back to life.

I phone her early; she's up by four and sometimes out

by six for the early commuter's meeting. If I miss her, it's her message that delivers exactly what I need. "I can't come to the phone right now, but God loves you and so do I. Have a great day, and I'll call you later."

Her couch is a haven to those in need. With barely enough for herself, she shares whatever she has with anyone ready to work a twelve-step program.

"Happy sixty-fifth birthday!" A few of the people she guides through the twelve steps of recovery organize an impromptu celebration for Judie. Janine, a close friend, hands her a diamond necklace.

"It's the circle of life," Janine gushes.

Judie's eyes open brightly and her mouth stretches into a wider smile. "This is too much," she says. "It's beautiful."

Janine tilts her head closer to Judie's. "It was meant for you." She lovingly pats her back.

Judie takes off the cross and gold chain that has glittered brightly around her neck since the day her mother gave them to her, not long before she passed. She hands the chain to one of her newly sober girls, then gives the cross to another. "That's the circle of life."

This is typical Judie, a grateful recovering alcoholic sharing every one of God's graces.

"I'm no Mother Teresa," she often says. But I'm not so sure. Whether we have less or more, it makes no difference to her. She makes no judgment, gives only love and acceptance.

I don't know where this tall, thin, gray-haired lady gets the strength to lift up so many. It's a tough world alcoholics come from, and Judie has lived to tell the tale. After twenty-eight years of working this program, she has become a power of example for many. The definition of courage, she lives with three cats in a studio apartment that sits atop a long flight of stairs. She defies the odds on a daily basis as she struggles against emphysema and poverty. "I may not have everything I want, but God always gives me what I need," she often says.

Yet, she has more to give than any ten people I've known. It's a language of love she communicates, one day at a time, every day of her life. Sharing her experience, strength, and hope, Judie is a testimony to faith and sobriety.

Once again it's Tuesday, and Judie is seated at her table. She's wearing a gray warm-up suit with cat hairs dangling precariously in every direction; between her hands sits a Styrofoam cup, the steam rising above the rim. A newcomer ambles through the door. Naturally, it's Judie who pushes her coffee aside and makes her way across the room to extend a hand and say, "Welcome." I smile because I remember a hundred years ago, or maybe it was yesterday, that new girl was me. She has no idea what she's in for. But I do. And for today . . . she's in good hands.

Pamela Hirson

Dream in Jeopardy

Hope is like a road in the country; there wasn't ever a road, but when many people walk on it, the road comes into existence.

Lin Yutang

Hurrying to meet Mama's bus, I could hardly contain my joy—my three-year plan had worked—my dream of entering nursing school was actually going to happen! Daddy had declined attending, but Mama was coming to share my big weekend, starting at my Friday night high school graduation and staying through my entry into St. John's Hospital's School of Nursing in Tulsa at noon on Monday.

For the past three years I had worked as a waitress during summers and weekends, mostly in Lester's Café, a little "mom and pop" place, to pay for my schoolbooks, clothing, and to put money into a savings account toward the five-hundred-dollar tuition to St. John's. After the first semester, no more tuition was charged at the three-year school, because students worked their way through at the hospital.

My high school graduation went off without a hitch, and the next morning, Mama walked proudly beside me to the bank to withdraw my savings for St. John's tuition. I'll never forget walking up to that tall mahogany counter and handing the teller my passbook. When I told the middle-aged woman I wanted to withdraw my savings, she looked at my passbook and then at me, puzzled. "I'm sorry," she said, "but your money has all been withdrawn—only yesterday, in fact."

My heart stood still, and I couldn't get my breath. Finally, I gasped, "There must be some mistake."

"I'm afraid not," the teller said, her voice kind, as she showed me a paper. "Right here it shows that you and your father came in three years ago and opened the account with both of your names on it. Yesterday, he came in and withdrew the money. Here's his signature."

I looked at Daddy's signature and my heart broke. But I was too stunned to cry. I was so stunned that Mama had to lead me away from the counter to a chair. Mama and Daddy had separated six months before and each had moved away. That's why I was staying with a girlfriend to finish my last semester of high school. *But why would he withdraw the money when he knew it would end my hopes for nursing school?*

As Mama and I walked away from the bank, she patted my hand. "Honey, your Dad must have done this awful thing to get back at me. You and he have always gotten along all right. If you call him, I'm sure he'll give you the money."

But he wouldn't. I pleaded with him but his only answer was a cold, "It's mine now, and if you're so smart, you get your precious tuition elsewhere!"

There wasn't an elsewhere. No bank was going to loan money to an eighteen-year-old without any hope of payback for three years, and none of my friends had that much money. What could I do? I thought about Lester, but he always put profits back into the café.

Five hundred dollars was a lot of money in 1948. No one in the whole world that I knew had that much money to lend . . . except maybe one of our customers at Lester's who always said I was a good worker—Mr. Smith of Jay Smith Plumbing

Mr. Smith was the only person who ever tipped me in that little café. Wearing a straw hat and clean, pressed cottons, he came into Lester's early every morning for breakfast. I'd hardly had time to exchange more than pleasantries with him while waiting on the brisk breakfast trade. I hadn't worked the breakfast shift since last summer. Would he even remember me? And wouldn't Lester be upset if I asked his customer for a loan? It was a crazy, embarrassing idea!

Saturday afternoon I called Lester anyway because it was my only hope for realizing my dream. When I told him my problem I figured he had every right to shut me down. Instead, he was understanding. "Mr. Smith still eats here every morning. Matter of fact, he asked about you recently. Come in Monday before seven and you're welcome to ask him. And good luck, Jeanne. I know that's playing it close to your noon deadline."

Monday morning I rode two buses to get there, but I walked into Lester's Café at ten minutes until seven. To my amazement, I'd visited with Mr. Smith only a few minutes when—not even waiting for me to ask—Mr. Smith said, "Lester told me your problem, Jeanne, and I'm happy to help." With those words, he handed me a check—already written to my name for five hundred dollars!

I was so stunned I just kept staring at the check and thanking him while he and Lester talked. They decided Mr. Smith would drive me to his bank to cash it because I didn't have a driver's license or other valid identification.

As Mr. Smith drove, he told me why he wanted to help. He understood my predicament, because as a youngster he had run away from his very difficult family and made his own way by hard work.

"You're a hard worker, too, so I know you'll make it!" he said. As we left the bank, he smiled at me and shook my hand and wished me good luck.

Because of his help, I did have good luck—the best. Upon graduation from St. John's, I was asked to join their staff to teach Nursing Arts. The day I graduated, Mama proudly brought me a money order for the amount I owed Mr. Smith, and we took it to him. He shook my hand and thanked me. "No, Mr. Smith," I said, "thank *you* for saving my dream. You'll always be my hero."

Jeanne Hill

The Jersey Blanket

By cultivating the beautiful we scatter the seeds of heavenly flowers, as by doing good we cultivate those that belong to humanity.

Vernon Howard

"Stella, I have to go back to work." Mac's face was white and strained from being a widower with a new baby. "I don't have anyone to help me with Billy. They told me at the hospital that without breast milk he'll die. They said he might die anyway. They said they've done all they can for him; he's just too small."

Stella was still nurturing grief and guilt having just watched her friend Sarah die after childbirth. At the age of forty, Stella had given birth four months previously to Lydia, her own healthy baby girl. Now Sarah's distraught husband, Mac, stood before her, holding his four-pound infant swathed in a jersey blanket. Billy's face, no bigger than Stella's hand, peered back into her eyes. How would she care for two babies? It was 1930; she had two other girls to feed, and Stella would have to ask for additional leave from her job in the hosiery mill. Her husband, Ed, had to move north to find work in the glass cutting industry. What would he say about another mouth to feed?

The steel in Stella's spirit could never be manufactured nor sold for profit. She put her fears aside to give Mac the answer she knew in her heart was the right one. "Yes, I'll take him and do my best to bring him around."

My grandmother, Stella, didn't allow the word "defeat" into her vocabulary. She ran a boarding house while working in a hosiery mill. This by itself would have been a challenge, but she was also willing to try to give this motherless baby the same start she was giving her own child.

The babies ate on different schedules; Stella seemed to always be feeding. Billy's mouth was so small she pumped her milk into a teacup and filled a medicine dropper with the liquid to feed him. By the time she was finished, little Lydia was howling for her turn to be fed. Lydia's diapers were much too large for a premature baby. Neighbors in the community donated men's T-shirts, and Stella used her sewing skills to fashion them into tiny diapers. The older girls became proficient in cooking and cleaning to enable the boarding house to maintain the income they so desperately needed for survival. Stella's oldest child, a teenager, watched the two babies while Stella pieced feed sacks together to make her daughters' school clothes.

Stella heard Mac's voice over the hum of her sewing machine as he walked in the door for a short visit. "Stella, he's looking so much better. I'd love to take him home, but I'd only have to bring him right back to you when I go to work." Mac's voice caught in a sob as he kneeled over the dresser drawer that held his tiny son. "One day you can come home with me, Billy-boy, I promise." Tears washed Mac's face as he kissed Billy's tiny head.

"Don't worry, Mac. You'll be able to take him home once you get a little more money ahead. If you have to be away from him, it's better now than when he really knows you're his daddy," Stella comforted.

Months passed into a year and a half, and Billy and Lydia began to toddle and play together. Any delay in development that Billy might have experienced was overcome through the attention he received from four females in the house. Billy mimicked Lydia's constant chatter to develop language skills of his own. Stella loved Billy as if he were her own son, convinced that nourishing a child with praise and affection was just as important as a good meal.

Billy had just turned four when Stella received the phone call she knew eventually would come. "Stella, this is Mac, I want to bring somebody over to meet you tonight."

After agreeing to the visit, Stella went to her bedroom and sobbed. "Dear God, this begins the end of my time with Billy. Show me how to face this loss, take me through this grief."

Stella liked Mac's friend, Margie, immediately. The couple planned to be married, and Billy would have a new mother.

As Stella packed Billy's clothes, she found the now-worn jersey blanket Mac had wrapped him in that first day. Holding it close, she decided to keep it. She knew that Billy's heavenly mother, Sarah, would be proud of her for nurturing Billy as her own. "Thank you, God, and now help Billy's new mama give him all the love he needs, and I pray you'd allow me to see him now and again."

In the years to follow, Mac made sure Billy never forgot Stella. They visited her on special holidays and birthdays. Some twenty years later, Stella received a phone call. "Mama Stella, there's somebody I want you to meet. Could we visit you tonight?"

Billy's voice was deep and confident.

"Sure, son, come on over." Stella enjoyed talking to Billy and his new fiancée. They were exactly right for each other. They married, and in a few years, they began to have children of their own. When Stella learned their first baby was Billy Jr., she threaded the needle on her sewing machine with light blue thread. Gradually, the worn jersey blanket took on new life, the tattered edges neatly trimmed with blue thread.

When her task was complete, Stella called Billy on the phone. "I have a gift for the new baby. Bring your family to see me." Proudly, Stella presented Billy and his wife with the blanket.

"You put it around him Mama Stella," Billy said as he handed his firstborn to the woman who had saved his life twenty-four years earlier.

Stella swaddled this precious newborn inside the jersey blanket and held him close to her heart, remembering another little Billy so long ago. Her steel blue eyes penetrated Billy Jr.'s brand-new parents. "Wrap this little boy with love warm as a blanket, and he'll always come back to you," she said as she passed Billy Jr. back to the arms of his devoted mom and dad.

Ann Coogler

Walkin' Down Main Street

Lives based on having are less free than lives based on doing or being.

E. Y. Harburg

The first time I saw Annie, she was huddled in the doorway of an abandoned building. She looked like a statue. Wrapped in her rubber raincoat, she stood out due to the bright orange color of her coat. Piles of garbage bags surrounded her as she sat on a sleeping bag. She stared at me and with one bony finger motioned to me to come.

I'd heard about Annie from my staff. They told me she was mute, so no one tried to communicate with her. *Why was she beckoning to me?*

I held a bag of warm blueberry muffins, dripping in butter, and a hot chocolate. *Would she be interested?* I wondered and stepped across the street.

"Hi, my name is Shirley. What's yours?" I asked as I stuck my hand out in front of her. "Are you interested in a blueberry muffin and some hot chocolate?"

Noticing there was room on her sleeping bag for another person, I sat beside Annie. As soon as I was seated, she snatched the bag of muffins, pulled one out, and began to eat. I held the hot chocolate until she was ready.

Stumbling right into the conversation, I told her my purpose for being in Pioneer Square.

"Annie, I'm an outreach worker, and I walk the streets in the Square, searching for people who need help. I work for a place called Safe House, but I also want to introduce you to a good friend of mine."

She only grumbled as I talked. I reached over and patted her hand, letting her know I wasn't talking to hear my own words. She turned her head toward me and pulled her raincoat hood back on her head. Smiling through jagged teeth, she looked at me straight on.

"Good day t'ya!" she spoke.

Laughing, I exclaimed, "Oh boy, people told me you could not speak!"

She grinned and nodded her head. "I speaks to who I want!"

Each day in the following weeks, I brought Annie a muffin and a hot chocolate. We would sit and talk for a few minutes before I left her to walk up the hill to work.

One morning she asked me, "How come you always tellin' me stories about God?"

"I didn't figure I had anything to lose, y'know. By the way, Annie, I want you to keep this little cross. I carry it in my pocket all the time to remind me of Jesus. You keep it. I think it glows in the dark!"

She wrapped her thin fingers around the cross, and then looked at me, and nodded. When I looked at Annie, I saw her wrinkled skin, her unwashed hands, and thought of her as someone's child. I don't know how she happened to live on the street.

After a few minutes of talking, I stood to say good-bye. It had become a ritual now, to go through this last-minute dialogue. I'd say, "Well, Annie, it's time for me to go to work, but if you happen to not be in this place tomorrow, I'll just look up Main Street and know that Jesus came a walkin' here to get you. And he will have called your name!"

"Right y'are."

For the next few weeks, I kept up the same routine. A muffin, a hug, and a cup of hot chocolate. She told me about street life in Pioneer Square. I shared with her about God.

One morning, as I was about to leave, she grabbed my arm.

"Wait. I'll say it today." She grinned.

I wasn't sure what she meant, but I said, "Okay, Annie."

Grinning at me through her broken teeth, she said, "We share a secret, you and I, don't we?"

Annie leaned forward, and with one bony finger she pointed up the street. "One day, Jesus is gonna walk right down Main Street up there, and he gonna call me name." She pointed at herself and smiled. A beautiful smile.

"Oh, Annie, yes, he is going to do that for sure, and what's better than that, he *will* take you home!"

"Yep! That he will, that he will!"

Annie looked away, caught up in some faraway dream.

"See ya tomorrow, Annie." I waved and walked up the hill to work.

"See ya tomorrow," she repeated.

In the following days, a heavy snowstorm fell on the Seattle area. Roads were blocked, stores were closed, and not too many street people ventured outside. I took the bus downtown as usual. It was a slower ride, but the metro was still running. It took me longer to walk down the hill where Annie's building was located. People had flocked into the muffin shop for their coffee, and I had to wait even longer than expected.

I was about to pay for the muffins when the owner placed his hand on my arm. "I have something to tell you about your bag lady."

He told me an emergency ambulance picked her up last night on the street corner. She had been mugged and beaten. He added that Annie didn't survive. "I'm sorry," he said. "She died right there on the street. I was there, and I kept something of hers. Is it yours? If so, I thought you might like to have it."

He placed the little plastic cross in my hand. Stunned, I could neither cry nor comment. I said thank you and slowly walked across the street.

I stood where Annie had spent her last days, and noticed her sleeping bag stuffed into the trashcan by the street. Now, the tears fell. "Oh, Annie, I will miss you," I cried.

An old man sat on a bench close by, trying to keep warm under layers of newspapers. He saw me standing in the doorway. "Hey, c'mere," he yelled. Walking out to the edge of the street, I stopped and looked at the old man. "Did you know her?" I asked.

"Who, Annie? Yeah. She tol' me about you. Wasn't nothin' anyone could do. But, I heard her say something after the thugs left."

"What . . . what was that?"

"Strange, but she kept sayin', 'There he comes. Right down Main Street!'"

I looked up the street and I knew. She's okay now.

I pulled the sleeping bag out of the garbage can and wrapped it around the old man. He smiled as if I'd given him a special present.

"Would you . . . would you like a muffin and a cup of hot chocolate?"

He nodded and flashed a toothless grin. I gave him the sack, then walked away. Before I crossed the street, I paused and looked up the street toward the business section of downtown.

"Well, Annie, I guess Jesus came a walkin' down the street last night. Wish I could have been here to hear him call your name!"

Shirley A. Reynolds

Going Home

The greatest thing in this world is not so much where we stand as in what direction we are moving.

Johann Wolfgang von Goethe

I'd about had it. Five hundred and fifty miles traveling in a twenty-four-year-old truck carrying cats, goats, and a dog pulling a trailer full of geese, sheep, and ducks. No power steering, no assisted brakes, and a top speed of fifty-two miles an hour, but that was only on good roads. I figured my average was about twenty-eight. To top it all, I was lost. I wanted to cry, needed to actually, but didn't want the tears to sap my last drops of energy.

The previous two years had been hell. I had sold my home with the intention of buying a small holding to house myself and animals. Like many others, I had a dream of the simple life, a haven away from the stresses and tensions of the modern world.

But the minute I sold my place, the housing market took off, and I landed slap-bang in the middle of the biggest housing boom the Western world had every seen. I ended up shifting from a variety of lousy rental accommodations to even lousier ones. I had packed up my belongings and animals and uprooted us all so many times that the prospect of relaxation, peace of mind, and security became a dim and distant memory.

After being a victim of greedy, manipulating landlords and watching "friends" disappear in an ever-increasing stream, I felt like the loneliest woman on the planet. My belief in fairness, democracy, and true friendship evaporated drop by drop with each passing day.

After spending nearly every waking moment scouring the Internet and agencies for a suitable property I could afford, I finally found one. After five months of legal wrangling, the house was actually mine. After two years of feeling like a dejected refugee in my own lands, I had finally secured a place. A place I may eventually call "home."

Once again I loaded up my belongings—the ones that hadn't been lost, damaged, disposed of, or stolen, in my frequent moves—and thirty-six animals of varying species and finally set off. There was no excitement, no air of anticipation, just tension, tiredness, and concern. I worried about how the animals would withstand the journey, how to unload all the stuff when I got there, if I got there— would the old truck stand up to the long haul? I worried about feeding the animals and bedding them down once we arrived: Would the pen doors be secure enough? Would foxes be in the area just waiting for an opportunity to attack? I glanced at myself in the rearview mirror. My features were stern and focused. I couldn't afford either mistakes or bad luck. If something went wrong, I was on my own.

The stick shift on the old truck was heavy and stiff. If I needed to brake, I had to practically stand on the pedal, my backside leaving the seat and my head nearly touching the roof. It plodded ponderously up the small, narrow, roads of the beautiful countryside. But ahead, even in the darkness, I could see the imposing mountains rising into the clear night sky. I stopped using my rearview mirror; all I could see were hundreds of headlights following me staunchly through the evening gloom. I lost count of the number of times I stopped at service stations to check the animals and take a nap. Then night started to turn into day and the rain came. Gray and metallic in the early October sky, it seemed to somehow complement my mood and appearance. I was filthy. My eyes avoided the reflection in the restroom mirrors and the inquiring stares of fellow travelers. I cursed the bright lighting and spotless, reflective interiors.

But finally, I was nearly home. An hour, one wonderful hour, and we would be there. I turned the page on my directions and my heart skipped a beat as I realized it had been ruined from some earlier spillage. I was lost on the steep hills on a busy Saturday afternoon.

People beeped their horns and shouted as the old truck and trailer struggled and plodded up the hills while I strained to see signs I might recognize. Eventually, I just went north; the one thing I knew was to go north. Finding a turnout on the other side of town, I reached for my cell phone. The battery was running low. I phoned the woman who had originally found the house for me; it was the first time we had ever actually spoken. "No, I don't know where I am, but I have a beautiful view of the sea," I told her. "Yes, I will take the next left and call back—provided my battery holds out."

I was panicking. It was turning dark and stormy, and the animals had been confined for a long time now and needed their freedom. The main road turned into a single-track country lane. The hills were steep, the truck lumbered on, rarely getting out of second gear. My arms screamed from fighting with the heavy steering. I had to reverse, many times, on narrow lanes and tracks. My phone battery beeped ever more urgently. It was another three hours before I finally found my way. Even as I drove the last half mile to what I knew would be our final destination, I felt only partial relief.

The big job was yet to come: unloading the animals, finding water buckets, feed, and securing their accommodations. My mind was overloaded with the coming practicalities of it, and the prospect seemed overwhelming. I turned in at a muddy track signposted with the name of our new home. The rain lashed the windshield, and the wind buffeted the big truck side to side.

Then I saw them. People. People I had never met before. People I had only known through the written word on the Internet. Strangers who had come to help. They had no vested interest, no reason to come; we had no past relationship, but they had come. The relief was unbelievable. Men jumped up on the roof rack and began unstrapping my worldly goods, deftly unloading tables, chairs, and chests. They had tools to mend doors and repair latches. They brought hay, straw, fuel for the fire, kindling to light it. Food for me—food for the animals.

Women made drinks and unpacked linens and clothing. They made the bed, started a roaring fire. Nothing, it seemed, had been forgotten.

The men unhitched the trailer and shifted it across the muddy ground with ease. The winds blew fiercely and the rain pelted down, making conversation difficult, but even in the dark they continued to mend fences and usher animals into their respective sanctuaries.

Still, I couldn't smile. A filthy, thin, bedraggled, middle-aged woman, who for two years had felt discarded by society, preyed on by vultures in human clothing, and betrayed by friends, couldn't truly comprehend this humanity from strangers. Their physical efforts, understanding, and compassion was too much for me to bear.

I felt like an alien watching the world from a distant planet. My emotions couldn't assimilate the contradiction between the people I had encountered for the past two years and these true humanitarians. It was as if they were a different species.

They cared, and what was more, they had shown they cared.

It was days before I could speak the words to thank them, but even those were a poor reflection of my gratitude, not only for their help, but also for reigniting my faith in the human spirit.

Betty Heelis

A True Work of Art

When love and skill work together, expect a masterpiece.

John Ruskin

All twelve of us huddled around a wooden post. I bent over the hole underneath the post, stirring cement mix and water, a piece of lumber for mixing in my hands, and the rocky New England dirt beneath my sneakers. I was in my third summer of work camp. Each summer my church's youth group traveled to a different city to help with various projects. The summer of 2003 we were in Ithaca, New York. Everyone in my crew (ten eager teenagers and two adult supervisors) was from a different state. I was the only non-New Englander. Even though I made a point to say that my hometown was in Northern Virginia, to them, I was the "Southern Belle."

My work crew was assigned to build an eight-by-twelve deck behind a tiny trailer for an older woman, Betty, who struggled to maneuver around her property. The long, jagged scars across her knees proved to me that just standing up caused her excruciating pain. When Betty introduced herself to us, her warm smile radiated gratitude.

We were twelve amateur carpenters at best, and the blueprints for our deck were simple, but the beauty of the deck was not in its structure, but in the emotion behind it. Blood and sweat went into the carpentry, and in my eyes, this work of art was just as fine as any of the Wonders of the World. My work crew began its construction as strangers, and we hammered the last nails as close friends.

During the week, I made an effort to befriend people I never would have met under normal circumstances. We prayed hand-in-hand with one another and with Betty. A robust and outspoken seventeen-year-old boy would squeeze my right hand, as a meager and timid fourteen-year-old girl held on to my right.

Complaints never slipped, even on our last workday when humid rain bathed our nearly completed deck. The boys with more tool experience always offered encouraging words to the girls who were operating power tools for the first time. I couldn't help but smile whenever I watched one sweet and poised girl, Amanda, rev up a powerful circular saw. Behind her work goggles, her eyes exuded newfound confidence.

When we finished building our eight-by-twelve masterpiece, all twelve of us stepped back to admire our work. One girl, Alicia, squealed with delight, while the youngest boy, Bernie, sighed with relief. Rachel looked down at her thigh, an open wound still evident from falling against a screw, and laughed good-naturedly at the memory.

I climbed onto the deck and jumped on it, testing its strength. When Betty saw our masterpiece, she wiped a tear from her eye. Twelve had come to her home every day for the past week with the express purpose of serving her.

I left Betty's home on our last day with high hopes for our deck's durability. I knew my memories of that week would also be everlasting. All the building materials were necessary for the creation of the structure, but the love and the willingness that went into it were even more crucial. The deck was a symbol of twelve strangers looking past geographical, economic, and superficial status to befriend one another and a disadvantaged woman.

Without a doubt, that week I gained a lot of carpentry knowledge. I learned the correct place to grip a hammer and to make sure a wooden post was level in the ground before securing it with cement. But most important, I learned that something doesn't have to be displayed in a museum for it to be a work of art.

Ashley Claire Simpson

Martha's Crayons

*Don't judge each day by the harvest you reap,
but by the seeds you plant.*

Robert Louis Stevenson

The phone call was expected, but it still left me feeling helpless and deeply sad. Martha's long battle against cancer was almost over—cancer was winning.

Friends for many years, Martha and I were sorority sisters in college, and then fellow teachers at a local junior high. As a novice teacher, I envied her boundless energy and amazing ability to successfully teach art to teenagers. I struggled to motivate them with music; she inspired winners. Later, she displayed her impressive watercolors in many shows where my husband exhibited.

Martha's family requested no visitors at the hospital. She simply didn't have the energy. I suspect they also knew that the ICU would be overwhelmed with the countless former students and friends coming to offer encouragement.

In lieu of visiting, I sent cards. Not fancy ones, just daily handwritten notes about anything but get well soon. I told her funny stories, described the weather, and gossiped about her fellow artists. Martha loved to enter juried shows, so I told her about art competitions, hoping against hope that she might get well enough to compete.

Late one afternoon, suffering writer's block about the next card, I sipped a cup of coffee and stared at the discarded wads of paper littering the kitchen table—my frustrated start and stop attempts at writing. Without warning, the kitchen door opened, and in waltzed Kate, a five-year-old neighbor girl who frequently dropped in to visit, because, as she put it, "I didn't have no fwiends."

"Whatcha' doing?" she asked, standing next to my chair, one foot propped on top of the other.

"I'm writing a card to a sick friend."

Her gaze roamed about the kitchen but stopped when she spied a large painting of Martha's leaning against the wall. She moved to it and bent down closer. Awarded first place in a recent show, the blue ribbon hung from the frame.

"I can draw," she said casually. Hands on her knees, she peered outside at "The Sentinel," a massive oak standing guard over my home. As if on alert, its huge leafless limb cast a protective shadow across the house.

Stooped, she looked at the painting a long time. Finally, she looked back at me over her shoulder. Her head cocked, her innocent blue eyes intense. "Who did this?" She emphasized each word.

"A friend. The same one I'm writing the card to."

"Oh, my. What kind of crayons does she use? I need to get some of them."

Eyes wide in sheer surprise, I laughed out loud. Kate had given me the thought for the next card. I grabbed her for a big hug. She looked bewildered when I plopped a kiss on top of her curly hair. "I don't know, Kate. I'll have to ask her."

Martha died a few days later. Her husband, Tim, pulled me aside at the funeral to thank me for the notes. "She loved the one about the crayons," he said. "It was the last time I heard her laugh."

Tears welled up as I squeezed his hand. "I hoped she would. I did," was my quiet reply. Turning to leave, I offered a silent prayer for the amazing innocence of a child. For Tim, time would remove the footprints of the day with all its care and sorrow. I was thankful that he would have the memory of the last laugh.

Barbara Ragsdale

From the Ashes

I am not a phoenix yet, but here among the ashes, it may be that the pain is chiefly that of new wings trying to push through.

May Sarton

"Mom! There's a fire in the basement!" my son, Jared, screamed as he pounded up the stairs. "I called 911! Get everyone out of the house. Now!"

Fire! Adrenaline pumped through my system as I hurried to get my elderly father, who lived in the upstairs apartment. "Paul, Ricky, do you hear me? Get out now." The boys flew out of their rooms just as I was coming out of the apartment with Dad. "Hurry! Everyone stay together." Smoke was already filling the house as we made our way out the front door.

I trembled in the chilly night air and stared in disbelief as flames licked at the windows of our home. Huddled in a soundless circle, I sent up a silent prayer of thanks that we'd all made it out safely. Suddenly, Jared broke away.

"I'm going to try and put it out Mom," he yelled, moving toward the house.

I grabbed him. "No, Jared, it's not safe."

"Mom, don't worry, I'm not going in." He shot forward and kicked in the basement window, sending shards of glass flying. Inky black smoke poured out as he raced for the garden hose. But as he turned on the faucet, the hose burst from the intense heat. Nothing but a thin stream of smoky vapor hissed out. Jared's shoulders slumped as he realized there was nothing more he could do.

Helplessly, I watched as flames crackled, consuming the home I loved. Back when we first moved in I'd wept over the loss of my husband, Richie. The words of the doctor played over and over in my head. "Mrs. Hoberg, we're terribly sorry, but your husband suffered a heart attack. He's . . . he's gone." Shocked and heartbroken, I returned home alone and struggled to raise our sons as best I could on my own.

Putting on a brave face, I would tuck the boys into bed with a story and a kiss goodnight. Afterward, I would sit at the dining room table, panicking over the growing stack of bills. *How would we manage?* It took a lot of hard work, but the boys and I slowly built a new life in this house. Dad even came to live with us. Happy times, like birthday parties in the backyard and popcorn and movie nights, replaced the sadness.

Swallowing hard, I blinked back tears. *I've already lost my husband; please don't take my house, too.* Would the firemen ever get here? We had a lifetime of memories inside, boxes of pictures that could never be replaced, Grandma's hand-crocheted doilies and my treasured Christmas decorations. The dated ornaments from the year each boy was born were so special to me. The furniture and other things could be replaced, but those things couldn't. Would any of it survive?

Screaming sirens cut into my thoughts as the fire trucks pulled to an abrupt stop at the curb. *Don't let them be too late.*

The hoses were reeled out and mighty arcs of water drenched the house.

Jared draped a blanket over my shoulders, tears coursing down his face. "Mom, I'm so sorry. It's my fault. I was cleaning my car collection for the show next week . . . the cleaner . . . I don't know how it happened. There were flames. I used the fire extinguisher right away. I thought it was out. But then the smoke started again." He wept as his shoulders shook.

"Come here, son," I gathered him in my arms as if he were a boy again, not the young man he was.

"It was an accident." I lifted his chin and looked straight into his eyes. "Do you hear me? It's okay, the important thing is that we all got out."

The chief approached me as the firefighters began winding up their hoses. I felt weak in the knees; not at all ready to hear what he had to say.

"We have the fire out, but I'm afraid the news isn't good. There's a great deal of structural damage and no floor just inside the front door." He handed me a slip of paper.

"We're putting you up at a hotel tonight. I've called ahead, so they'll have your rooms ready by the time you get there."

I hadn't even thought of where we would stay! "Thank you," I stammered as I tucked the paper into my pocket.

The days that followed were chaotic. I spent hours on the phone with my insurance company. Claims adjustors took photographs, and the contractor stopped by to assess the damage. The whole interior was blackened, and as I followed behind him, the acrid smell made my eyes and nostrils sting. Everything inside was destroyed and would need to be rebuilt. Tears clogged my throat as I reached down and touched the charred remains of our photo albums, it was clear that all of our keepsakes were lost forever.

Until the renovation was completed, we lived in a temporary trailer that was set up on the front lawn. Fitting me, the boys, and Dad into such a small space made for really cramped quarters. Going back to work was almost a relief, and besides, we needed the money. Even working two jobs, I could barely meet our bills. I had to stock our empty trailer. We needed everything, but for now, clothing and groceries would have to do. After a final stop at the pharmacy to pick up Dad's prescription, I returned to the trailer to set up our new "home."

I plodded into the tiny kitchen and plunked the groceries on the counter. *Everything always lands on my shoulders.* That's when I saw it. A covered dish with a pink sticky note perched on top. "My famous lasagna. Enjoy! If there's anything else you need, don't hesitate to call. Love, Mary."

I lifted the lid and inhaled the delicious, spicy aroma. She had also included two loaves of garlic bread and a salad, too. I popped a ripe cherry tomato into my mouth and smiled for the first time in days. I wouldn't have to cook tonight.

Then I spied the stack of fluffy new towels my neighbor had dropped off last night. And what about the overnight bag my friend Mary Joan from down the street had put together for us the night of the fire? We didn't even have to ask. I'd been overwhelmed at her thoughtfulness. In fact, that same night our lawn had been dotted with friends and neighbors. They'd wrapped jackets around us to keep us warm and handed us cups of hot coffee from a thermos. One couple took Dad to their place for a cup of tea and to rest up.

Long after that night, I felt supported and loved. Greeting cards filled the mailbox. One in particular made me smile. Sprigs of flowers and a little bluebird graced the front and inside a simple handwritten note, "Thinking of

you, don't forget we're here for you. Love, Charlene."
Some folks dropped by just to give me a hug.

See, Linda, you really aren't alone, whispered a still, small voice.

All along, caring friends and neighbors had surrounded me; I just hadn't realized it until now. I *wasn't* alone after all. Deep gratitude filled every corner of my heart. Right then and there I stopped thinking about what I'd lost and started counting all that I still had. Sure, we'd suffered a major setback, but we still had our lives, one another, and friends who cared enough to see us through.

The boys and I, along with my dad, would face the future together. And I was certain God would help us to build a beautiful new life from the ashes of the old.

Linda Hoberg
as told to Susan A. Karas

The Colton Camaro

Three grand essentials to happiness in this life are something to do, something to love, and something to hope for.

Jose Addison

Killeen is the gateway to the Hill Country of Texas. It's also Army country, home of Fort Hood. In Killeen, people wear their patriotism and pride with honor. It's a town where folks go beyond the call of duty, whether it's serving their country, their community, or keeping their promises. Sadly, Shane Colton never had a chance to keep one of the promises he made to his eleven-year-old son, Lance.

Shane was only thirty-two when his Apache helicopter was shot down on Easter Sunday, April 11, 2004, while providing cover for a fuel convoy heading to Fallujah, Iraq. Before Shane's deployment with the 1st Calvary Division, 227th Aviation Regiment, he and Lance were in the process of dismantling a 1968 Camaro they had planned to rebuild. The car was in pretty bad shape and Shane wanted to do a ground-up restoration, which meant hours of work. Since Shane loved cars and Lance loved doing anything with his dad, it was a perfect project for this father-and-son team. Then the duty call came, and they stored the Camaro under a tarp in the hot Central Texas sun, awaiting Shane's return.

On September 1, 2004, Shane's service and sacrifice was profiled on a "Fallen Heroes" segment of the *Evening News with Dan Rather* that I happened to be watching with my wife. We own a company that supplies rubber details and weatherstripping to gearheads restoring cars. We specialize in Camaros, so when I heard, "Camaro," it caught my attention. Not only was I greatly moved by the loss of this brave and honorable man in service to our country, I was equally moved by his young son's desire to honor his father by finishing that car. It's an Army tradition . . . finishing the job.

While my wife, Donna, went to work finding Lance and his mother, Inge, I got in touch with people in the car community to see if we could put our heads and hearts together to help this young man. And help they did.

With Inge's blessing and our promise to involve Lance in the restoration process, we took the car to Central Texas College in Killeen where the rebuild process began. ARMO, the Automotive Restoration and Marketing Organization, exercised its marketing muscle, and word of the Colton Camaro project quickly spread throughout the car world. People all over the country—from guys who just loved cars, to businesses in the automotive aftermarket industry—were donating money and parts. Websites and bulletin boards devoted space to the project. People offered advice from their own restoration experiences, while others wanted to know what the plans were: would Lance keep it stock, or modify it?

Shane and Lance had put together a detailed notebook on ideas for the car, and that guided the effort. However, everything did not go smoothly. Soon, nearly all of the students who were working on the restoration were themselves deployed to Iraq, and work stopped. The Colton Camaro sat.

Once again, the car community rose to the challenge. Jim Barber of Classic Automotive Restoration Specialists contacted Forsythe Technical Community College in Winston-Salem, North Carolina, to ask if the automotive shop students would be willing to pick up where Central Texas left off. They quickly agreed.

It was barely six weeks until the keys to the fully restored Camaro were to be presented to Lance at the November 2005 Specialty Equipment Market Association (SEMA) show in Las Vegas. The car shell arrived at Forsythe, eighteen hundred miles from Killeen, on Monday, September 19. FedEx delivered the rest of the car parts—in pieces—soon after. More than sixty volunteer students and faculty challenged themselves by working nights and weekends to complete the project. Miraculously, at the end of October 2005, the fully restored Camaro was on its way to Las Vegas.

During the SEMA show, the canary yellow Camaro with black rally stripes turned heads. "This is exactly how Dad wanted it, but he would have done it in way more time with me," Lance told the reporter covering the show. "It's amazing that so many people could be so selfless; like, you see all this evil and greed in the world, then this bunch of people got together for this one project."

When I handed Lance the keys and he sat in the driver's seat, surely Shane was in heaven beaming. No one who was there will ever forget it. This was a restoration made possible by many compassionate and generous people, with some divine intervention from one very proud dad.

Lance is now a motivated teenager and one of only seventeen, out of thousands of students in his school district, selected for the International Baccalaureate program. He also made the National Junior Honor Society. After the completion of the Camaro restoration project, we moved the remaining money to a new fund set up for Lance's college expenses. The fund continues to grow and is now in excess of $10,000.

My parents taught me at an early age that life is short, and if you can make a difference in some way, do it. I have a feeling Shane lived by the same philosophy. I'm just glad we were in the right place at the right time to help a family who had given the ultimate to us all.

Lance is looking forward to getting his learner's permit next year, another test I'm sure he'll ace. But he'll have to wait a little while to be presented the keys to the Camaro again, this time by Inge, who plans on turning them over when Lance heads off for college—his goal is to attend MIT.

Gary Anderson
as told to Theresa Peluso

The Long Way Home

The ultimate measure of a man is not where he stands in moments of comfort and convenience, but where he stands at times of challenge and controversy.

Dr. Martin Luther King Jr.

Walking through the World Trade Center at 8:30 AM on Tuesday, September 11, 2001, I debated stopping at the bank. After all, I had plenty of time to catch a PATH train to my office just on the other side of the Hudson River.

But for some reason, I decided to skip the bank and instead descended the long escalator in the middle of the Trade Center to catch my train. Before proceeding through the turnstile, I stopped to buy another PATH ticket. After all, I had plenty of time.

The train came quickly and brought me and my fellow commuters to our station just on the other side of the river. I rode the elevator up to my office and looked out the picture windows that framed the beautiful Manhattan skyline. It was 8:45 AM.

In disbelief, I watched as the first plane crashed into the North Tower of the World Trade Center at 8:46 AM. In horror, I watched as the second plane hit.

We evacuated our building.

"Leave the area and go home!" The police officer wielding a bullhorn repeated this directive to the crowds spilling out of the office buildings on the New Jersey side of the Hudson River. "Get away from this area." The war planes flying overhead gave added urgency to his message as we were herded away from the Hudson.

I desperately wanted nothing more than to follow the policeman's order and get home safely to my family in Westchester, New York, but all access routes from New Jersey to New York were immediately shut down. Stopping a few blocks away, stunned groups of people comforted one another. Trying to process what was happening all around us, we stared at the New York skyline in disbelief. Disbelief turned to devastation as we witnessed both the sacred and mundane evidence of human life jettisoned from the exploding twin towers.

We frantically tried to reach loved ones. Periodically turning on my cell phone to try to raise a signal, I feared losing the little battery power I had left. I tried to convince myself that it was a good thing I couldn't reach my older son, who was away at college, since I wouldn't want to worry him. As I would learn when he was finally able to reach me, the whole world was watching.

The neighborhood was enveloped in a "loud silence." Because cars were no longer able to enter our immediate area, the normal background noise of daily life was gone, replaced by the wail of emergency vehicle sirens and the roar of military planes overhead. Evacuees from New York, covered in ash and missing shoes, began streaming off the ferries. If only we could wake up and discover that we were just extras in a very bad "B" movie—but no director yelled, "Cut!" We were trapped in a horrific reality no civilized human being could imagine.

A throng hungry for information gathered around a parked car and turned the radio volume up as loud as it would go. The latest update on the attack was broadcast to a stunned crowd. The Pentagon had been hit.

Still absorbing this shock, we watched the World Trade Center as the South Tower collapsed in a massive cloud of dust before our eyes. Shortly thereafter, the North Tower would suffer the same fate.

Desperate to get home, but with no idea how to do it, my coworkers and I began to head north. Making our way to Hoboken, a main transportation hub, we were hopeful that some access route to New York would open up. But the news was not encouraging. In the controlled chaos at Hoboken, everyone wanted to help, but options were limited. The tunnels were closed, the PATH trains were shut down, and no rental cars were available. We waited . . . and waited . . . and waited. I asked an overwhelmed transit worker if any buses were heading to Leonia, a New Jersey town in which my sister lived. Shaking his head, he suggested, "Why don't you take that bus over there—it's heading for Teaneck."

Although I had no idea where Teaneck was, I needed to keep moving. I bid farewell to my coworkers and joined the orderly line waiting to get onto the bus. No fares were collected—many of us hadn't been able to gather our personal belongings before evacuating. Once the last passenger was aboard, the somber group headed out onto the highway.

My seatmate was a young woman who was talking in hushed tones with her fiancé. I still had my cell phone, but the battery was dangerously low from all the futile attempts to speak with my husband and younger son. Finally able to get an outgoing signal, I was disappointed I couldn't get through the switchboard at my husband and son's school. I tried my home number. My seatmate must have overheard the tearful message I left on the answering machine and the promise that I would try everything possible to get home to them.

I asked this stranger if she had heard if the Tappan Zee Bridge to New York was open. She called her fiancé, who told her that he didn't think it was, but he would keep checking. She asked if I wanted to hitch a ride with them. "My fiancé is meeting the bus in Teaneck—you can ride with us." Thankful they were going my way, and grateful for their generosity, I eagerly accepted.

Upon reaching Teaneck, we still didn't know if the bridge was open, but we hopped into the car and took off. Unfortunately, many of the roadways to get to the bridge were now closed. Undaunted, my new acquaintances took a series of detours. It was dark, but we finally arrived at the Tappan Zee Bridge. Happy to join the congested caravan of cars, we slowly made our way across the Hudson River, back to New York. I asked this wonderful couple to leave me on the other side of the bridge so they could continue on their way; but they insisted on taking me all the way to my home, another thirty minutes south of the bridge.

Pulling onto my street, I gave my new friends my heart-felt thanks for bringing me "Home Sweet Home." Although eager to get inside, I questioned them to be sure they knew how to get back to the highway so they could continue on their journey to their own home.

They smiled and assured me that, yes, they knew how to get there. They would retrace their route and head back toward the Tappan Zee Bridge. But instead of heading to upstate New York, as I had assumed, they would be joining the long line of cars heading back over the bridge. Why on earth would they do that? Because my heaven-sent angels lived in a house only a few short blocks from where the bus dropped us off many hours ago—*in Teaneck, New Jersey.*

Pamela Hackett Hobson

More Chicken Soup?

We would love to hear your reactions to the stories in this book. Please let us know what your favorite stories were and how they affected you.

Many of the stories and poems you have read in this book were submitted by readers like you who had read earlier Chicken Soup for the Soul books. We publish at least five or six Chicken Soup for the Soul books every year. We invite you to contribute a story to one of these future volumes.

Stories may be up to 1,200 words and must uplift or inspire. You may submit an original piece, something you have read, or your favorite quotation on your refrigerator door.

To obtain a copy of our submission guidelines and a listing of upcoming Chicken Soup books, please write, fax, or check our websites. Please send your submissions to:

Chicken Soup for the Soul
P.O. Box 30880
Santa Barbara, CA 93130
Fax: 805-563-2945
Website: www.chickensoup.com

Just send a copy of your stories and other pieces to the above address. We will be sure that both you and the author are credited for your submission.

For information about speaking engagements, other books, audiotapes, workshops, and training programs, please contact any of our authors directly.

Supporting Others

The publisher and authors of *Chicken Soup for the Soul, Celebrating People Making a Difference* are pleased to donate five cents for every book sold, up to $1 million, to the Modest Needs Foundation.

Founded in 2002, ModestNeeds.org is an award-winning 501(c)3 nonprofit organization that works to stop the cycle of poverty before it starts for low-income workers struggling to afford emergency expenses, like those we've all encountered before: the unexpected auto repair, the unanticipated trip to the doctor, the unusually large winter heating bill.

ModestNeeds.org believes every person has the power to make a difference. So, by choice, the work done by ModestNeeds.org is funded exclusively by the "small change" donations of people just like you.

Since 2002, Modest Needs' "small change" donors have stopped the cycle of poverty for thousands of individuals and families who stood to lose everything over a short-term financial emergency.

We hope you'll enjoy *Chicken Soup for the Soul, Celebrating People Making a Difference* and help ModestNeeds.org reach even more of the hardworking people who need our help the most. Because Modest Needs has earned the highest possible charity rating from the Better Business Bureau's Wise Giving Alliance, you can give with confidence, knowing that they won't abuse your kindness.

But more importantly, simply by working together in this very modest way, we can make sure that no hardworking person is ever forced to choose between taking a child to the doctor or putting food on the table.

ModestNeeds.org
Dr. Keith Taylor, President and Founder
Modest Needs Foundation
115 East 30th Street, Fl 1
New York, NY 10016
Website: www.ModestNeeds.org
E-mail: questions@modestneeds.org

Who Is Jack Canfield?

Jack Canfield is the cocreator and editor of the Chicken Soup for the Soul series, which *Time* magazine has called "the publishing phenomenon of the decade." The series now has 105 titles with over 100 million copies in print in forty-one languages. Jack is also the coauthor of eight other bestselling books, including *The Success Principles: How to Get from Where You Are to Where You Want to Be, Dare to Win, The Aladdin Factor, You've Got to Read This Book,* and *The Power of Focus: How to Hit Your Business, Personal and Financial Targets with Absolute Certainty.*

Jack has recently developed a telephone coaching program and an online coaching program based on his most recent book, *The Success Principles.* He also offers a seven-day Breakthrough to Success seminar every summer, which attracts 400 people from fifteen countries around the world.

Jack is the CEO of Chicken Soup for the Soul Enterprises and the Canfield Training Group in Santa Barbara, California, and founder of the Foundation for Self-Esteem in Culver City, California. He has conducted intensive personal and professional development seminars on the principles of success for over 900,000 people in twenty-one countries around the world. He has spoken to hundreds of thousands of others at numerous conferences and conventions and has been seen by millions of viewers on national television shows such as *Today, Fox and Friends, Inside Edition, Hard Copy,* CNN's *Talk Back Live, 20/20, Eye to Eye, NBC Nightly News,* and *CBS Evening News.* Jack was also a featured teacher on the hit movie, *The Secret.*

Jack is the recipient of many awards and honors, including three honorary doctorates and a Guinness World Records Certificate for having seven Chicken Soup for the Soul books appearing on the *New York Times* bestseller list on May 24, 1998.

To write to Jack, or for inquiries about Jack as a speaker, his coaching programs, or his seminars, use the following contact information:

The Canfield Companies
P.O. Box 30880 • Santa Barbara, CA 93130
Phone: 805-563-2935 • Fax: 805-563-2945
E-mail: info@jackcanfield.com • Website: www.jackcanfield.com

Who Is Mark Victor Hansen?

In the area of human potential, no one is more respected than Mark Victor Hansen. For more than thirty years, Mark has focused solely on helping people from all walks of life reshape their personal vision of what's possible. His powerful messages of possibility, opportunity, and action have created powerful change in thousands of organizations and millions of individuals worldwide.

He is a sought-after keynote speaker, bestselling author, and marketing maven. Mark's credentials include a lifetime of entrepreneurial success and an extensive academic background. He is a prolific writer with many bestselling books, such as *The One Minute Millionaire, The Power of Focus, The Aladdin Factor,* and *Dare to Win,* in addition to the Chicken Soup for the Soul series. Mark has made a profound influence through his library of audios, videos, and articles in the areas of big thinking, sales achievement, wealth building, publishing success, and personal and professional development.

Mark is the founder of the MEGA Seminar Series. MEGA Book Marketing University and Building Your MEGA Speaking Empire are annual conferences where Mark coaches and teaches new and aspiring authors, speakers, and experts on building lucrative publishing and speaking careers. Other MEGA events include MEGA Marketing Magic and My MEGA Life. He has appeared on television (*Oprah,* CNN and *Today*), in print (*Time, U.S. News & World Report, USA Today, New York Times,* and *Entrepreneur*), and on countless radio interviews, assuring our planet's people that "you can easily create the life you deserve."

As a philanthropist and humanitarian, Mark works tirelessly for organizations such as Habitat for Humanity, American Red Cross, March of Dimes, Childhelp USA, and many others. He is the recipient of numerous awards that honor his entrepreneurial spirit, philanthropic heart, and business acumen. He is a lifetime member of the Horatio Alger Association of Distinguished Americans, an organization that honored Mark with the prestigious Horatio Alger Award for his extraordinary life achievements. Mark Victor Hansen is an enthusiastic crusader of what's possible and is driven to make the world a better place.

Mark Victor Hansen & Associates, Inc.
P.O. Box 7665 • Newport Beach, CA 92658
Phone: 949-764-2640 • Fax: 949-722-6912
Website: www.markvictorhansen.com

Who Is Peter Vegso?

Peter cofounded Health Commumnciations, Inc. (HCI Books) in 1978 after immigrating from Canada to South Florida.

Twice recognized by *Publishers Weekly* as the #1 Self-Help Publisher, Health Communications' first *New York Times* bestseller, *Adult Children of Alcoholics* by Dr. Janet Woititz, appeared on the list in 1985 and remained there for fifty-one weeks.

Since then, HCI Books has been the home of dozens more national, *USA Today*, and *New York Times* bestsellers in the areas of mental health, recovery, spirituality, and self-help, including *A Child Called It* and *The Lost Boy* by Dave Pelzer.

With the debut of the first book in the phenomenal Chicken Soup for the Soul series in 1993, HCI Books began an expansion of their publishing interests to include the inspirational genre.

HCI Books continues to "publish people, not books." Peter's personal goal became the company's mission statement, to "make a difference in the lives of our readers and the people they come in contact with."

Diversification within Peter's businesses includes magazine publishing and a conference management division, which is an approved source for Continuing Education credits for professionals working in the mental health and social work community.

Peter enjoys spending (rare) spare time at his successful Thoroughbred breeding and training facility in Ocala, Florida, with his wife, Anne, and his two daughters, Melinda and Hayley. One of the few goals he has not yet realized, but certainly will, given his track record of success in anything he tackles, is to win the Kentucky Derby and the Triple Crown.

Peter Vegso
Health Communications, Inc.
3201 S.W. 15th Street • Deerfield Beach, FL 33442
Phone: 954-360-0909• Fax: 954-360-0034
Website: www.hcibooks.com

Who Is Theresa Peluso?

Theresa has always felt drawn to a page and the power of words. Books represent knowledge, expression, freedom, adventure, creativity, and escape—so it's no surprise that her career has revolved around books.

Theresa's career began over thirty years ago in a large publisher's book-club operation. In 1981, she joined Health Communications, Inc. (HCI Books), then a fledgling publisher, that grew to become the country's #1 Self-Help Publisher and home to groundbreaking *New York Times* bestsellers and the series recognized as a publishing phenomenon, Chicken Soup for the Soul.

After more than twenty years spent in the day-to-day operations of a thriving publishing company, Theresa began developing books as a writer, compiler, and editor.

She is the coauthor of *Chicken Soup for the Horse Lover's Soul*, *Chicken Soup for the Horse Lover's Soul II*, *Chicken Soup for the Recovering Soul*, *Chicken Soup for the Recovering Soul Daily Inspirations*, *Chicken Soup for the Shopper's Soul*, *Chicken Soup for the Dieter's Soul*, *Chicken Soup for the Coffee Lover's Soul*, and *Chicken Soup for the Wine Lover's Soul*.

She enjoys life in South Florida with her husband, Brian, and looks forward to the many adventures ahead.

Theresa Peluso
Health Communications, Inc.
3201 S.W. 15th Street • Deerfield Beach, FL 33442
Phone: 954-418-0844 • Fax: 954-418-0844
Website: www.hcibooks.com
E-mail: teri@soulofthepeople.com

CONTRIBUTORS

The stories in this book are original pieces or taken from previously published sources, such as books, magazines, and newspapers. If you would like to contact any of the contributors for information about their writing or would like to invite them to speak in your community, look for their contact information included in their biography.

Diana M. Amadeo is an award-winning author. She lives in New England with her husband and three grown children close to her heart. Diana has in excess of 450 publications as books, magazine articles, and essays. Yet she humbly, painstakingly tweaks her thousand or so rejections with the eternal hope that they may, too, see the light of day.

Gary Anderson has owned collector and race cars since his teens. He turned his hobby into a successful business as an automotive rubber supplier, which has expanded into making rubber products for a wide range of industries. Semiretired, Gary still enjoys his cars and spending time with his wife, Donna, and their kids, grandkids, and many friends around the country. To donate to Lance Colton's college fund, e-mail soffseal @soffseal.com, or visit www.soffseal.com for contact information.

Elizabeth Atwater lives in Pfafftown, a lovely, quiet little village in North Carolina. While all her spare time is devoted to writing, her heart is devoted to her soul mate, best friend, and wonderful husband, Joe.

Nancy Baker resides in College Station, Texas, with her husband and golden retriever. She enjoys traveling, reading, and walking. After retirement she pursued her lifelong love of writing and has been published in anthologies, national magazines, and devotionals. She is a hospital and a hospice volunteer.

Nancy Bennett has had her work published in various places including *Chicken Soup for the Soul in Menopause*, the *Christian Science Monitor*, and *Reunions Magazine*, as well as many mainstream publications. Her pet projects include reading and writing about history and creating ethnic dinners to test on her family. She lives near a protected salmon stream where the deer and the bears often play.

Judy A. Bernstein is coauthor of the Christopher Award–winning memoir *They Poured Fire on Us from the Sky: The True Story of Three Lost Boys of Sudan.* She continues her work with the International Rescue Committee in San

Diego, California, while speaking to schools and organizations and working on her next book.

Corey Binns is a science writer based in New York City. She's contributed to publications including *Popular Science, Scientific American,* and the *New York Times*. Currently, she's working on a book for third and fourth graders called *Poo Power*. You can read more of Corey's work and contact her at coreybinns.com

Pamela R. Blaine writes "Pam's Corner" for her local newspaper. Many of her stories have been published in magazines, newspapers, and books. She is a church pianist and has a CD of songs she has written. Her goal in writing is to encourage and to preserve family history for her children. Visit Pam at www.blaines.us/PamyPlace.htm, or e-mail her at pamyblaine @blaines.us.

Ellen Bolyard is an office administrator in Morgantown, West Virginia, where she resides with, Bob, her husband of twenty-eight years. They are the parents of three grown children. She has read the Chicken Soup series for years and this is her first work to be published.

LaRonda Bourn lives with her husband, John, and her two amazing girls, Sophie and Maggie, in a beautiful Minnesota town dedicated to preserving its German heritage. She feels blessed to be working in marketing, where she can do what she loves most: being creative and encouraging her coworkers.

Ellie Braun-Haley lives in Central Alberta. She has a number of stories and books published and is the author of *A Little Door, A Little Light,* a book she was challenged to write following the death of her seventeen-year-old son, Jason. Ellie speaks on the material from the book, hoping to help ease the pain of others who have lost someone they love.

Carolyn Brooks is president of Carolyn Brooks Ministries, the National School of Protocol, Simply Divine Communications, and Bella-Mia Skin Care by Beauty for Ashes Cosmetics. Carolyn is the author of *Conversations on Faith,* and her work has appeared in many other anthologies. Her future releases will include *Breaking the Silent Addiction of Abuse—Breaking Free from Your Past,* and *Moving Up the Corporate Ladder God's Way.* To find out more about Carolyn, please visit www.carolynbrooks.com.

Renie Szilak Burghardt is a freelance writer who was born in Hungary. She has been published in over fifty anthologies, including several Chicken Soup for the Soul books, the latest of which have been: *Chicken Soup for the*

Child's Soul, and *Chicken Soup for the Soul: Celebrating Brothers and Sisters.* She lives in the country and loves nature, animals, and spending time with her friends and family. She can be reached at renie.burghardt@gmail.com.

LindaCarol Cherken's career began with an interview with the Beatles for her Lankenau School newspaper. She has written for national newspapers, including the *Philadelphia Daily News,* and coauthored with her daughter, Carolyn, a syndicated advice column called "Mother and Daughter." LindaCarol is Communications Director for the Porter Institute of Valvular Heart Disease at Abington Memorial Hospital, Abington, Pennsylvania. She also enjoys writing essays for the Chicken Soup for the Soul books.

Cynthia Hope Clark is a retired government director and now a full-time freelance writer, penning stories on the banks of Lake Murray, South Carolina. She is the founder of FundsforWriter.com, an award-winning website recognized annually in *Writer's Digest* magazine. She's writing a mystery series based on her escapades with the federal government.

Ann Coogler, a native of North Carolina, enjoys life in Salem, South Carolina, with husband, Bill. Her writing can be seen in: *God Allows U-Turns: American Moments, Chicken Soup for the Recovering Soul: Daily Inspirations, Chocolate for a Teen's Dreams,* and *Bereavement Magazine.* To learn more about Ann, visit www.anncoogler.com.

James Robert Daniels has written fiction and nonfiction since 1975 and is published in books, magazines, newspapers, and online internationally. To find out more about Modest Needs and to make a contribution, please visit http://www.modestneeds.org.

Paul J. DiLella teaches English, speech, and drama at Pahrump Valley High School in Pahrump, Nevada. Previously, he taught at Solomonville Elementary in Solomonville, Arizona. It was during a trip in 2002 to Solomonville that this road incident happened. A published playwright, Paul attends the Utah Shakespearean Festival in Cedar City, Utah, each summer.

Lawrence D. Elliott is a nationally published author and has been a realtor in Southern California since 1989. He lives with his wife, Lisa, and his dog, Lacie, in Ontario. He also runs a network of real estate. To find out more about Lawrence, please visit www.LawrenceElliott.com.

Patricia Cena Evans is a nurse-midwife in Southern California where she lives with her husband and the youngest of their five children. She is a prolific writer, and the coauthor of the upcoming *Chicken Soup for the Empty Nester's Soul,* due for release in 2008. To find out more about Patricia, please visit www.emptynesterssoul.com, or contact her at pattevans@aol.com.

Peggy Frezon is a writer from New York whose publishing credits include *Guideposts, Sweet 16, Positive Thinking, Angels on Earth,* and *Teaching Tolerance.* Her stories have also appeared in *Chicken Soup for the Soul, Soul Matters,* and other publications. To find out more about Peggy, please visit http://peggyfrezon.googlepages.com.

Rick and Virginia Hawthorne's Valley View Vaulters have won championships against all odds. Lessons stop only when weather makes it impossible to practice in an open arena. If you can help the Hawthorne's with their campaign to cover the arena, or to find out more about Valley View Vaulters located at Independence Ranch in Lakeview Terrace, California, please visit www.valleyviewvaulters.com.

Betty Heelis still enjoys the simple life on her rural small holding. She is surrounded by her animals, wildlife, and stunning open countryside, all of which contribute toward a state of mind that allows Betty to recount her exploits or escape into fantasy through writing.

Dorothy Hill is a writer and a retired educator. Many of her stories concern her experiences as a single parent, a foster parent, and an adoptive parent. *Chicken Soup for the Christian Woman's Soul* and *Chicken Soup for the Single Parent's Soul* are two books that feature her work.

Jeanne Hill is an author, an inspirational speaker, and a contributing editor to *Guideposts* magazine. Her award-winning short stories and articles are often chosen for anthologies. She has also authored monthly columns in magazines and published two inspirational books: *Daily Breath* (Word Books) and *Secrets of Prayer-Joy* (Judson Press).

Miriam Hill is coauthor of *Fabulous Florida* and a frequent contributor to Chicken Soup for the Soul books. She's been published in the *Christian Science Monitor, Grit, St. Petersburg Times,* and *Poynter Online.* Miriam's manuscript received Honorable Mention for Inspirational Writing in the 75th Annual *Writer's Digest* Writing Competition.

Pamela Hirson lives with her son, daughter, and bichon frise, Roxy Rose. She is a passionate writer who finds gratitude in delivering a positive message. As the facilitator of a monthly writer's workshop, she volunteers her time, hoping to inspire other writers in their work. She can be reached at: awriterslife@optonline.net.

Pamela Hackett Hobson is a banker and author. Pam's first novel, *The Bronxville Book Club*, was featured in the *New York Times* article "Buzzzz, Murmurs Follow Novel." The sequel is entitled *The Silent Auction*. To find out more about Pam, please visit www.pamelahobson.com, or e-mail her at author@pamelahobson.com.

Rose M. Jackson authored two leader's guides for Donna Partow Ministries and worked with Dr. Walt Kallestad on five books, including *Be Your Own Creative Coach*. Rose enjoys speaking at women's retreats, dancing and camping with her husband, and traveling, especially with their two sons and grandchildren. To find out more about Rose, please visit http://www.donnapartow.com/Rose_Bio, or e-mail her at ecrmjackson @msn.com.

Susan A. Karas's work has been published in *Chicken Soup for the Shopper's Soul, Guidepost's Sweet 16, Positive Thinking,* and *Plus Magazine,* among others.

Mimi Greenwood Knight is thrilled to have her work included in a dozen Chicken Soup for the Soul books as well as seeing 300 of her articles and essays published in national parenting magazines, Christian websites, and a smattering of anthologies. She lives with her hubby and four kids in South Louisiana where she enjoys butterfly gardening, Bible study, and the lost art of letter writing.

Karen Kosman is an inspirational speaker and author of *Wounded by Words* (New Hope Publishers, 2007). Karen's joy and zest for life warms hearts. She has authored stories in several compilations and magazine articles. She can be reached at ComKosman@aol.com.

Cheryl M. Kremer lives in Lancaster, Pennsylvania, with her husband, Jack, and teenagers, Nikki and Cobi. Her father told her this story a few months before he passed away in December 2006. Cheryl's work has appeared in quite a few Chicken Soup for the Soul books. She can be reached at j_kremer@verizon.net.

Joyce Laird is a freelance writer who juggles her time between industrial and consumer feature writing, creative nonfiction, and fiction. She is a regular contributor to *Woman's World* and *American Fitness* magazines and became one of the Chicken Soup authors with *Chicken Soup for the Dog Lover's Soul*.

Kathryn Lay is a full time author and speaker living in Texas. Her books include *Crown Me!* a novel for children, and *The Organized Writer is a Selling Writer.* She and her husband have been helping immigrants and refugees for thirty years. To find out more about Kathryn, please visit www.kathrynlay.com or e-mail her at rlay15@aol.com.

Celeste Leon lives near Lake Tahoe, California, where she enjoys the outdoors with her husband of fourteen years and their five-year-old daughter. Celeste is a physical therapist and has written stories for www.heartwarmers.com and *Daily Inspiration*, the newsletter for www.beliefnet.com. Celeste is currently writing a family biography, including stories about her father's incredible life and accomplishments.

Jaye Lewis is an award-winning writer, who looks at life from a unique perspective, celebrating the miraculous in the everyday. Jaye is currently editing her book, *Entertaining Angels*, which she hopes to submit to a publisher soon. To find out more about Jaye, please visit www.entertaining angels.org, or e-mail Jaye at jayelewis@comcast.net.

Patricia Lorenz is an art-of-living writer and speaker and the author of ten books. She's one of the top contributors to the Chicken Soup for the Soul books with stories in over thirty editions. To find out more about Patricia and to inquire about her speaking for your group or community, please visit website www.PatriciaLorenz.com, or she can be reached at patricialorenz@juno.com.

Priscilla Miller is a freelance writer and is published on a regular basis in several northern Michigan newspapers. Never having had any formal training, she has always loved to write. She realized her life's dream of having her work published at the same time she was diagnosed with "wet" macular degeneration, which threatens to rob her of her eyesight.

Ava Pennington is a writer, Bible study teacher, public speaker, and former human resources director. With an MBA from St. John's University in New York, and a Bible Studies Certificate from Moody Bible Institute in Chicago, Ava divides her time between teaching, writing, speaking, and volunteering. She can be reached at rusavapen@yahoo.com.

Beth Pollack, a recent graduate of University of Pennsylvania, has written for everything from *Newsweek* to *Chicken Soup for the Gardener's Soul*. She is currently looking to publish her first novel—a historical fiction mystery about a crime with clues spanning continents and generations back to WWII.

Claudia Porter is an inspirational speaker, author, composer, and music teacher. In addition, Claudia and her husband, Bruce, of Torchgrab Ministries, Inc., have been a part of bringing comfort to hurting people ravaged by tragedy and terrorism around the world. Claudia is also published in *Chicken Soup for the Christian Soul 2.* She can be reached at claudia@torchgrab.org.

Barbara J. Ragsdale majored in music education and English in college, plays piano and organ, and has directed children's choirs. Barbara is a certified land and water aerobics instructor and works for a company that specializes in custom-made ocular prosthesis for children and adults. Also published in *Chicken Soup for the Girl's Soul,* she is a winner in a nonfiction writing contest sponsored by a branch of National Pen Women.

Shirley A. Reynolds is a freelance writer and retreat speaker, who recently moved from big city suburbia. She enjoys writing, photography, solitude, four-wheeling, and the beauty of a mountain environment. With one grandson, she has a never ending source of material. She has published several stories and is presently working on a book about her work with street youth.

Rhonda Richards-Cohen is a graduate of Greenville College and Stanford University. She resides in Dallas with her stepchildren and husband, Todd. She is still going through Gertrude's stuff and is writing a memoir about her great-aunt and their years together. Gertrude died two days after her eighty-seventh birthday. Her memory is a blessing.

Sallie A. Rodman is an award-winning writer living in Los Alamitos, California, with her husband. Her children are grown, and she has two grandchildren. She looks back with fond memories of the Good Samaritans and has a framed picture in her cowgirl outfit to remind her of that adventuresome trip. She can be reached at sa.rodman@verizon.net.

Kim Rogers is a freelance writer who lives with her husband and sons in Oklahoma. A journalism graduate of the University of Central Oklahoma, her work has appeared in *Chicken Soup for the Girl's Soul, Guidepost's Sweet 16,* and many other publications.

Harriet May Savitz is the award-winning author of twenty-six books, including *Run, Don't Walk,* an *ABC Afterschool Special* produced by Henry Winkler. Her essays appear in seventeen of the Chicken Soup for the Soul books. Several of her books (children and young adult) have been reissued by AuthorsGuild/iUniverse and can be found at www.iUniverse.com. To find out more about Harriet or her books, please visit www.harriet maysavitz.com or e-mail her at hmaysavitz@aol.com or at Essay Books at www.authorhouse.com.

Michael Jordan Segal, who defied all odds after being shot in the head, is a husband, father, social worker, author, and inspirational speaker. His "miraculous" comeback story was first published in *Chicken Soup for the Christian Family Soul.* Since then he's had numerous stories published. To find out more about Mike, please visit www.InspirationByMike.com, or www.sterlingspeakers.com/segal.htm.

Alexandera Simone (pen name) is a graduate from the Biological Sciences program at the University of Guelph in Ontario, Canada. She enjoys writing online articles, essays, and short stories, usually relating to environmental conservation or political debates. She hopes to one day become a published novelist in the fantasy or science fiction genre.

Ashley Claire Simpson is a fourth-year student studying Politics and History at the University of Virginia. She is from Herndon, Virginia, and she wrote this story about one of the mission trips she took in high school with her home church. About to graduate and enter the "real world," she would like to thank her loving family for their infinite love and support.

Jami Smith resides in Baton Rouge, Louisiana, where she is a student at Louisiana State University, majoring in communication studies. She currently works as the marketing manager for LSU Student Media. In her spare time, Jami enjoys writing and attending LSU football games.

Nick Sortal is a senior writer for the South Florida *Sun-Sentinel.* In 2001, he authored *Basketball Tip-Ins, 100 Drills and Tips for Young Players* (McGraw-Hill) and has been recognized for outstanding journalism by the Florida Press Club and the Florida Recreation and Park Association. But he is proudest of his parents, Violet and Mike Sortal of Herrin, Illinois, his wife, Robyn, and his children, Diane, Michelle, and Aaron.

Morgan St. James splits time between Marina Del Rey, California, and Las Vegas, Nevada. She met Rick and Virginia Hawthorne in 1995, became part of their family of friends, and has written several articles about them. Morgan coauthors the *Silver Sisters Mystery* series with her sister, Phyllice Bradner, and is the author of several short stories published in anthologies and on Amazon Shorts. She belongs to Sisters in Crime and Henderson Writer's Group. To find out more about Morgan, please visit www.silversistersmysteries.com.

Gloria Cassity Stargel writes for *Guideposts, Decision, Today's Christian,* and others. Her award-winning book, *The Healing,* a cancer-survival story, gains value with age like a fine antique. You can read portions of it at www.brightmorning.com. To order ($11.95 per copy), please visit the website, call 1-800-888-9529, or write to Applied Images, 312 Bradford St., N.W., Gainesville, GA 30501.

Pamela Strome-Merewether and her husband live in New Mexico with their very beautiful children, Taylor and Alexis. The entire family is very involved in the local community and enjoy spending time together doing family activities.

Scot Thurman has served as both a campus minister at the University of Arkansas's Baptist Collegiate Ministry and a minister of pastoral care at University Baptist Church in Fayetteville, Arkansas. He and his wife, Robyn, own Thurman's Lodge in Eureka Springs, Arkansas, and have two children, Lila Claire and Matthew Scot.

Colleen Tillger did finish college and is working as a women's counselor. However, her father always encouraged her to pursue her dreams, so she is also working on her first novel and has recently started a small business designing edgy apparel for dogs (www.punkrockdogg.com), inspired by her spaztastic Boston terrier, Murphy.

Nancy Viau is the author of the middle-grade novel, *Samantha Hansen Has Rocks in Her Head* (Amulet, Fall 2008). She has contributed stories, poems, and essays to: *Highlights for Children, Highlights High Five, Babybug, Ladybug, Hopscotch for Girls, Fun For Kidz, The Writing Group Book, Family Circle, FamilyFun, The Philadelphia Inquirer,* and many other magazines and newspapers, in print and online. To find out more about Nancy, please visit www.nancyviau.com.

Mirna Whidden is an educator and is pursuing a Ph.D. in education. She enjoys traveling and spending time with her family. Naomi Whidden is now in high school, enjoying sports, and is very involved with her local church. In Naomi's spare time, she enjoys reading and playing the guitar.

Kathy Whirity is a newspaper columnist who lives in Chicago with her husband of twenty-eight years, Bill, their daughters, Jaime and Katie, and her two loyal golden retrievers, Holly and Hannah. The love of writing is what motivates Kathy to share her joy with others. She feels it is a gift from above and feels blessed for the privilege to touch others with her words. You can reach Kathy by e-mail kathywhirity@yahoo.com.

Vickie Williams-Morris is a performance, visual, and literary artist from northeast Ohio. She was awarded an Ohio Arts Council Individual Excellence Award (2007) for a collaborative work of nonfiction, *Pam I Am: A*

Felon's Story. She gives thanks to God and her family and friends. To find out more about Vickie, please visit www.wilmorcreations.com.

Kerry M. Wood, retired teacher of English and foreign languages, textbook coauthor, and freelance writer, is the author of *Past Imperfect, Present Progressive,* a self-published memoir. To find out more about Kerry, please visit Kerry at www.kerrymwood.com.

Acts of kindness

Code #1592 • $14.95

Code #0146 • $14.95

Love of family

Also Available

Chicken Soup African American Soul
Chicken Soup African American Woman's Soul
Chicken Soup Breast Cancer Survivor's Soul
Chicken Soup Bride's Soul
Chicken Soup Caregiver's Soul
Chicken Soup Cat Lover's Soul
Chicken Soup Christian Family Soul
Chicken Soup College Soul
Chicken Soup Couple's Soul
Chicken Soup Dieter's Soul
Chicken Soup Dog Lover's Soul
Chicken Soup Entrepreneur's Soul
Chicken Soup Expectant Mother's Soul
Chicken Soup Father's Soul
Chicken Soup Fisherman's Soul
Chicken Soup Girlfriend's Soul
Chicken Soup Golden Soul
Chicken Soup Golfer's Soul, Vol. I, II
Chicken Soup Horse Lover's Soul, Vol. I, II
Chicken Soup Inspire a Woman's Soul
Chicken Soup Kid's Soul, Vol. I, II
Chicken Soup Mother's Soul, Vol. I, II
Chicken Soup Parent's Soul
Chicken Soup Pet Lover's Soul
Chicken Soup Preteen Soul, Vol. I, II
Chicken Soup Scrapbooker's Soul
Chicken Soup Sister's Soul, Vol. I, II
Chicken Soup Shopper's
Chicken Soup Soul, Vol. I-VI
Chicken Soup at Work
Chicken Soup Sports Fan's Soul
Chicken Soup Teenage Soul, Vol. I-IV
Chicken Soup Woman's Soul, Vol. I, II

To order direct: Telephone (800) 441-5569 • www.hcibooks.com
Prices do not include shipping and handling. Your response code is CCS.